contents

Introduction

Employment law continues to change and expand, with the introduction every year of new legislation and judgments that affect the way the law is interpreted.

Since the last edition of *Law at work* was published in May 2009 the *Equality Act 2010*, which overhauls and extends discrimination law, has been approved by Parliament and received Royal Assent. The government has also introduced a right to request time off for training and outlawed the blacklisting of trade unionists, as well as detailed legislation which (in 2011) will give new rights for agency workers, and the option for fathers to take additional paternity leave.

Furthermore, there have been a large number of important judicial decisions on subjects such as the taking of holiday, what kinds of beliefs are protected by the religion and belief regulations, the right to legal representation at disciplinary hearings, redundancy consultations in multi-nationals, the use of "last in, first out" as a redundancy selection criterion, and the status of collectively agreed terms and conditions following a TUPE transfer.

Now in its 22nd year, *Law at work 2010* explains the key areas of employment law so that representatives and individuals can identify their legal rights. Unlike most other publications on employment law, it examines the law from the perspective of workers and trade unions.

Law at work 2010 provides the basic information that will help establish your rights in the workplace and decide whether there is a legal claim. It is not intended that this booklet on its own should enable an individual or union rep to take a claim through the legal procedures, but it shows where the relevant law can be found and gives examples of the areas that are covered.

LRD's *Case law at work* series of booklets provides summaries of many more cases and should be read in conjunction with this booklet.

Most trade unions offer their members a comprehensive legal service and any member or union rep contemplating taking a legal case should contact their union first. In many unions, tribunal cases will be handled internally at district, regional or even head office level.

Differences in law across the UK

This booklet refers to the legislation as it applies to England, Wales and Scotland (although there are some minor variations in Scotland). However, the principles also apply in Northern Ireland which has its own legislation but a similar structure.

In England and Wales, decisions from the employment tribunal go to the EAT in England, and from there to the Court of Appeal in England and then the Supreme Court (formerly referred to as the House of Lords).

In Scotland, appeals from the employment tribunal go to the EAT in Scotland, and from there to the Court of Session and then the Supreme Court.

A significant difference between the Northern Irish legal system and those in England and Wales and Scotland is that tribunals in Northern Ireland are still called industrial tribunals and there is no Employment Appeal Tribunal (EAT). Appeals from industrial tribunals go straight to the Northern Irish Court of Appeal (and from there to the Supreme Court).

Decisions from the two EATs are binding on each other and on employment tribunals in England, Wales and Scotland, and are strongly persuasive in industrial tribunals in Northern Ireland.

Judgments of the Court of Session and the two Courts of Appeal are not binding on each other, but bind all courts and tribunals below them.

Legislation

Most employment rights are statutory rights, so called because they come from a statute (another name for a piece of legislation). Anyone bringing a claim in a tribunal should acquaint themselves thoroughly with the appropriate sections of the statutes which are always given.

Where, for example, this booklet mentions "section 1, ERA", it means that the relevant law is to be found in the first section of the *Employment Rights Act 1996*. (See "Further information" at the end of this booklet for details of where to obtain copies of the statutes).

Relying on the exact wording of the statute and showing its relevance to your argument is essential to a successful tribunal claim.

The volume of legislation governing employment relationships has grown dramatically over the last 20 years or so. In 2004, the government decided to introduce legislative changes only twice a year, on 6 April and 1 October. However, some legislation originating from European Union (EU) law may be introduced on other dates.

Case law

The law also changes constantly as a result of decisions made by judges. This is known as "case law" and examples — with their case references — can be found throughout this booklet.

European law

UK employment law is heavily influenced by European law. Judgments from the European Court of Justice (ECJ), even where the case is brought from another EU state, bind the UK courts.

Public sector workers, including those in the former public industries like gas and water, can bring claims in the UK based on EU law. This process is known as "direct effect" and gives direct access to the

Reading a case reference

Gibson v East Riding of Yorkshire Council [2000] IRLR 598 tells you that the claimant was called Gibson; the case was brought against East Riding of Yorkshire Council; and the judgment was reported in the law reports for 2000. The letters IRLR stand for Industrial Relations Law Reports, and the case was reported on page 598. Other law reports include the Industrial Cases Reports (ICR).

If the case has not been reported in the law reports, or if it is also available free of charge online, the case number is generally quoted. For example, a case reference beginning "EAT" or "UKEAT" is from the Employment Appeal Tribunal; Court of Appeal decisions will include "EWCA". For details of how to find cases, see "Further information" at the end of this booklet.

benefit laid down in European law. To claim direct effect, however, the right under EU law has to be precise.

Mr Gibson brought a claim for holiday under the European Working Time Directive, which had not been implemented in the UK by the date set by the EU. The Court of Appeal held that the wording of the Directive was not sufficiently precise about the situations when the right would apply, and Gibson's claim failed. *Gibson v East Riding of Yorkshire Council [2000] IRLR 598.*

The ruling of the ECJ in *Francovich v Italian Republic [1992] IRLR 84* gave **private sector workers** the right to sue their own state if it fails to properly implement European law. In the UK, such claims must be initiated in the High Court, not the employment tribunals. The claim would be for damages resulting from the state's failure to introduce the right under European law, rather than a claim for the right itself.

Civil liberties and employment law

The *Human Rights Act 1998* implemented the European Convention on Human Rights into UK law. It gives citizens the right to challenge **public authorities** where they act in conflict with human rights, including the right to freedom of association, expression and assembly, the right to a private life and the right to be protected from discrimination.

Claims against a public authority for a breach of human rights law can be taken in the UK courts. It should also be possible to use the Act to challenge the actions of public sector employers where these infringe human rights principles. So far there have been few employment law cases using the Act.

In the case of *O'Flynn v Airlinks EAT/0269/01*, the EAT held that a company policy of zero tolerance on alcohol and drugs, which made it clear that the employer would randomly test employees and dismiss anyone who failed the test, was unlikely to be a breach of the *Human Rights Act*. The policy was reasonable, it said, taking account of the employer's legitimate safety concerns.

In the case of *X v Y EAT/0765/02 [2003] IRLR 561*, the EAT held that a person who was dismissed for failing to inform his employers that he had been charged with gross indecency did not have the right to protection under the *Human Rights Act*. The activities for which he had been charged had occurred in a public place and his dismissal as a result of the charge could not be said to have breached his right to a private life.

The case of *Pay v United Kingdom (Application No. 32792/05)* involved a probation officer who specialised in the rehabilitation of sex offenders. Following an anonymous tip-off, photographs of Mr Pay engaging in sadomasochistic activities were found on the internet. Mr Pay, having declined to cease these activities and terminate the associated business that he ran, was dismissed.

The European Court of Human Rights decided that although Mr Pay's right to respect for his private life and right to freedom of expression had been breached, due to the sensitive nature of his post those breaches and the decision to dismiss were justified.

In *McGowan v Scottish Water UKEAT/0007/04 [2005] IRLR 167*, the EAT held that the employer (a public corporation) investigating what was effectively criminal activity (the alleged falsification of time sheets) had the right to protect the assets of the company and surveillance was not disproportionate, and therefore did not amount to a breach of Article 8 rights.

But in the case of *Copland v UK (application 62617/00)*, the European Court of Human Rights said that monitoring an employee's telephone calls, emails and internet use was a breach of her human rights as she had not been warned that this would happen and had a reasonable expectation of privacy at work.

The **EU Charter of Fundamental Rights**, although not legally binding, has been adopted by EU member states including the UK. It recommends that member states guarantee the right to equality and non-discrimination and the right to freedom of thought and expression, including the right to take strike action.

The *Regulation of Investigatory Powers Act 2000* also limits the extent of employers' rights to **intercept employees' emails, faxes and phone calls**. Regulations accompanying the Act state that the right to intercept messages only exists where consent has been given, where there is a legitimate business interest, or in cases where the employee is off work sick or on holiday.

Employees also have rights under the *Data Protection Act 1998*, which cover information stored in electronic form and paper files or documents. Employees can ask to see any stored personal information held by the employer.

You may see copies of your job application, references, bonus assessments, sickness and other attendance records and any email communications which are about you, or even simply refer to you.

Employers can charge a fee for access, which is currently set at a maximum of £10 for each request. The employer must abide by certain data principles designed to ensure that the information stored is not excessive and is kept securely.

The Information Commissioner's Office provides information as well as Codes of Practice covering privacy and electronic communications and data protection, which are available on their website at www. ico.gov.uk/tools_and_resources.aspx.

More information: See the LRD booklet *Monitoring and surveillance — a guide to privacy at work* (£4.00). The LRD magazines *Labour Research* and *Workplace Report* update readers every month on legal changes. And LRD Booklets look at specific areas of the law in more detail (see "Further information"). Relevant publications are highlighted at the end of each Chapter.

1. The employment law system

Employment rights in the UK come from two main sources. The first is legislation enacted by Parliament in the form of Acts of Parliament or Regulations; this is referred to as **statutory law** (from "statute", which is another word for a piece of legislation). The second is **common law** (also referred to as case law), which has developed over the years from decisions made by judges in specific cases.

The system of **legal precedent** means that lower courts are bound by the decisions of higher courts. This means that employment tribunals must follow decisions that have been made by the Employment Appeal Tribunal (EAT), which must follow those of the Court of Appeal (or Court of Session in Scotland).

In Northern Ireland, appeals from industrial tribunals go straight to the Court of Appeal. However, judgments of the UK EAT are strongly persuasive on the tribunals, which mean they can still be used to support a claim. The Supreme Court (formerly referred to as the House of Lords) is the highest court in the UK, so the principles decided here will apply to all courts and tribunals.

The UK must also comply with **European law**, and its legislation must be interpreted so as to comply with European law as far as possible. The European Court of Justice deals with the interpretation of European law, and its decisions are binding on all courts and tribunals in the UK.

Most employment claims are dealt with by employment tribunals but there are cases that have to be brought in the **ordinary courts** (the County Court or High Court) — principally breach of contract claims and applications for injunctions.

Employment tribunals

Employment tribunals (industrial tribunals in Northern Ireland) were set up under the *Industrial Training Act 1964* as an informal, accessible, quick and inexpensive way of resolving employment disputes, although they have become increasingly legalistic — it is more likely than not that the parties in a case, particularly the employer, will have legal representation at a tribunal. They are not part of the court system and have **separate rules of procedure**; these are set out in the amended *Employment Tribunals Act 1996* and the *Employment Tribunals (Constitution and Rules of Procedure) Regulations 2004*, which came into force on 1 October 2004.

A full tribunal consists of a legally qualified chairperson (now called an **employment judge**) and two **lay members**, one drawn from a panel of employer representatives and one from a panel of employee reps. Certain types of claim (for example, pay claims under the *Working Time Regulations*), and case management discussions, can be heard by an employment judge sitting alone.

Tribunals, like all other judicial bodies, must, where possible, interpret the law to give effect to the European Convention on Human Rights which was implemented in the UK by the *Human Rights Act 1998* (see "Civil liberties and employment law" on page 12).

This includes the **right to a fair trial**. Tribunals have to demonstrate an absence of bias and give both parties the right to state their case and respond to any allegations made against them.

The EAT has held that a tribunal which excluded relevant witness evidence acted unfairly (*Kilduff v MIND in Bradford EAT/0568/04*), and that if a member of the panel becomes unavailable part way through a hearing, the parties are entitled to know whether that member was drawn from the employers' or employees' panel (*Rabahallah v BT plc EAT 0382/04 ([2005] IRLR 184)*).

Most claims that can be heard by an employment tribunal are **statutory claims**, meaning that they involve rights given by employment legislation rather than the employment contract.

These include claims for unfair dismissal, unlawful deduction from wages, redundancy pay, discrimination, equal pay, claims relating to parental rights, claims arising from the *Working Time Regulations*, and many trade union rights.

An employment tribunal can also hear a claim for **breach of contract** (see "Contract changes" in Chapter 3), which is a common law claim, but only where the breach is arising or outstanding on dismissal.

This means that a worker who wants to pursue a breach of contract claim while they are still employed will usually have to do this in the

County Court or High Court. The maximum amount that a tribunal can award in a breach of contract claim is £25,000.

Anyone who has been declared **bankrupt** can only take a claim if approved by the trustee in bankruptcy.

To pursue a tribunal claim, you must now submit the claim on the specified Claim form (ET1) and complete all the **required information** on the form. If the claim is not submitted on the correct form or some of the required information is missing, the claim will not be admitted.

The claim form can be obtained from Jobcentres, most advice agencies and benefit offices, or can be downloaded from the Employment Tribunals Service website at www.employmenttribunals. gov.uk. You should specify on the form all the claims that you wish to bring.

For example, if you think that you were unfairly dismissed and that your dismissal was discriminatory on grounds of your sex, you should state that you are claiming both unfair dismissal and sex discrimination as these are separate claims.

The form must be sent to the correct employment tribunal office, which is determined by the postcode of your normal workplace and can be found on the Employment Tribunals Service website (www. employmenttribunals.gov.uk) or by phoning its enquiry line on 0845 795 9775 (minicom 0845 757 3722).

When the tribunal receives your claim form, it will send a copy to your employer and invite the employer to respond by completing the Response form (ET3).

Time limits

The application must be submitted within the time limits laid down for each piece of employment legislation.

Time generally runs from the date of the act complained of (for example, the date of dismissal in an unfair dismissal claim). Although there are exceptions, the time limit for most employment claims is three months.

Please note that where an individual's employment was terminated without notice (i.e. taking immediate effect) on 10 January, the time limit for lodging a claim will be 9 April and not 10 April. Union reps should be aware that the time limit for an application for interim relief (see "Victimisation" in Chapter 5) is only **seven days**.

If a claim is issued out of time, the tribunal has no jurisdiction to hear it and it will be dismissed. A tribunal does have discretion to **extend the time limits** in some circumstances, but these are very specific and the power is rarely exercised.

A claim sent by first class post at least two working days before the expiry of the time limit (four days if second class) will be within the limit, even if it is not received until after the date.

In the case of *Consignia v Sealy [2002] EWCA Civ 878 ([2002] IRLR 624*, the Court of Appeal refused to extend the time limit for a postal worker who posted his application a day before the time limit expired. The court said that he should not have relied on next day delivery, knowing that the Royal Mail does not guarantee that all first class post will be delivered the next day.

In unfair dismissal cases, the time limit can be extended if it was **not reasonably practicable** to present the claim in time. In discrimination cases, it can be extended if it is **just and equitable** to do so.

Failure of machinery, such as printers or faxes, is not enough to justify an extension, according to an EAT ruling in a case where the claim arrived 11 minutes late because of problems with the claimant's printer. The EAT held that this was a relatively common occurrence and did not mean it was not reasonably practicable to comply with the time limit (*Fishley v Working Men's College EAT/0485/04*).

A late claim of unfair dismissal and disability discrimination from a claimant who had been hospitalised during part of the three-month limit was also refused. Although it was not reasonably practicable for the claimant to submit his claims when he was in hospital, he had not provided medical evidence about his medical conditions after his discharge (*Chouafi v London United Busways [2006] EWCA Civ 689*).

Mr Wadher, who had been off work with stress, lodged his tribunal claim five weeks out of time (in April 2008). At a pre-hearing review (which Mr Wadher, due to ill-health, was unable to attend as a witness) the tribunal decided that it would be just and equitable to allow the late claim. The EAT endorsed this decision. The EAT stated that there was plenty of material (e.g. medical certificates) from which the tribunal could conclude that Mr Wadher was suffering from stress and depression from September 2007 onwards. Although the evidence did not specifically indicate why, if Mr Wadher was well enough in April 2008 to present his claim, he was not well enough in March or February, the EAT thought that would have been too rigid an approach. Depression can delay and impair decision-making, without making it impossible. *Accurist Watches Ltd v Wadher UKEAT/0102/09*.

A police officer, suffering from mental ill-health, instructed solicitors to pursue a claim against her employer. Unfortunately, due to a misunderstanding, the individual's claim was lodged six weeks out of time. The employer's argument that the case should not proceed, was rejected by the tribunal.

The tribunal decided that the individual's ill-health caused her failure to give full information to her lawyers and was the reason for the late submission of the ET1. The Court of Appeal upheld the tribunal's ruling, commenting that whether a claim will be accepted is a matter to be determined by individual tribunals which have heard the relevant facts. *Chief Constable of Lincolnshire Police v Caston [2009] EWCA Civ 1298*.

If you have not received an acknowledgement of your claim or you submit it very close to the deadline, you should check with the tribunal office that it has been received.

In general, ignorance of the time limit is not a valid reason for extending the time limit. And if a claim is submitted late because the claimant has received the wrong legal advice, or has not been advised of the time limit by their solicitor, this will not be treated as a sufficient reason to extend time (although the claimant may be able to bring a negligence claim against the solicitor).

In one case (*Opare-Addo v Wandsworth BC EAT/0740/01*), the fact that the claimant was represented by her union was one of the reasons why the tribunal thought it was reasonably practicable for her to have lodged her claim in time.

However, the Court of Appeal did allow an extension of time in a case where the claimant had sought advice from the Citizens Advice Bureau but had not been told about the time limits (*Marks & Spencer v Williams-Ryan [2005] EWCA Civ 470 ([2005] IRLR 562)*).

Pre-hearings and deposits

Before the claim reaches a full hearing, an employment judge may hold a **case management discussion** to deal with matters relating to the procedure and management of the proceedings, such as clarification of the issues in dispute and the provision of additional information or documents that are relevant to the claim.

A tribunal can also call for a **pre-hearing review** (PHR), which deals with more fundamental issues, such as whether the tribunal has jurisdiction to hear the claim (including whether the claim has been submitted in time).

At a PHR, an employment judge, or a full tribunal in some cases, also has the power to order a party to **pay a deposit** if it believes that they are arguing a case that has little prospect of success but is still arguable. The deposit can be for a sum of up to £500. This is usually refunded after the claim or can be used to offset any order for costs (see below).

A tribunal can also strike out a claim, or an employer's response, that is "scandalous, vexatious or has no reasonable prospect of success" or which has been conducted in a "scandalous, unreasonable or vexatious manner". Claimants who fail to actively pursue their claims — for example, by failing to comply with directions or orders given by the tribunal — are also at risk of having their claims struck out.

And it is also now possible for an employment judge to issue a **default judgment** if the respondent has not issued a valid response form in time or does not intend to oppose the claim. This is a judgment made without a hearing, but it cannot go ahead if the respondent has asked for a review of the decision not to accept its response.

If either party wants documents from the other side that are necessary to support their claim, but has been refused access to them, it can ask the tribunal for an order to provide the documents. This is known as **discovery** or **disclosure**. "Privileged" documents, which are primarily communications between legal representatives or between lawyers and their clients, do not have to be disclosed.

However, if both parties have waived their right to privilege (meaning they have shown that they are prepared for the information to be made public), without prejudice documents or discussions can be referred to in the case (*Brunel University v Webster & Vaseghi [2007] EWCA Civ 482*).

Also, the cases of *New Victoria Hospital v Ryan [1993] IRLR 202* and *Howes v Hinckley Borough Council UKEAT/0213/08* state that legal professional privilege does not extend to communications to and from a firm of employment consultants.

The hearing

Once any preliminary issues have been resolved, the claim proceeds to a **full hearing**. This usually takes place in public, although there are exceptional cases where a hearing can be conducted in private — for example, if there is an issue of national security. In cases involving allegations of sexual misconduct or disability cases involving evidence of a personal nature, the tribunal may issue a **restricted reporting order**; depending on the nature of the allegations, this may apply permanently or just until the date of the judgment.

Some claims (involving unlawful deduction of wages, for example) can be dealt with by an employment judge sitting alone, but most are heard by a full tribunal. If the facts are in dispute, the case should be decided by a full tribunal.

It is important to present all of the case law that could be relevant to your case, as well as focusing on the words of the legislation. If the tribunal is aware of a relevant case that it wants to take into account, it must ask both parties to make representations on it. If it fails to do so, the hearing will be unfair (*Albion Hotel (Freshwater) Ltd v Maia e Silva EAT/375/00 [2002] IRLR 200*).

You have the right to be **represented** by an individual of your choice (*Bache v Essex CC [2000] IRLR 251*), or to represent yourself. If the tribunal disapproves of the behaviour of your representative, it can warn you that it believes that the representative's behaviour is inappropriate and that you risk rejection of your claim. On the basis of this, you can decide whether you want to keep or change your representative.

You can call **witnesses** in support of your claim, and if necessary you can ask the tribunal to issue a "witness order" compelling them to attend. This might be necessary, for example, if an employer is unwilling to give a witness time off work to attend the hearing.

Once an order has been issued, an employer has to concede the time off. The tribunal has discretion over whether to grant a witness order, and can take into account whether the witness's evidence is relevant to the issues (*Noorani v Merseyside TEC [1999] IRLR 184*).

If you need to request an **adjournment**, you must make an application to the tribunal, and you should provide any necessary evidence in support of your application. If the application for an adjournment is on medical grounds, the tribunal must consider the medical evidence provided and not jump to its own conclusions, as the EAT held in the following case:

The day before her hearing, Ms Fadina requested an adjournment because she was unwell and sent a sick note stating that she was suffering from stress and anxiety. The tribunal rejected the request and said there was no physical reason why Fadina could not attend. The EAT noted that the tribunal had not contacted Fadina or her representative before considering the adjournment, and had made assumptions about her medical condition without investigating it. It had jumped to conclusions that were not supported by facts, and Fadina's case was sent to a different tribunal for hearing. *Fadina v Government Car and Despatch Agency EAT/0264/04.*

Once the case has been heard, the tribunal will issue its judgment with reasons. Either it will do this at the end of the hearing or, if there is no time or the tribunal wishes to consider the case further, it can "reserve" its judgment and issue it at a later date. If the judgment is reserved, the tribunal must put its reasons in writing. If it gives its reasons verbally at the end of the hearing, the parties can request that they are provided in writing.

As a rule, each party has to **meet its own legal costs**, but there are limited circumstances in which costs may be awarded (see below). Essentially there is no right to legal aid for employment tribunal cases (although in Scotland, claimants with complex cases.may be eligible for assistance). However, legal aid is available for claims in the County Court or High Court — provided the individual qualifies under the income rules.

Claimants, witnesses and volunteer representatives at employment tribunals may be able to claim travel expenses, accommodation costs, loss of earnings (up to £45 a day) and child or adult care costs. Details of expenses that can be claimed can be found on the Employment

Tribunals Service website: www.employmenttribunals.gov.uk or by
phoning the service's enquiry line on 0845 795 9775 (minicom 0845
757 3722).

Costs orders

In limited circumstances, a tribunal has the power to issue an order
for costs (in Scotland they are called expenses) against a party. This
will generally be where that party or its representative has acted
"vexatiously, abusively, disruptively or otherwise unreasonably", or
where its proceedings were "misconceived" (interpreted as having
no reasonable prospect of success).

A **wasted costs** order can be made against a legal or any other
representative who has caused another party, including their own
client, to incur costs through their "improper, unreasonable or
negligent act or omission". This only applies where costs have
actually been incurred, and will not therefore apply to voluntary or
not-for-profit sector representatives or trade unions.

Preparation time orders can be awarded in favour of a party who
has not incurred any legal costs. This means that unrepresented
parties or those presented by voluntary or not-for-profit sector
representatives can recover costs for their time spent preparing.
These are made in the same circumstances as other costs orders.

The amount of costs that can be ordered are:

◆ a fixed sum of up to £10,000;
◆ a sum agreed by the parties; or
◆ the whole or a specific part of the costs incurred.

Employment Appeal Tribunal

Either side can appeal against a tribunal decision, but only if there
has been an **error of law** or the decision was **perverse** (meaning that
no reasonable tribunal could have come to that decision).

If the conduct of the hearing is such that a party was deprived of the
right to a fair trial (for example, because the tribunal showed bias or
there was an unreasonable delay in coming to its decision), this will
amount to an error of law (*Bangs v Connex South Eastern [2005]
EWCA Civ 14 ([2005] IRLR 389)*).

Appeals from employment tribunals go to the EAT in England, Wales and Scotland (which has a separate EAT); in Northern Ireland, appeals from industrial tribunals go to the Court of Appeal. The appeal must be lodged **within 42 days** of the tribunal sending out its decision, not the date when you received it (*Gdynia American Shipping Lines v Chelminski [2004] EWCA Civ 871 [2004] IRLR 725*).

The EAT has discretion to **extend the time limit** but this is exercised only in rare and exceptional cases (*Aziz v Bethnal Green City Challenge [2000] IRLR 111*). If you have submitted an appeal and not had it acknowledged it is important to check that it has been received. You should contact the EAT office to make sure.

EAT procedure is governed by the Employment Appeal Tribunal Rules 1993 (as amended) and the Employment Appeal Tribunal Practice Direction 2004, which came into force on 1 December 2004.

It is not the function of the EAT to conduct a rehearing of the facts. New evidence and **new points of law cannot be raised** on appeal if they were not raised at the tribunal hearing, unless there are exceptional circumstances.

The EAT can order **costs** (**expenses** in Scotland) against a party if its appeal proceedings were unnecessary, improper, vexatious or misconceived, or if there is unreasonable conduct. It can also order costs for a failure to comply with an order. It is recommended that you get legal advice before contemplating an appeal.

Other courts

Some cases go to the ordinary courts rather than to the tribunals. For example, police prosecutions for offences to do with **picketing** (see Chapter 9) go to either the Magistrates' Court or the Crown Court, depending on the severity of the charge. Claims for breach of contract if the employee is still employed go to the County Court or the High Court.

There is a legal principle that, if you bring a claim in one court, you cannot then take the same claim to another. However, in the case of *Sajid v Sussex Muslim Society [2001] EWCA Civ 1684 ([2002] IRLR 113)*, the Court of Appeal held that the High Court could hear a claim that initially had been lodged with an employment tribunal, because Mr Sajid had made it clear that he was only withdrawing his breach of contract claim from the tribunal proceedings because it was in excess of the £25,000 limit and he intended to pursue it in the High Court.

Compromise agreements

Legally binding settlements, in which the parties refrain from issuing or continuing proceedings, can be agreed before a case reaches a tribunal. This can happen through the services of an **Acas** conciliation officer (see below), in which case the agreement will usually be put in writing on a form COT3, or through a compromise agreement reached following advice from a relevant **independent advisor**, such as a lawyer, union official or advice worker. If an advice centre worker is providing the advice, there must have been no payment for it.

By signing a compromise agreement, the employee is barred from bringing or continuing with a claim in relation to the issues specified. Compromised claims can include present and future claims if these are, or could have been contemplated at the time of the agreement (*Byrnell v BT EAT/0383/04*).

However, in the case of *Hinton v University of East London [2005] EWCA Civ 532 ([2005] IRLR 552)*, the Court of Appeal said it was not enough for an agreement to refer to "all claims" in order to compromise any claim the employee might have.

The agreement must clearly indicate the particular proceedings it is compromising. Dr Hinton's claim for whistleblowing was not compromised because there was no mention of public interest disclosure or description of those facts. He could therefore pursue his claim.

If a representative enters into an agreement on an individual's behalf, that individual must have given them authority to do so. In the case of *Gloystarne & Co Ltd v Martin EAT/1008/00 ([2001] IRLR 15)*, Mr Martin was not bound by a settlement agreement made by a union official through Acas because he had not given his consent.

In the case of *Collidge v Freeport [2008] EWCA Civ 485 (2008 IRLR 697)*, the claimant proposed terminating his employment through a compromise agreement. As part of the agreement, the employee warrantied that the company need only pay the sum due if, at the date of signing, he was not aware of conduct on his part that might constitute a breach of contract. The company subsequently refused to pay and began an investigation into Mr Collidge's misuse of expenses and company resources. The Court of Appeal decided that the warranty was a condition precedent of making the payment, and that the company was therefore justified in not making the payments due.

Although the facts of this case are extreme (the employee was a former executive chairman and the sum sought was £500,000), reps are advised to ensure that such warranties are excluded from compromise agreements.

Settlements through Acas

The Advisory, Conciliation and Arbitration Service (Acas) has a general duty to **promote good industrial relations**. It provides advice and guidance on employment issues (particularly through its Codes of practice), runs training events and provides arbitration in collective and individual disputes. Acas also offers a **conciliation** service in employment tribunal claims. When a claim is made to a tribunal, it is copied to Acas; a conciliator then contacts the parties and tries to help them resolve the dispute without the need to go to a hearing.

The *Employment Act 2008* removed set periods of conciliation and Acas will now attempt to settle cases right up to hearing. Acas operates in England, Scotland and Wales. In Northern Ireland, conciliation is through the Labour Relations Agency, and the same set periods for conciliation apply.

Binding arbitration

Acas also operates a voluntary but binding **arbitration scheme**, available as an alternative to taking a tribunal claim in unfair dismissal and flexible working claims.

If a claimant decides to enter into arbitration, they waive their right to pursue the claim in the tribunal or through the courts. The arbitration scheme can only be used **if both parties agree in writing** to resolve the dispute in that way, and if this agreement has been reached either through a conciliation officer or by way of a compromise agreement following independent advice. Both parties must also complete a **waiver** form.

The arbitrator cannot deal with any jurisdictional issues — for example, whether the claimant is an employee, whether they had the necessary continuous service or whether the claim is submitted in time. All these issues are waived.

The arbitrator can make the same awards as a tribunal in unfair dismissal and flexible working claims. However, with arbitration the hearing is **in private** and the outcome **confidential**. There is also **no right to appeal**. The fact that the outcomes of arbitration are private means that it is difficult to compare the results with those achieved through the tribunal system.

More information: See the LRD booklets *Disciplinary and grievance procedures* (£4.20) and *Employment tribunals — complying with the new procedures* (£4.00). *Workplace Report* has regular updates on cases concerning procedural issues.

2. Categories of worker

Employment status

There are legal distinctions between an **employee**, a **worker** and someone who is genuinely **self-employed**. These distinctions are important because individuals have **different statutory employment rights** according to their employment status.

While **contractual rights** can be enforced by anyone who has a contract, regardless of whether or not the contract is in writing, **statutory rights** (which come from a particular statute or piece of legislation) only apply to those specified in that statute.

Individuals who are **self-employed** have few statutory employment rights, but may be covered by anti-discrimination legislation if they have a contract to personally carry out work for someone else.

In addition, **part-time workers** and **fixed-term employees** are protected by specific legislation from less favourable treatment because of their employment status. This is discussed below.

Determining an individual's employment status is far from straightforward, largely because the particular circumstances under which someone agrees to work can be so varied. As a result, there is a large and constantly growing body of case law on the subject.

It is rare that the cases consider each definition. If someone brings an unfair dismissal claim, they need to show that they are an employee; the focus might be on whether they are an employee or self-employed. The list on page 25 sets out the main employment rights applying to workers and employees.

Employee, worker or self-employed?

Definitions of employee and worker vary, and it is important to check the precise definition in the legislation you are relying on to see to whom it applies. Generally, the law defines an employee as someone who works under a **contract of service** (or contract of employment) and a worker as someone who works under a **contract for services**. However, these definitions are not explained so it has been up to judges to explain the difference through case law.

Rights covering all workers

◆ National Minimum Wage (unless excluded on grounds of age or training)
◆ Protection against unlawful pay deductions
◆ Equal pay
◆ Working hours and breaks
◆ Holidays
◆ Right not to be refused work because of union membership
◆ Right to be accompanied at a disciplinary/grievance hearing
◆ Protection against discrimination on all unlawful grounds
◆ Protection against detriment for whistleblowing

Rights covering employees only

◆ Itemised pay statement detailing gross net pay and deductions
◆ Written statement of particulars
◆ Statutory minimum notice
◆ Protection from unfair dismissal
◆ Implied terms (such as mutual trust and confidence)
◆ Time off for union duties and training
◆ Time off for union activities
◆ Time off for safety reps
◆ Time off for public duties
◆ Time off for antenatal care
◆ Statutory maternity pay and leave
◆ Statutory paternity pay and leave
◆ Statutory adoption pay and leave
◆ Parental and dependency leave
◆ Right to request flexible working
◆ Right to request time off for training
◆ Protection in business transfers (TUPE)
◆ Redundancy pay and rights
◆ Guarantee pay on layoffs
◆ Medical suspension pay

The courts have established the concept of **mutuality of obligation** between an employer and an individual who works for the employer.

There must be some obligation on the individual to carry out work, and an obligation on the employer to pay for or provide that work. For example, where an agency worker could decide not to turn up for work any time it suited him and the organisation could dispense with his services whenever it chose to, there was no mutuality of obligation (*Craigie v LB Haringey EAT/0556/06*).

Mutuality of obligation is necessary for there to be any contract at all, so it must be present for both workers and employees. The presence of a mutuality of obligation therefore does not tell you whether someone is an employee or a worker, but if there is no mutuality of obligation then the individual is neither — they could be a casual worker (see "Casual workers" below) or self-employed.

The obligation on the worker/employee is only to provide some work. In the case of *Cotswold Developments Construction Ltd v Williams EAT/0457/05 ([2006] IRLR 181)*, the EAT confirmed that the right to refuse work or to choose to withhold work does not prevent there being mutuality of obligation, as long as there is some obligation on an individual to work and some obligation on the other party to provide or pay for that work.

However, the ability to refuse to work at all indicates a lack of mutuality, as found by the EAT in the case of *Khan v Checkers Cars Ltd EAT/0208/05*:

Mr Khan worked for a company that provided a taxi service at Gatwick Airport. He had his own car and paid his own tax and National Insurance, but had to use set routes and charge set fares. He paid the company a commission and could choose whether or not he wanted to work and what hours to work.

The EAT held that the obligation on an employee is to provide some minimum work and not necessarily to accept work whenever it is offered. However, Khan could choose whether to work at all and therefore was not under an obligation to provide any work, which meant there was no mutuality of obligation. Khan was therefore not an employee.

For both workers and employees, there is also a requirement for the individual to **personally** carry out the work. If they are able to provide a **substitute** to carry out the work, this points to them being self-employed rather than a worker or employee.

In the case of *Real Time Civil Engineering Ltd v Callaghan EAT/0516/05*, the EAT held that a lorry driver was not an employee because he had signed a contract just 18 months previously that said he could send in a substitute — even though he had never exercised that right.

And in *Stevedoring and Haulage Services Ltd v Fuller and others [2001] EWCA Civ 651 ([2001] IRLR 627)*, a term in the contract specifically stating that there was no mutuality of obligation led the Court of Appeal to rule that the dockers could not be employees.

Having established that there is a mutuality of obligation and a requirement to carry out the work personally (which are essential to both), the crucial factor in deciding whether someone is a worker or an employee is likely to be the **degree of control** exercised over them.

This includes, for example, whether the employer stipulates the hours worked and when holidays can be taken; how much direction or supervision the employer exercises; whether the individual is subject to disciplinary and grievance procedures; and whether the individual is entitled to work for anyone else.

In the case of *Younis v Trans Global Projects Ltd & another EAT/0504/05*, a business consultant was found to be a worker but not an employee:

Fathi Younis entered into a three-year consultancy contract, which involved him getting overseas business contacts for the company. He was paid £100 for each day that he carried out such work, and a bonus for any contracts that were secured as a result, but there was no requirement that he worked a specified number of days. In fact he submitted monthly invoices of £3,200, which were always paid. He was free to carry out his own business interests.

Although accepting that Younis was paid a daily rate only when he was actually working for the company, the EAT held that — as the opportunity to work was unlimited and the company had paid the monthly invoices without question — there was the necessary mutuality of obligation for there to be a contract for services.

However, a number of factors, including the lack of control over his work, meant that Younis was not employed under a contract of service. This meant he was a worker and could pursue claims for deduction of wages, holiday pay and race discrimination, but was not an employee so could not claim unfair dismissal or breach of contract.

Where there is a **specific term in the contract** indicating what the employment relationship is, this will be a strong factor in the decision (and was the deciding factor in the Callaghan case on page 26) — but it will not necessarily be conclusive.

Independent contractors

Sometimes the issue is not whether the individual is a worker or an employee, but whether they are **employed** or **self-employed**. Many of these cases arise over claims for **holiday pay**: someone who is genuinely in business on their own account is an independent contractor and has no statutory entitlement to holiday pay, whereas a worker is entitled to paid annual leave under the *Working Time Regulations 1998*. It is therefore in the employer's interests to argue that an individual is self-employed.

Again, there are a number of factors that identify someone who is self-employed as opposed to a worker, or even an employee. Factors that the court or tribunal will take into account include:

◆ what the paperwork says (this could be a job advertisement as well as a contract);

◆ whether the workers provide their own equipment;

◆ whether they can provide a replacement to carry out the work;

◆ whether they have any helpers;

◆ whether they have taken on any financial risk;

◆ whether they receive sick pay or holiday pay;

◆ whether they are responsible for their own expenses; and

◆ whether they are responsible for their own tax and National Insurance.

These all relate to the essential questions the tribunal has to answer, which are whether there is a mutuality of obligation, whether the worker is required to carry out the work personally and what degree of control they have over the way they carry it out. Without those, the individual cannot be a worker, as explained above.

A yacht skipper who exercised a level of control and freedom over how he worked, and who was treated as self-employed for tax and National Insurance purposes, was an independent contractor and not an employee. *Haine v Rolls Royce EAT/0028/04*

But a gym worker who asked to be self-employed and paid tax on a self-employed basis was an employee on account of the control exercised by her employer, which included setting her hours and disciplining her (*London Fitness Consultancy v Hickson EAT/0160/05*).

The one factor that might prove conclusive by itself is whether the individual can provide a replacement to do the work, because this means they are not required to carry out the work personally. If an employer asks an employee to sign a contract with a clause saying that the employee is able to provide a substitute, this could deprive them of statutory employment rights.

In the case of *R J Prentice Brickwork v O'Brien EAT/1086/02*, the EAT accepted that the law allows employers to avoid having to pay for holidays simply by inserting the right to hire a substitute:

Mr O'Brien was a bricklayer whose contract gave him an absolute right to provide a substitute to do his work. When he was made up to chargehand, he argued that this meant in practice that he could no longer engage a substitute; therefore, he said he was a worker and entitled to holiday pay. But the EAT held this was not the case: it said that the express term in his contract was clear and was not overruled by his becoming a chargehand.

Check to make sure that your employer is not inserting a clause in your contract allowing you to provide a substitute as a way of avoiding having to provide some employment rights. However, if the contract says that you can arrange for a substitute but only with the employer's approval, this does not give you a blanket right to send someone else to do the work and therefore you can still be a worker (*Byrne Brothers (Formwork) Ltd v Baird and others EAT/542/01 ([2002] IRLR 96)*).

The Court of Appeal ruled that bricklayers working for the Redrow group were workers, despite the employer's argument that they did not have to carry out the work personally and therefore were self-employed. They had been issued with standard subcontractors' contracts that said they "must at all times provide sufficient labour", but the court held that this was not a right to provide a substitute. It pointed out that they were paid weekly and given individual contracts, which suggested that they were expected to carry out the work personally. They were workers and so were entitled to holiday pay. (*Redrow Homes (Yorkshire) v Wright; Redrow Homes (North West) v Roberts [2004] EWCA Civ 469 ([2004] IRLR 720)*).

Autoclenz contracted with (supposedly self-employed) individuals to clean cars for British Car Auctions. The individuals were paid on a piecework basis and were responsible for their own tax and National Insurance Contributions. The company supplied cleaning materials and group insurance, in respect of which it deducted sums from the weekly pay. The valeters wore overalls, originally with the company's logo, but latterly with that of BCA. The individuals' claim that they were employees was rejected by the EAT. Specifically, the EAT found that there was no evidence that the contractual clauses which set out that the individuals could substitute themselves with another and weren't required to accept offers of work, were a sham. However, the EAT did find that the claimants were workers and they were therefore entitled to the national minimum wage and holiday pay.

The Court of Appeal decided that the claimants were employees as well as workers in the wider sense. Legally it is not necessary to show both parties intended to mislead anyone in order to prove a written contract is a sham. It is not a question of what happened in practice (though this may be an indicator), but a matter of looking at all the evidence to decide what the intentions of the parties and the true legal position actually were. The employment judge had decided on the facts that there was a mutual obligation to offer and undertake work, and an obligation of personal service without substitution. Autoclenz also exercised a high degree of control over the work. The elements of a contract of employment were therefore proved and the claimants were employees. (*Autoclenz v Belcher UKEAT/0160/08/DA*).

Casual workers

Individuals who work on a casual basis may find it difficult to argue that they have "worker" or "employee" status, because there will not be a mutuality of obligation. In the case of *Carmichael v National Power [1999] UKHL 47 [2000] IRLR 43*, the House of Lords held that casuals working as guides for National Power were self-employed because their contracts referred to them working "on a casual, as required basis". The same principle was applied in the case of *Kendal & others v Caley Fisheries EAT/0507/04*:

Mrs Kendal and her colleagues worked as scallop-cutters, a job in which the amount of work varied from day to day and week to week. The employer would leave a message on an answerphone, which the workers could phone to find out whether there was work available for the following day; they could then decide whether or not they wanted to do it. The EAT rejected the argument that Kendal and her colleagues had been continuously employed on a series of contracts of employment, each lasting for a day. There had been no mutuality of obligation, it said, because they had not been obliged to accept work that was available. Therefore, they had not been employed under a contract of service.

But a casual worker who had worked part of every week for three years **was** found to be an employee and had the right to claim unfair dismissal (*Vernon v Event Management Catering Ltd UKEAT/0161/07*). And in the following case, the EAT held that a relief area manager was an employee even though his contract stated there would be times when no work was available and he was not paid during these periods:

William Wilson was required to cover for holidays and sickness absences. His contract said that there would be occasions when no work was available. It also contained overtime, holiday and sickness provisions and provided a pension scheme. It provided grievance and disciplinary procedures and required both parties to give notice and had provisions for exclusivity and confidentiality. The EAT said that a number of factors pointed to an employment relationship — for example, Wilson was integrated into the organisation and was paid net of tax and National Insurance, and the company exercised a substantial degree of control over the way he carried out his work. The EAT held that, if there was work available, the employer had to offer it and Wilson had to do it. This made him an employee. *Wilson v Circular Distributors Ltd EAT/0043/05 ([2006] IRLR 38)*

Homeworkers

There is nothing in principle that prevents a homeworker from being a worker or an employee. Their employment status will be decided on the same basis as set out above. However, it may be particularly difficult to demonstrate that there is the necessary control to establish employment status, as was shown in the long-running case of *Bridges and others v Industrial Rubber EAT/0150/04*:

Mrs Bridges and seven other women brought claims including unfair dismissal and redundancy against Industrial Rubber, for whom they had worked at home trimming excess rubber from moulded products. In January 2003, Industrial Rubber had issued a new contract to the homeworkers, stating that the company was under no obligation to offer work and the homeworker would be under no obligation to accept any work offered. The EAT was critical of the way the contract had been introduced, but held that the homeworkers were bound by its terms. The contract was the deciding factor on the issue; however, the EAT said that, even if this had not been the case, Industrial Rubber had not had enough supervisory control over the work for there to be a relationship of employer and employee.

Volunteers

Volunteers are not employees if they do not receive any pay or benefits other than their expenses. The EAT held in the case of *SE Sheffield CAB v Grayson EAT/283/03 ([2004] IRLR 353)* that volunteer advisors could not be employees because their lack of payment in return for offering their work meant that there could be no contract of employment. And the EAT reached a similar conclusion in the case of *Melhuish v Redbridge CAB EAT/0130/04*:

Mr Melhuish was an unpaid voluntary worker for a Citizens Advice Bureau and brought a claim of unfair dismissal. The EAT held that there was no contract at all because there was no "consideration". The legal principle that a promise made for nothing is not binding requires both parties to a contract to bring something of value to it — this is what is known as "consideration". In an employment context, consideration is usually wages on one part and the supply of work on the other. Although consideration does not have to be money, the EAT said the opportunity to attend training courses was not consideration.

Voluntary workers are specifically excluded from the *National Minimum Wage Regulations* (see "National Minimum Wage" in Chapter 4).

Young workers

The *Working Time Regulations 1998* give young workers (those under 18 but above school leaving age) the right to a **rest break** of at least 30 minutes, consecutive if possible, after four-and-a-half hours' work, in addition to a **daily break** of at least 12 hours and at least two days off a week. In most cases, young workers are prohibited from working **nights**; where they are allowed to do so, the employer has to undertake a health assessment.

Young workers' working time must not exceed eight hours a day or 40 hours a week. These hours cannot be averaged over a longer period, and young workers cannot individually opt out of the requirements. In addition, where a young person works for more than one employer, working hours are aggregated and must be within the overall maximum.

Those aged under 18 who work with dangerous machines and substances have limited statutory protection under the *Factory Acts*. When carrying out risk assessments and deciding what work is suitable for them, employers are legally obliged to take particular account of young people's inexperience.

Apprentices

An employer takes on an **apprentice** to provide that person with the training and work experience necessary to qualify in a particular trade, usually over a number of years. An apprentice is in a special position in respect of employment rights: an employer **cannot dismiss** them before the end of that contract except in very limited circumstances. Unlike an individual with an ordinary employment contract, an apprentice cannot be dismissed for redundancy or for misconduct.

An apprentice who is dismissed before the end of their contract may be able to claim damages for loss of training and status as well as loss of earnings for the remainder of the apprenticeship.

The Court of Appeal was called upon to decide whether a **"modern apprenticeship"** — where training is provided by an external provider and work experience by an employer — fits the traditional apprenticeship criteria. The court held that it did:

Liam Flett signed up to an individual learning plan (ILP) to become a qualified electrician: his employer would pay him wages and would give him work experience and access to training by a government-funded external trainer over a period of four years.

Flett was dismissed without notice before the end of his training and claimed that, having been denied the opportunity to become a qualified electrician, he was entitled to loss of earnings for the remainder of his apprenticeship as well as damages for the loss of training and status. He estimated these losses at £50,000.

The Court of Appeal held that a modern apprenticeship is not fundamentally different from a traditional apprenticeship. It appeared (although the tribunal would have to consider some additional evidence) that Flett was working under an apprenticeship that could only be ended if he was unable to meet the standard necessary to progress (*Flett v Matheson [2006] EWCA Civ 53 ([2005] IRLR 412)*).

Children

Children under the age of 13 years cannot be employed in any capacity. Thirteen-year-olds can do **light work** that is not harmful to their health and safety, school attendance or other factors, and which is permitted under local authority bye-laws.

There are strict limits on the **working hours** of children under 16. Fourteen-year-olds can work up to five hours on weekdays and Saturdays during the school holidays. In all, they cannot do more than 25 hours a week.

Fifteen-year-olds can do up to eight hours a day and 35 hours a week, again during the school holidays. A child under the age of 16 cannot work more than two hours on a school day or Sunday. They cannot work in **industrial undertakings**, including transport, street trading, merchant shipping or mining. Employers must have carried out a risk assessment before offering employment to a child or young person.

Children have the right to a **rest break** of at least an hour in any shift lasting more than four hours, and to a **two-week break** from any work during school holidays. Bye-laws regarding the employment of children should be available from your local authority.

Part-time workers

The *Part-Time Workers (Prevention of Less Favourable Treatment) Regulations 2000* (PTWR) define a part-time worker as any worker whose hours are less than those of a full-time worker. This definition would even cover workers on **"zero hours"** contracts who have no fixed hours at all.

Anyone defined as a part-time worker has the right to be treated no less favourably than a comparable full-time worker. This includes the right to the same **contractual benefits**, such as pay and holiday (although these can be made pro rata to the hours worked), and the right not to be subjected to any other detriment.

If the reason for the less favourable treatment is unrelated to the worker's being part-time, there is no protection under the regulations (*Gibson v The Scottish Ambulance Service EAT/0052/04*).

If an employer can show that its less favourable treatment of part-time workers is **justified on objective grounds**, this will provide them with a defence against a claim under the PTWR.

When considering claims of less favourable treatment, tribunals consider the following questions:

◆ what is the treatment complained of?
◆ is it less favourable than that of a full-time worker?
◆ is the treatment less favourable because the worker is part-time?
◆ is there any objective justification for the less favourable treatment?

A claim under the PTWR is based on a comparison with an equivalent full-time worker known as the **comparator**. (The decision in *Carl v University of Sheffield UKEAT/0261/08/CEA* established that hypothetical comparators cannot be used for claims under the PTWR).

The case of *England v The Governing Body of Turnford School*

EAT/438/02 shows that it is important to make sure that the comparator works equivalent full-time hours:

Ms England claimed that she was treated less favourably than full-time workers. The workers whom she had identified as her comparators worked nearly twice as many hours as she did: she worked 18 hours a week while they worked 35. However, the employer was able to show that contractual "full-time" hours were actually 37, even though no one worked those hours; the workers were therefore not suitable comparators.

As well as being full-time, the comparator must be employed under the **same type of contract** and be engaged in **the same or broadly similar work** as the part-time worker who is bringing the claim. Guidance on this was given by the House of Lords in early 2006, in a case brought by the FBU firefighters' union on behalf of its retained firefighters:

The Lords said it was wrong to focus on small differences between the full-time and part-time roles when overall the jobs were substantially the same; a tribunal must always look at the roles as a whole, and should also only take qualifications, skills and experience into account in so far as they are relevant to the work undertaken at the time. In that case, the Lords held that the work done by retained and whole time firefighters is comparable for the purposes of the PTWR (*Matthews and others v Kent and Medway Towns Fire Authority and others ([2006] UKHL 8 ([2006] IRLR 367)*)

Part-time workers have the right to the **same pension arrangements** as full-time workers. In the case of *Preston v Wolverhampton Healthcare NHS Trust EAT/1069/02 [2004] IRLR96*, the EAT held that excluding part-time workers from joining an occupational pension scheme was unlawful.

However, the ruling makes it clear that employers can make it necessary for part-time workers to take steps to exercise their option to join the pension scheme, even though entry may be automatic for full-time workers without them being required to take any action. Trade union representatives need to be aware of this ruling, and to ensure that part-time workers are told what their rights are and how to exercise them.

The European Court of Justice (ECJ), in the case of *Steinicke v Bundesanstalt für Arbeit C-77/02 ([2003] IRLR 892)*, held that European law does not prevent pension rights for part-time workers being **calculated pro rata**, as long as the way that the calculation is done does not mean that the part-time worker gets proportionately less. However, in the case of *Trustees of Uppingham School Retirement Benefits Scheme for Non-Teaching Staff v Shillcock [2002] EWHC 641 ([2002] IRLR 702)*, the High Court ruled that the exclusion of workers earning less than the National Insurance threshold was justified, even though the outcome was to exclude proportionately more part-time workers.

Part-time workers attending union training should get paid for all the hours on the course (see "Rights to time off" in Chapter 5). However, part-time workers are not necessarily entitled to pay if the course occurs on their days off (i.e. on days when they would not have been at work): *Calder v Secretary of State for Work and Pensions UKEAT/0512/08/LA*.

In relation to **overtime pay**, it is not contrary to equal treatment laws to pay enhanced rates only when the part-timer has completed the full-time hours (*Stadt Lengerich v Helmig [1995] IRLR 216*).

Nor are part-time workers entitled to have account taken of previous years they had worked full-time when their redundancy pay is calculated (*Barry v Midland Bank [1997] EWCA Civ 3037 [1999] IRLR 581*). However, in one case where a part-time worker had to work proportionately more hours than a full-time worker before qualifying for overtime pay (the *Elsner-Lakeberg* case, see below), the ECJ held that this amounted to sex discrimination.

Edeltraud Elsner-Lakeberg was a part-time teacher. All teachers' contracts said that they did not get paid for the first three hours of overtime in a month. As a result, Elsner-Lakeberg had to do proportionately more work before being entitled to overtime pay. The ECJ held that this amounted to unlawful discrimination. *Elsner-Lakeberg v Land Nordrhein-Westfalen C-285/02 ([2005] IRLR 209)*

A part-time worker who claims to have received less favourable treatment has the right to ask the employer for a **written statement** of the reasons for the difference in treatment, and may take a claim of less favourable treatment to an employment tribunal. Less favourable treatment of part-time workers can also amount to indirect **sex discrimination** (see Chapter 6) or unequal pay if it adversely affects more of one sex than the other.

A claim for the right to work part-time could be taken under sex discrimination law or under the *Flexible Working Regulations* (see "Flexible working" in Chapter 8). However, each case will depend on its facts. In the case of *MoD v MacMillan EAT/0003/04*, the EAT held that refusing an employee the right to work part-time did not amount to sex discrimination. But another employee who was denied the right to work part-time succeeded in her sex discrimination claim because her employer had failed to show that her job could not have been done as a job share (*Hardys & Hansons plc v Lax [2005] EWCA Civ 846 ([2005] IRLR 7261)*).

Temporary employees

Employees on **fixed-term contracts** (also known as temporary employees) are entitled to equivalent rights and treatment as permanent employees under the *Fixed-term Employees (Prevention of Less Favourable Treatment) Regulations 2002* (FTER).

Fixed-term employees are those working for a **specified period of time** or those employed to undertake and complete a **specified task**. The UK regulations apply only to employees, and agency workers are specifically excluded (regulation 19). A contract is still for a fixed term even if it contains a clause that would give either party the option to end it earlier:

Fixed-term employee Mr Allen was dismissed, but his employer did not follow the procedures that would have applied to a permanent employee. His contract had a clause that said the contract could be terminated by notice. The employer argued that the regulations could not apply to this contract, since its termination clause meant it was not really for a fixed term. However, the EAT disagreed (*Allen v National Australia Group Europe EAT/0102/03 ([2004] IRLR 847)*).

Fixed-term employees have the right to **paid holidays**, pro rata to the length of their contract. In cases where they work on more than one fixed-term contract, their service is added together to assess rights to holiday pay. The regulations cover all **contractual terms**, including pay and pensions. However, each particular term does not have to be the same as for a permanent employee, as long as the **overall employment package** is no less favourable.

Fixed-term employees have the right to a written statement of their main contractual terms, and to guarantee pay and medical suspension pay (see

Chapter 4), in the same way as permanent staff. The right to no less favourable treatment extends to qualifying periods for employment benefits and opportunities for training and permanent employment. Fixed-term employees also have the right not to be subjected to **any other detriment** because of their temporary employment status.

Fixed-term employees can compare their treatment with that of permanent staff employed by the same employer, so long as they are doing the **same or similar work** and are working at the same establishment. If there is no comparable employee at that establishment, a comparison can be made with the pay and benefits package of comparable employees at other locations.

Employers can legally **justify less favourable treatment** if they have a good reason. For example, they may be able to justify excluding a fixed-term employee from the occupational pension scheme on the grounds that the contribution would be too low to be viable.

Controversially, Department for Business, Innovation and Skills (BIS) guidance states that it would not be necessary for the employee to be paid the value of the pension contribution that the employer would have made.

Fixed-term employees who believe they have been less favourably treated have the right to ask for a **written statement** explaining the difference in treatment. This can be used as evidence in a tribunal.

If a temporary employee has been working continuously under a single contract that has been renewed at least once, or under a series of contracts, for four or more years, they will become a permanent employee unless the employer can justify continuing to employ them on a temporary basis.

Temporary employees who are employed for a short period can lose out on employment rights that are dependent on length of service, such as unfair dismissal rights that apply only if the employee has worked for at least a year. But those who work on a series of temporary contracts with short gaps between each may be able to establish continuity of service (see "Qualifying for unfair dismissal rights" in Chapter 10).

The dismissal of fixed-term employees on the grounds of having asserted their rights under the regulations is automatically unfair, and the employee can bring a claim even if they have worked less than a year and would thus be excluded from normal unfair dismissal claims. However, the ending of a fixed-term contract does not, of itself, amount to less favourable treatment.

In the case of *Webley v Department for Work and Pensions [2004] EWCA 1745 ([2005] IRLR 288)*, the Court of Appeal held that a decision not to renew a 51-week fixed-term contract (i.e. a contract designed to prevent an employee gaining sufficient service to be able to claim unfair dismissal) was not unlawful under the FTER.

Less favourable treatment of fixed-term employees can also amount to **indirect sex discrimination** (see Chapter 6) or unequal pay if it adversely affects more of one sex than the other:

Karen Whiffen, a schoolteacher employed on a series of temporary contracts, did not have her contract renewed. The school wanted to make redundancies and decided to get rid of the temporary staff first. It was only after that stage that they applied the redundancy selection criteria. The Court of Appeal held that the policy of dismissing fixed-term contract holders had a greater impact on women teachers in the school than on men, and was therefore indirectly discriminatory (*Whiffen v Milham Ford Girls' School [2001] EWCA Civ 385 ([2001] IRLR 468)*)

Temporary employees also have the same protection as permanent staff against discrimination on the grounds of **pregnancy and maternity**. A temporary employee cannot be dismissed, refused renewal of her contract or refused employment for these reasons, according to the ECJ in the cases of *Tele-Danmark v Handels C-109/00 ([2001] IRLR 853) and Jimenez Melgar v Ayuntamiento de Los Barrios C-438/99 ([2001] IRLR 848)*.

Employers can no longer require employees to sign a waiver of dismissal or redundancy rights when beginning or renewing a temporary contract. A temporary employee who is made redundant and who has worked for the employer for two or more years is entitled to redundancy pay.

Agency workers

The **conduct of employment agencies** is governed by the *Employment Agencies Act 1973* and the *Conduct of Employment Agencies and Employment Businesses Regulations 2003*. These laws make it unlawful for an agency to charge a worker to find them work (with a very few exceptions, including performers, models and professional sports people), and place limits on the right of agencies to charge fees where a temp placed by the agency is offered a permanent job with the employer. They also require an agency to inform its workers of the method and calculation of pay and holiday entitlement, and make it unlawful for an agency to withhold pay if a worker cannot produce a **time sheet**.

Most agency workers will meet the statutory definition of a worker (see page 24) and will be entitled to the statutory rights given to **all workers** — including protection against discrimination and victimisation on grounds of trade union membership.

Also, the *Working Time Regulations 1998* and *National Minimum Wage Act 1998* include special provisions to cover agency workers who would not meet this definition, making sure that all agency workers are entitled to these basic rights including holidays. Furthermore, since 27 October 2008, under the *Fixed-term Employees (Prevention of Less Favourable Treatment) (Amendment) Regulations 2008*, agency workers on contracts of up to three months duration, are entitled to Statutory Sick Pay (SSP).

It is possible for an agency worker to be deemed to be an employee, either of the agency or the end user, giving them much greater employment rights — including the right to claim unfair dismissal — but recent case law illustrates that this will be unusual.

The principle that an agency worker can be an employee of the end user was endorsed by the Court of Appeal in the case of *Brook Street Bureau (UK) Ltd v Dacas [2004] EWCA Civ 217 ([2004] IRLR 358)*, concerning a cleaner who had worked for a local authority for four years until she was replaced while on sick leave.

The Court of Appeal said that although she was not an employee of the agency there could have been an implied contract of employment between Dacas and the council. Unfortunately, as Dacas had not appealed on that point no decision on that was made.

But the EAT has said it will be "rare" for a contract of employment to be implied between an agency worker and the end user, and its judgment was upheld by the Court of Appeal (*James v London Borough of Greenwich [2008] EWCA Civ 35*). In that case, the court found there were clear contractual terms between the worker and the agency and none with the council and said it was only necessary to imply terms when none existed.

This is most likely to happen in a case where agency arrangements are set up as a sham to disguise a continuing contractual relationship, or where the parties have intended to change the contractual relationship but not succeeded in doing so.

This happened in the case of Patrick Muscat, who was dismissed and re-engaged as a contractor in order to reduce staffing levels; the Court of Appeal held he was still an employee (*Cable & Wireless v Muscat [2006] EWCA Civ 220 ([2006] IRLR 354)*).

Future rights

The *Agency Workers Regulations 2010* (which implement the Agency Workers Directive) are expected to come into force on 1 October 2011 — although they remain subject to amendment. Under the current regulations, agency workers who have worked in the same post for 12 weeks for the same end-user, will acquire important new rights. Specifically, they will be entitled to benefit from the same principle working conditions as a comparable employee who has been recruited by the end-user.

The definition of an agency worker in the regulations, covers someone who is an employee of an agency and someone who personally carries out work for the agency. It does not extend to someone who is self-employed, employed on a managed service contract, or employed via their own company.

Although there is a twelve week qualifying period, in order to deter abuse, how this amount of service is calculated has been broadly drafted. Where there is a break between the work the agency worker carries out for one particular end-user, the separate periods may be aggregated and counted towards the twelve week qualifying period. Specifically, the agency worker's work shall be treated as continuous if the break is for less than six weeks or is due to the individual taking sick leave (for up to 28 weeks), leave for a reason connected to pregnancy or childbirth (including maternity leave and maternity suspension), paternity leave, adoption leave, seasonal shutdown, closure due to a strike or lock-out, or jury service.

Also, even if the agency worker changes role, their period of continuous service is not necessarily broken. In particular, work in the new role will only be treated as part of a separate qualifying period from the previous role in certain circumstances. Firstly, the role must be substantially different from the previous role, and secondly, the agency will need to have written to the worker explaining the work they will be performing in the new role.

Additionally there is an anti-avoidance provision (regulation 9). Where there is a deliberate attempt to prevent an agency worker from acquiring the right to equal treatment with directly employed colleagues, the agency worker will be deemed to have met the qualifying conditions.

For example, where an agency worker is hired for a period of 11 weeks, then dropped for seven weeks, then rehired for 11 weeks — they will be treated as being entitled to equal treatment. Furthermore, the entity responsible for such an arrangement (i.e. the agency and/or end-user) could be ordered to pay compensation to the individual concerned (additional to any other award due) of up to £5,000.

Where an agency worker does meet the qualifying conditions, s/he will be entitled to the same principle conditions, as his or her directly hired colleagues. This right to parity extends to working time issues (i.e. a right to the same breaks and rest periods, the same night work protection, as well as a right to the same contractual holidays — the above statutory entitlement portion being payable in lieu.

Pay which is related to the individual's performance is also covered (e.g. shift allowances, commission and overtime). However, pay not related to performance (e.g. company sick pay, maternity pay, paternity pay, redundancy pay, and pension contributions) are excluded. Also, there won't be an entitlement for an agency worker to insist on working the same number of hours as a directly hired colleague.

However, certain rights are not dependent on any qualifying conditions and will accrue from the beginning of an agency worker's assignment. Specifically, pregnant workers will be automatically entitled to paid time off for antenatal care, to be the beneficiary of a risk assessment, and to be offered alternative work if suspended on maternity grounds. Agency workers will (irrespective of their length of service) also be entitled to access collective facilities such as a workplace crèche or canteen — unless the refusal of the employer to share these facilities is objectively justified.

All agency workers will also have the right to have the end-user keep them informed about any suitable vacancies that the end-user has (regulation 13).

If an agency worker (who has met the qualifying conditions) believes that s/he is receiving less favourable principle working conditions than someone directly hired by the end-user, s/he is entitled to challenge the agency (and if no response is forthcoming, subsequently the end-user).

Specifically, if s/he submits a written request for an explanation of his or her treatment, the agency/end-user must respond within 28 days. The agency/end-user's response, or lack of it, will be taken into account by a tribunal examining a subsequent claim on this matter brought by the individual. The time limit for lodging a complaint with an employment tribunal will be three months.

Crown employees

Crown employees (those who work for government departments and agencies including civil servants) are entitled to most of the statutory rights set out in the *Employment Rights Act 1996* except for redundancy and collective consultation rights, minimum notice and insolvency payments. Instead they have equivalent or better rights under agreements within their own employment.

Certain categories of Crown employees have, in some circumstances, alternative avenues for pursuing legal claims. For example, if prison officers and the police (including British Transport Police) are dismissed, the remedy lies not through the tribunals but by way of a special complaints body.

They are entitled to be treated no less favourably than they would have been by the employment tribunals, or to be given the reasons why they were not (*R v Civil Service Appeal Board ex parte Cunningham [1991] IRLR 297*).

The *Criminal Justice and Public Order Act 1994* places prison officers in the same category as the police, and section 127 of that Act removes their right to strike. Although section 127 was disapplied in the public sector in England, Wales and Scotland, the government has re-introduced a strike ban for prison officers in England and Wales and it still applies in Northern Ireland and in the private sector everywhere.

Scotland still has a voluntary agreement that prison officers will not take industrial action.

Working outside the UK

With closer ties developing between European states, more workers will find themselves working outside the UK at some point. Under the European Posting of Workers Directive 1996, which came into force in the UK at the end of 1999, all workers temporarily working in a EU state have the right to the same statutory minimum terms and conditions as those permanently working in that state.

Employment disputes are brought in the courts of the place where the employee habitually carries out their work, in accordance with the Brussels Convention.

In the case of *Weber v Universal Ogden Services C-37/00 ([2002] IRLR 365)*, the ECJ held that this is the state where the employee has worked the longest, except where the employee had worked in a number of states but had recently settled in one.

The sex, race and disability discrimination Acts were amended by the *Equal Opportunities (Employment Legislation) (Territorial Limits) Regulations 1999* so that they now include workers who work some of their time outside Great Britain.

A ruling by the House of Lords in January 2006 made it possible for some employees working outside Great Britain to bring claims of unfair dismissal in the UK. The ruling was made in relation to three separate cases heard together.

The Lords said that, although it is unusual for an employee who works abroad to come under UK law, there are exceptions — such as when an employee is posted abroad for a business carried on in Great Britain, or when someone is working in a British enclave in a foreign country:

Stephen Lawson worked as a security supervisor at an RAF base on Ascension Island, John Botham was a youth worker at Ministry of Defence bases in Germany, and George Crofts was an aircrew member for Hong Kong airline Cathay Pacific who was based at Heathrow.

The Lords held that Lawson and Botham were "expatriate" employees whose work abroad had strong connections with Great Britain, and Crofts was a "peripatetic" employee whose work constantly took him to different places but whose tour of duty always began and ended in London.

In all cases, they said, the focus must be on where the employee works at the time of dismissal. All three were entitled to bring their claims in the UK. *Serco Ltd v Lawson; Botham v MoD; Crofts & others v Veta Ltd & others [2006] UKHL 3*

More information: See the LRD booklets *Contracts of employment* (£4.70), *Temporary workers* (£3.70) and *Part-time workers* (£3.40). *Workplace Report* has quarterly updates on contracts.

3. Starting work and the employment contract

References and employer checks

Most employers require a reference before they will employ someone. Young workers starting work for the first time are likely to come with references from school or college, plus examination results. But from then on, job offers will generally rely on employer references.

An employer generally has no obligation to provide a reference, but an employer that does provide one has a duty of care to make sure it is **accurate and not misleading**. If it is not accurate because the employer has not taken proper care, the worker can bring a claim for **negligence** in the civil courts for any resulting financial loss (*Spring v Guardian Assurance [1994] IRLR 460*).

It is not fair and reasonable for a reference to include information about complaints against an employee if these have not been brought to the employee's attention — and this also gives grounds for **constructive dismissal** (see page 203), if the reference is provided by an employer for a current employee (*TSB Bank v Harris [2000] IRLR 157*). However, the reference does not need to be comprehensive (*Kidd v Axa Equity [1999] EWHC QB 184 [2000] IRLR 301*).

There is no legal obligation on the employer to provide a **good reference**. If a poor reference means that an individual does not obtain employment, there is no breach of the duty of care, provided the employer has ensured that the reference is accurate, not misleading and not malicious (*Kirk v Legal and General [2001] EWCA Civ 1803 [2002] IRLR 124*).

Although an employer does not have to give a reference, they may be breaking the law if they refuse to do so **because the worker has made a claim** against them. In the case of *Jones v 3M Healthcare and others EAT/0714/00*, the EAT held that three disabled workers denied or given poor references by their ex-employers because they had previously brought discrimination claims had been unlawfully discriminated against. The failure to provide a reference amounted to **victimisation** (see Chapter 6).

But it is not unlawful for the employer to refuse to provide a reference because it wants to protect its position in legal proceedings, according to the House of Lords in the case of *Chief Constable of West Yorkshire Police v Khan [2001] UKHL 48 ([2001] IRLR 830.* It held that the reason the police refused to provide a reference was not because Khan had brought a discrimination claim, but because they were trying to protect themselves in the litigation of that claim. Even though this was less favourable treatment, the Lords said, it was not victimisation because the evidence was that the police would provide a reference after the case had finished.

If an employer has made a **job offer subject to a satisfactory reference** being obtained, the contract will not take effect unless or until this happens. The prospective employer can decide whether the reference is satisfactory; the test is a subjective one (*Wishart v NACAB [1990] IRLR 393*). There is nothing to prevent an employer asking for references from people other than those the employee has nominated (*Purvis v Luminar Leisure Ltd t/a Chicago Rock Cafe EAT/1332/99*).

Although it is usually for the employer to decide whether or not the reference is satisfactory, this cannot be used as an excuse to dismiss an employee for a discriminatory reason.

In the case of *Halai v Integrated Asian Advice Service EAT/0855/03*, a female outreach worker was ostensibly dismissed as the result of a poor reference provided after she had begun work, but the Employment Appeal Tribunal (EAT) said the real reason was that she had claimed that she should be paid equal pay with a man doing the same job.

Since 1997 it has been a criminal offence for an employer to employ someone who has no legal right to work in the UK under the Asylum and *Immigration Act 1996*, which required employers to check a person's entitlement to work before employing them. The government introduced stricter controls through the *Immigration, Asylum and Nationality Act 2006* (IANA) which apply to the recruitment of workers. This law means that employers will continue to ask potential recruits for documentation that proves their right to live or work in the UK, which can include a passport, birth certificate or certificate of registration. However, it introduced two new offences for employers: one of negligently employing an illegal worker, which is a civil offence with financial penalties; and one of deliberately employing an illegal worker, which is punishable by a fine and/or imprisonment.

Employers should ask all job applicants to prove their entitlement to work in the UK, as selecting only some individuals based on assumptions about their right to work may amount to race discrimination.

It has been quite common for employers to state that a job offer is subject to receipt of a satisfactorily completed health questionnaire. However, under section 60, *Equality Act 2010* (expected to come into force in October 2010) it will be unlawful for employers to continue this practice. Specifically, job applicants won't be able to ask job applicants disability or health-related questions (except in certain circumstances). The Equality and Human Rights Commission is responsible for enforcement.

Criminal convictions

The *Rehabilitation of Offenders Act 1974* says that individuals whose convictions are regarded as "spent" after a period of rehabilitation do not have to declare those convictions when applying for a job, unless they work in certain specified areas of work such as nursing or teaching. Section 4(3)(b) of the Act also makes it unfair to dismiss someone because of a spent conviction, or to prejudice their employment in any way.

The **period of rehabilitation** varies according to the sentence and the age when convicted, although sentences of at least 30 months served in a prison, youth custody or a young offenders' institution are never spent. The different periods of rehabilitation are set out in section 5 of the Act: for example, a conviction of less than six months' imprisonment would be spent after seven years:

In the case of *Wood v Coverage Care [1996] IRLR 264*, an employee with past convictions was made redundant. The EAT held that her employer was entitled to refuse to consider her for alternative employment in a residential home for the elderly, an area of employment where convictions were never spent. The fact that her duties were only administrative was not relevant.

Although in most cases it is unfair to dismiss someone because of a spent conviction, an employee will still need to meet the normal qualifying conditions for unfair dismissal (see Chapter 10) in order to bring a claim. If a conviction is not spent, but the employer has not asked for details of convictions, there is no obligation on the employee to disclose it.

Under the *Police Act 1997*, employers have the right to ask job applicants to disclose criminal record certificates. There are two types of **disclosure** — "enhanced" where checks are needed on job applicants working with children, the elderly or vulnerable, and "standard" for other types of work. Checks are carried out by the Criminal Records Bureau, whose Code of Practice on disclosure of information is available at: www.crb. gov.uk/PDF/Code%20of%20Practice.pdf.

The employment contract

The employment contract is fundamental in any employment relationship because it sets out the terms and conditions under which the work is to be done. Employees should know what those terms are and how to enforce them.

Once an employer has offered a job and the employee has accepted it, there is a legal contract, even if there is **nothing in writing**. If the employer subsequently withdraws the offer, the employee may be able to claim damages for breach of contract (*Sarker v South Tees Acute Hospitals [1997] IRLR 328*).

In most cases, damages are limited to the length of notice required to terminate the contract legally. But if the contract is for a fixed period of time and there is nothing allowing for it to be ended earlier, damages could be recovered for the whole period, as the High Court ruled in *Gill and others v Cape Contracts [1985] IRLR 499*.

Although a verbal offer and acceptance can still be binding, proving it may be difficult. In the case of *Wright v Canterbury Christ Church University College EAT/0428/04*, the EAT held that an offer is binding if a "reasonable person" would infer from the words that the employer intended to be bound by the offer once it was accepted — whether or not this was actually the employer's intention.

To enforce the contract, you need to know **who the employer is**. This should be given in your written statement (see below). Employees of charities and voluntary organisations are likely to be employed by the management committee, although the individuals on that committee may change (*Affleck v Newcastle Mind [1999] IRLR 405*). A company that argued it was not an individual's employer in an attempt to avoid liability for unpaid wages was given short shrift by the EAT, as its name appeared on the wage slips (*Alternative Welding Services Ltd v Knox EAT/0099/04*).

Local authorities generally employ teachers, even though there may be local management of schools (*Askew v Governing Body of Clifton Middle School [1999] IRLR 708*). But school governing bodies can be the employer in some cases. Local authorities are liable for the actions of elected councillors where these affect the ability of employees to carry out their duties (*Moores v Bude-Stratton EAT/313/99 ([2000] IRLR 676)*).

Under sections 1 and 2 of the *Employment Rights Act 1996* (ERA 96), employees have the right to a **written statement of particulars** of their employment. This must be given to the employee no later than two months after their employment begins, and must include:

◆ the names of the employer and the employee;
◆ the date on which employment began and the period of **continuous employment**;
◆ the scale and rate of **remuneration**, pay intervals and the method of calculating pay;
◆ terms and conditions relating to **hours of work** and **holiday entitlement** (including public holidays);
◆ the **job title or description**; and
◆ the employee's **place of work**.

These must all be detailed in a single document. However, provided that they are given within the two-month deadline, other employment particulars can be documented by instalments. These are:

◆ whether employment is **permanent** or for a **fixed term**;
◆ details of **sickness**, **pensions** and **notice**;
◆ details of the employer's **disciplinary and grievance procedures** (see "Disciplinary procedures" in Chapter 10);
◆ details of **collective agreements** affecting employment; and

◆ details of any requirements regarding **work outside the UK**.

The written statement can refer the employee to another document (provided there are opportunities for reading it at work) for employment particulars relating to **sick leave and pay** and **pension schemes**.

The section 1 requirements make no specific mention of **overtime**. However, in the case of *Lange v Georg Schunemann GmbH C-350/99 ([2001] IRLR 244)*, the European Court of Justice (ECJ) ruled that, if overtime is an essential element of the contractual relationship so that employees should normally do it if requested, a reference to it must be included in the written statement.

According to the ECJ in the case of *Kampelmann and others v Landschaftsverband Westfalen-Lippe* and other cases C-253/96 to C-258/96 ([1998] IRLR 333), just putting the job title without any further description is not sufficient.

As far as **notice requirements** are concerned, it is sufficient for the statement to refer the employee to the law on the matter (see "Termination with/without notice" in Chapter 10) or to a collective agreement, providing there are opportunities to see it at work. If there are no terms relating to any of the above items, this has to be stated.

The right to a written statement does not apply only to new employees — **existing employees** can ask for a statement of their particulars if they do not have one.

If the employer does not provide a written statement, the employee can refer the matter to a tribunal at any time while they are working for the employer or within three months of the employment ending (or later, if a tribunal decides it was not reasonably practicable for them to do so within the three months).

A tribunal can determine what terms and conditions have been agreed, based on whatever evidence is available, but it cannot change terms that have been agreed (*Eagland v BT [1992] IRLR 323*).

If the particulars of employment change, the employer must give the employee a **written statement of the change** within one month of the change (section 4, ERA 96).

Terms of the contract

The contract sets out the rights and obligations of the employee and the employer. Contractual terms can be written down or verbally agreed. They can be **express** or **implied**, and can include terms agreed in a collective agreement or through custom and practice.

Express terms

Express terms are those that have been **specifically agreed** by the employer and employee. These take precedence, and an express term can usually only be overridden if it attempts to take away a statutory right. For example, an express term saying that a worker is entitled to two weeks' holiday would be overridden by the *Working Time Regulations 1998*, which give a right to 5.6 weeks' holiday (see "Holidays" in Chapter 4).

If a contract term is **ambiguous**, the tribunal will look at what has happened in practice to interpret it. In *Cook and others v Diageo EAT/0070/04*, the EAT held that the employer was entitled to change the dates of additional holidays so that they no longer coincided with bank holidays, because the contract said that it could set them according to local circumstances.

However, employees of another company successfully argued that they were entitled to triple pay on bank holidays, despite a written agreement that suggested they should receive only double time. This was because the practice of paying triple time had operated for more than 30 years and was continued after the new agreement was introduced.

The Court of Appeal said this made the term ambiguous, and it could therefore take account of what had happened in practice to decide what employees were entitled to (*Dunlop Tyres v Blows [2001] EWCA Civ 1032 ([2001] IRLR 629)*).

But if the term is too **uncertain**, the tribunal may be unable to enforce it. In the case of *Fontana v Fabio EAT/140/01*, a contractual term which obliged the employer to pay pension contributions but did not specify the amount, was held to be too unclear to enforce. There was no way of assessing what might be a reasonable amount, since different employers pay different levels of contributions. Furthermore, the EAT noted that the employee had never suggested to the employer what he thought might be a reasonable contribution.

Private health insurance, where available, is almost always an express term (*Marlow v East Thames Housing [2002] EWHC 1460 [2002] IRLR 798*).

An **equal opportunities policy** can, in certain circumstances, amount to an express term (*Taylor v Secretary of State for Scotland [2000] UKHL 28 [2000] IRLR 502*). But some company policies may only amount to **statements of principle**, rather than of contract. In the case of *Wandsworth LB v D'Silva [1998] IRLR 193*, the Court of Appeal ruled that the authority's sickness absence procedure was not contractual and could therefore be changed unilaterally without causing a breach of contract.

Implied terms

If terms have not been expressly agreed, they can be "implied" through conduct or custom and practice. If the conduct of the parties demonstrates that they have agreed a certain term, it may be implied into the contract. However, it is not enough to show that something has happened for a certain length of time — there must be evidence that both parties intended it to be part of the contract. For example, in the case of *North Lanarkshire Council v McDonald & another UKEATS/0036/06*, the fact that workers had worked half an hour of overtime every day for a year did not make the extra hours a contractual right.

In the same way, terms that have been regularly adopted in a particular trade or industry or in a particular area and have become standard practice are said to be implied through **custom and practice**. The term must be "reasonable, notorious and certain" (notorious meaning that it is well known).

If a term is truly **discretionary** it cannot be regarded as a contractual right through conduct or custom or practice — but the employer must be able to demonstrate that it exercised its discretion whenever that term was applied. In the case of *Horkulak v Cantor Fitzgerald International [2004] EWCA Civ 1287 ([2004] IRLR 942)*, which concerned an employee's entitlement to compensation in respect of a discretionary bonus following his successful claim for wrongful dismissal, the Court of Appeal held that where a term is discretionary there is an implied term that the employer will exercise its discretion genuinely and rationally. There is no implied term that on promotion an employee should be better off:

Mr Fisher accepted promotion to a managerial post. Custom and practice said that on promotion he would receive an increase on his basic pay of at least 5%. This happened, but his new grade did not pay unsocial hours' payments and Fisher found that he was actually out of pocket. He went to a tribunal, arguing that there must have been an implied term that his actual earnings would increase by at least 5%, but the EAT held that there was no such implied term (*London Underground v Fisher EAT/0104/04*).

An employee's implied terms include **fidelity and good faith** — for example, not giving away trade secrets (*Ticehurst & Thompson v BT [1992] IRLR 219*). The terms of a contract can also be implied if there would be no workable contract without them. These can be terms that both parties would have agreed to, had they thought about it, or terms that have been held to be **essential to all contracts of employment**.

Well-established implied terms include the duty not to destroy **mutual trust and confidence**, which binds both employer and employee. Neither party should, without "reasonable and proper cause", act in a manner that is likely to destroy the trust or confidence that exists between employer and employee.

An employer's failure to deal properly with an employee's grievance is a breach of trust and confidence (*Sodexho v Busfield EAT/0890/02*). So is offering an employee money to leave, as the case of *Bates Wells & Braithwaite v MacFarlane EAT/0616/02* demonstrates:

Because Wendy MacFarlane's baby had cerebral palsy, she asked to change her working arrangements. Her employers instead offered her £5,000 to leave, prompting her to resign and claim constructive dismissal. The EAT held that the offer of money to leave amounted to a breach of mutual trust and confidence.

The High Court held that a senior manager's behaviour, which included asserting authority using **foul and abusive language** and not giving the employee a chance to respond, was a breach of mutual trust and confidence which gave the employee the right to sue for wrongful dismissal (*Horkulak v Cantor Fitzgerald International [2003] EWHC 1918 (QB) ([2003] IRLR 756)*). The **unreasonable behaviour** of a manager also amounted to a breach of contract in the case of *Morrow v Safeway Stores EAT/0275/00 ([2002] IRLR 9)*:

Supermarket employee Marjorie Morrow was publicly reprimanded by her manager in full view of customers and staff, in a manner which the EAT found was humiliating. This amounted to a breach of the implied term of trust and confidence, giving Morrow the right to resign and claim constructive dismissal.

Treating an employee in an **arbitrary or capricious manner** by not offering the same benefits as are available to other workers can also be a breach of trust and confidence (*BG plc v O'Brien EAT/1063/99 ([2001] IRLR 496)*).

In the case of *Malik v BCCI [1997] UKHL 23 [1997] IRLR 462*, the House of Lords ruled that the Bank of Credit and Commerce International (which had gone bust) was responsible for its former employees' inability to secure new employment because of its reputation, based on dishonesty or corruption. The employees were entitled to "stigma damages", based on a breach of the implied term of mutual trust and confidence.

However, the stigma must have a "real or substantial effect" on the employee's ability to get a new job and must have caused actual financial loss, according to the Court of Appeal in a later case. *BCCI v Ali (No 3) [2002] EWCA Civ 82 ([2002] IRLR 460).*

Employers can also be in breach of an implied term if they **negligently misrepresent** a situation, as a result of which employees take or accept a course of action which they would otherwise have rejected. In the case of *Hagen v ICI Chemicals [2002] IRLR 31*, employees agreed to transfer under TUPE (see Chapter 12) because they had been told their pension rights would be more or less the same, but this was not the case and some employees lost out substantially. The High Court held that this was a breach of contract and that the employees could sue their old employer for damages.

Employers also have the implied **duty of care** towards their employees to provide a safe system of work and a suitable working environment. In *Walker v Northumberland CC [1994] EWHC QB 2 [1995] IRLR 35*, the High Court held that this extends to a duty not to cause an employee psychiatric damage by reason of the volume or character of the work that they are required to perform, where it is **reasonably foreseeable** that the employee might become ill as a result.

A breach of the duty of care can entitle an employee to claim constructive dismissal in an employment tribunal. But it can also give rise to a claim for damages in the civil courts as a personal injury claim, if the employee can show that the injury was foreseeable. In 2002, the Court of Appeal set out the principles for dealing with psychiatric injury claims arising from **stress at work**. Its ruling covered appeals in four separate claims, but is known by the lead case, *Sutherland v Hatton [2002] EWCA Civ 76 ([2002] IRLR 263)*.

The emphasis in Sutherland was on the test of **foreseeability**, which is key to establishing liability for any sort of work-related injury. The court said the question to be asked was whether that kind of harm to that particular employee was foreseeable by a reasonable employer.

When one claimant — teacher Alan Barber — appealed, the House of Lords upheld the court's reasoning but said it had been wrongly applied in his case. Because Barber had already been off sick once with a stress-related illness, the Lords held that his school could have reasonably foreseen that he would become ill if work pressures continued, and should have taken steps to prevent this. Barber's claim therefore succeeded (*Barber v Somerset CC [2004] UKHL 13 ([2004] IRLR 475)*).

The *Sutherland* test has been specifically approved again in the case of *Hartman v South Essex Mental Health and Community Care NHS Trust and other adjoined cases [2005] EWCA Civ 6 ([2005] IRLR 293)*. Here the Court of Appeal stressed that an employer is not automatically liable simply because an individual suffers stress at work. It also held that an employer cannot be assumed to be aware of a **pre-existing condition** if this was disclosed confidentially to occupational health as part of a pre-employment health screening.

Equally, employers accused of bullying are only likely to have breached the implied duty of care if they had notice or information alerting them to the risk to the employee's health. If they are aware of the risk and refuse to do anything about it, they could be in breach of their duty of care.

In *Dickens v O2 plc [2008] EWCA Civ 1144*, Ms Dickens was promoted in the space of 10 years, from being a secretary to a management accountant and on to Finance and Regulatory Manager. Ms Dickens, who had no formal accountancy training, was latterly assigned to conduct audit work with which she struggled (having not received enough training and support). Ms Dickens had a crisis at work causing her to go home. She said that she could not cope and was suffering from stress and depression including Irritable Bowel Syndrome, she was frequently late to work and was asked to take a sabbatical. Her employer referred her to its confidential counselling helpline and only subsequently to occupational health.

The Court of Appeal decided that Ms Dickens' illness was reasonably foreseeable and that O2's failure to address her work issues had aggravated her pre-existing depressive condition. The court found that O2 should have sent Ms Dickens home and instructed occupational health to investigate earlier. Therefore the employer was liable for failing to do anything of substance.

In the case of *NWT Freight Forwarding v Owen EAT/0643/01*, a requirement for a driver to work without a reasonable break was found to be a breach of contract:

Immediately on his return from a nine-day overseas driving job, Mr Owen was told to do another long-distance job. He refused on the grounds he had not had enough time off between trips, and was dismissed. The EAT agreed that there was an implied term entitling Owen to a reasonable break before he undertook more driving duties. The requirement to work another long shift with inadequate time off was an unreasonable order and amounted to a breach of contract.

Employers are also liable if their employees act in a way that would breach a contract and as a result cause harm to a **third party** to whom the employer owes a duty of care.

Where a term has not been negotiated with an individual employee, the House of Lords has held that the employer has an implied duty to take reasonable steps to bring that term to their attention (*Scally and others v Southern Health Board [1991] IRLR 522*). The ruling came in the case of four doctors who were unaware of their right to purchase additional years towards their pension entitlement.

The extent of this duty was considered by the Court of Appeal in the case of *Ibekwe v London General Transport Services Ltd [2003] EWCA Civ 1075 ([2003] IRLR 697)*:

Bus driver Daniel Ibekwe was off sick during a period when he would have had to exercise an option regarding his pension scheme. His employer had informed employees of the available options through letters sent with their pay slips and placed notices on workplace notice boards. Ibekwe had called into work each week to pick up his pay slip, but claimed that he had not seen the notices. The Court of Appeal ruled that the employer had complied with its duty to take reasonable steps to inform, and there was no obligation to check whether individual employees had received the notice.

The duty to inform does not oblige the employer to advise employees of their best choice (*University of Nottingham v Eyett [1999] IRLR 87*) or to protect their economic well-being (*Crossley v Faithful & Gould Holdings [2004] EWCA Civ 293 ([2004] IRLR 377)*).

In the case of *Reda v Flag Ltd [2002] UKPC 38 ([2002] IRLR 747)*, the employment contract gave the employer the right to choose how to terminate it: either at the end of its term or with pay in lieu. There was no implied term that the choice would be exercised in a way that would be most beneficial to the employee.

Works rules and collective agreements

Works rules, guidelines or rules about how work should be carried out can be part of the contract, even if the employee has no option but to accept the rule.

Although most collective agreements are not legally binding on the parties who have concluded them (the employer and the union), items within the agreement that can be incorporated into the individual's contract become binding conditions of that contract.

A company reached an agreement with the T&G general union giving workers the right to 20 days' leave plus bank and public holidays. The company then published a staff handbook which said that bank and public holidays were part of the 20 days. The EAT held that the collective agreement's effect was to amend existing contracts, and the employer could not unilaterally change them. *Wood Hall Personnel & Transport v Harris and Gonsalvez EAT/156/02.*

Tribunals have to look at the "contractual intention" of the parties, when deciding whether the terms of a collective agreement are incorporated. In the case of *Kaur v MG Rover [2004] EWCA Civ 1507 ([2005] IRLR 40)*, the Court of Appeal held that the term in a collective agreement which stated that there would be no redundancies was "aspirational" and did not amount to a contractual term.

However, in *Harlow v Artemis International [2008] EWHC 1126*, an employee successfully obtained access to a collectively agreed enhanced redundancy policy. The High Court noted that the policy was identifiable as an entitlement, the method of calculating payment was clearly set out and the policy was referred to in individuals' contracts.

Changes agreed in negotiations are **binding on all employees**, even if they might not like what has been negotiated, particularly where a considerable amount of time has passed before they voice their objections (*Henry v London General Transport Services [2002] EWCA Civ 488 ([2002] IRLR 472)*).

In the case of *Trotter v Grattan EAT/0179/03*, a collectively agreed stop and search policy was incorporated into the contracts of every employee, even if they had not all individually agreed to the policy:

Objecting to a new company policy of random searches, Mr Trotter resigned and claimed constructive dismissal. The EAT held that while the policy change did amount to a fundamental breach of contract, the constructive dismissal was fair. The policy had been introduced after consultation with the unions, so was not imposed arbitrarily, and it would not be reasonable for the employer to have to differentiate between employees who had agreed the change and those who had not.

If a workplace rep has apparent authority to negotiate, the employer can reach a deal at that level, even if the procedures say that a full-time official should be informed of any deals concluded (*Harris v Richard Lawson Autologistics [2002] EWCA Civ 442 ([2002] IRLR 476)*). However, if a change has not been agreed by all recognised unions, it may well be the case that it is not universally incorporated:

A local authority wanted to change holiday terms, but only reached agreement to do so with one of its two recognised unions; nevertheless it introduced the change. The EAT noted that collective bargaining "rests upon a foundation of consensus and process" and that the processes for voting agreed between the unions had not been followed. This meant there had been no local agreement to the change, which therefore had not been incorporated into employees' contracts. *South Tyneside MBC v Graham EAT/0107/03.*

Once a change is incorporated into an employee's contract, it becomes a binding contractual term. The employee cannot revert to the previous contractual arrangement without a further agreement.

Illegal clauses

If the employer proposes something illegal in the contract, such as a method for non-payment of tax by paying "cash in hand", or paying part of the salary as "expenses", employees need to be wary — it may mean that they cannot enforce any part of the contract, including statutory rights under it.

For an employee to be barred from enforcing their employment rights on the grounds of illegality, a tribunal must identify the facts that made performance of the contract illegal, and must establish that:

♦ the employee knew that it was illegal; and

♦ the employee actively participated in the illegality (*Kaid v Gruppo EAT/0546/03*).

In *Wheeler v Qualitydeep [2004] EWCA Civ 1085*, the Court of Appeal considered the case of a Thai employee who had only received two pay slips in three years. Although Ms Wheeler's husband was a native Englishman, she barely spoke English and was unaware of what the Revenue's requirements were. The Court of Appeal found that there was insufficient evidence that Ms Wheeler was aware of the employer's tax fraud. Accordingly the employee was not prohibited from bringing a claim.

In *Blue Chip Trading Ltd v Helbawi UKEAT/0397/08*, the EAT examined a claim made by a foreign student who worked nights as a security guard:

Mr Helbawi worked more hours than he was permitted to under the terms of his visa. When he complained that the pay that he had received was less than that permitted by the *National Minimum Wage Regulations*, his employer argued that his tribunal application should not be heard because his contract was illegal. The EAT decided that a tribunal could hear the parts of Mr Helbawi's claim that related to the weeks during vacation time that he was permitted to work. In other words the fact that Mr Helbawi had breached the terms of his visa did not mean that he was prevented from bringing any claim at all.

An employee who participates in an illegal contract **may not be able to bring a claim of unfair dismissal**. The High Court has held that this is not a denial of the right to a fair trial under human rights law (*Soteriou v Ultrachem [2004] EWHC 983 (QB) ([2004] IRLR 870)*).

However, employees have been allowed to bring unfair dismissal claims in cases where:

♦ the employer refused their request to make arrangements to pay their tax and National Insurance (*Warp Technologies Holdings v Nunoo and Vermani EAT/0527/04*); or

♦ they were paid occasional sums cash in hand (*Annandale Engineering v Samson [1994] IRLR 59*).

Although there have been cases where employees have been denied employment rights even though they had not known what they were doing, in the joined cases of *Enfield Technical Services Ltd v Payne UKEAT/0644/06* and *Grace v BF Components Ltd UKEAT/0367/06*, the EAT said this had only happened because they had misrepresented the situation in some way by, for example, declaring part of their wages as "expenses".

Employers cannot usually avoid **discrimination** claims on the grounds that the contract is illegal (*Leighton v Michael [1996] IRLR 67*). But if the illegality is entirely due to the employee's actions, it may remove their right to bring a discrimination claim.

In the case of *X v Governing Body of Addey and Stanhope School [2004] EWCA Civ 1065*, the Court of Appeal held that an employee's decision to work in the UK without documents was criminal and meant that he could not pursue a discrimination claim.

Unfair contract terms

In some circumstances, it may be possible to challenge a term in an employment contract under the *Unfair Contract Terms Act 1977* (UCTA), although this is rare.

A term is unfair under UCTA if it tries to restrict the employer's liability as a result of a breach of contract, or if it entitles one of the parties to exercise the term in a way that is substantially different from what was expected of them.

In the case of *Peninsula Business Services Ltd v Sweeney EAT/1096/02 [2004] IRLR 49*, a sales executive challenged the terms of his contract after he had resigned. Because the contract stated that commission would only be paid to employees who were still employed at the time that the commission became due, the claimant's resignation cost him over £20,000.

But the EAT said the term was valid, because the claimant had agreed to it by signing the contract; it would be wholly unacceptable if a party signed a contract and then claimed they could not be bound by its terms.

UCTA did not apply because the claimant was entirely aware of the arrangements for paying commission when he entered into the contract, and it could not be said that the employer had behaved in a substantially different way from what could reasonably be expected of it.

Restrictive covenants

If an employer wants an employee to be bound by terms after their employment has ended — for example, to restrict who they can work for or to protect confidential information — they must include a specific term in the contract. This is called a **restrictive covenant**.

There are limits on the extent to which an employee can be bound by a restrictive covenant. A clause that is a **restraint of trade** is unenforceable, but a clause that protects an employer's **legitimate business interests** is allowed.

A person could set up in competition with a former employer, but a restrictive covenant may prevent them from soliciting or having dealings with the former employer's customers or from taking similar employment for a period of time.

A restrictive covenant will only be enforced if it is **reasonable**. This will depend on:

◆ the extent to which it tries to limit the employee's activities;
◆ the geographical area covered; and
◆ how long it lasts for.

If a term is too wide it will not be enforced:

The Court of Appeal ruled that a clause preventing an employee from working in any capacity in any business within the UK for anyone who was in competition went beyond what it was legitimate to protect and was unenforceable (*Wincanton v Cranny [2000] IRLR 716*).

However, in *Kynixa Ltd v Hynes [2008] EWHC 1495*, the High Court considered the enforceability of restrictive covenants (contained within shareholder agreements) against three high-level executives. The executives left to work for a competitor but concealed the identity of their new employer from Kynixa Ltd. Given their seniority, even though the restrictive covenants were very wide (lasting 12 months from date of termination), they were found to be reasonable and enforceable.

Employees who are dismissed in **fundamental breach of contract** (see below) are released from their obligations under that contract and any restrictive covenants cannot be enforced (*Rock Refrigeration v Jones [1996] EWCA Civ 694 [1996] IRLR 675*).

The Court of Appeal held that a clause entitling an ex-employee to receive commission payments as long as he did not work for a competitor for a year was an unreasonable restraint of trade (*Marshall v NM Financial Management [1997] EWCA Civ 1237 [1997] IRLR 449*).

Even if a restrictive covenant is valid, an employer wishing to enforce such a clause will still have to show that a breach will do it some harm. In the case of *Jack Allen (Sales & Service) Ltd v Smith [1999] IRLR 19*, the Court of Session refused to enforce restrictive covenants because the employer had been unable to identify any real loss.

Contract changes

Employers should never introduce contract changes without consulting either the union, other employee reps (if there is no recognised union) or the individual employee.

Contracts may be changed lawfully:

◆ where the **contract allows for a change** — for example, if there is a reasonable mobility clause (which has been recently exercised) allowing the employer to change the place of work;
◆ if the **parties agree** to the change;
◆ through **collective bargaining**; or
◆ by **terminating the existing contract** and offering new terms (although this could amount to an unfair dismissal — see "Breach of contract" below).

If an employer insists on changing terms without agreement, this is a unilateral variation of contract and the employee may be able to pursue a claim for breach of contract (see below).

Agreement to a change of contract can either be **"express"** (the employee verbally consents or signs a new contract, for example) or **"implied"** by the employee's conduct. If an employer announces that the hours of work will change from a 9.30am start to a 9.00am start and the employees come in at 9.00am the next day and carry on coming in at 9.00am without objecting, this is an implied agreement to change their hours to a 9.00am start — even if they have not said "yes" or "no" to it.

It is important that employees are made aware that a failure to oppose a change could mean that they will be taken to have accepted it and may not be able to challenge it at a later date.

However, this is not necessarily the case if the proposed change does not take immediate effect:

Ms Aparau was given a new contract which said she might be required to move to a different location at any time. She did not sign it but continued to work. The EAT held that, where a new term is introduced unilaterally (without agreement) but it does not take effect immediately, a tribunal should take care before concluding there had been an implied acceptance. *Aparau v Iceland Frozen Foods [1996] IRLR 119.*

If the terms change, the employer must issue a **new statement** of employment particulars (see Chapter 3) detailing the changes within a month (section 4, ERA 96). There is no provision for statements by instalment, as is the case with the initial statement. If the employer changes its name, a new statement must be provided, which must include the date on which the employee's continuity of service began.

In workplaces with a recognised union, contractual changes usually occur through **collective bargaining**. Collective agreements typically are incorporated into individual employees' employment contracts by a specific reference to the agreement in the contract.

But if changes have always been made through collective bargaining in the past, this might be taken as implied agreement to changes made in that way (see "Works rules and collective agreements" above).

Sometimes the contract of employment itself may seek to allow for changes to the terms and conditions. For example, it may include a **mobility clause** purporting to permit the employer to change the place of work, or a **flexibility clause** allowing it to change employees' duties.

If there is an express clause allowing for a change, there is no implied term that this must be exercised in a reasonable way. However, the employer can only impose it in such a way that the employee can comply, and it must not do so in a way that destroys trust and confidence (*White v Reflecting Roadstuds [1991] IRLR 331*).

Also, a change which doesn't offer any consideration (something in exchange), or results in too much being asked of the employee, may be a breach of the implied term of trust and confidence (*St Budeaux Royal British Legion Club v Cropper EAT/39/94*).

In the case of *Land Securities Trillium Ltd v Thornley EAT/0603/04 ([2005] IRLR 765)*, the EAT held that a flexibility clause did not require the employee to do whatever the employer asked:

Architect Jane Thornley brought a constructive dismissal claim after her role was changed from a hands-on architectural role to a managerial one. The EAT upheld her claim, saying that the imposition of the new job description was a fundamental breach of her contract which had the effect of de-skilling her by taking her away from the hands-on role.

A flexibility clause stating that she must perform "any other duties which may reasonably be required" of her did not give her employer the right to require her to do anything it asked. In fact, it imposed a requirement of reasonableness, which the employer had not shown. In any case, the tribunal had been entitled to look at how she had carried out her duties in practice, not just how they were described in a job description (which is not a prescriptive document).

An employer may be able to force employees to move to another location instead of making them redundant if there is a mobility clause in their contract (*Home Office v Evans & Laidlaw [2007] EWCA Civ 1089*). However, the place at which a person can be asked to work, is where they have consistently worked in reality — and not where a contract clause (which has not recently been exercised) states that they might be required to work from: *High Table Ltd v Horst & ors [1997] IRLR 513; [1998] ICR 409.*

There is no entitlement to be paid to relocate unless the contract says so. But in the case of *United Bank v Akhtar [1989] IRLR 507*, a requirement for an employee to relocate from Leeds to Birmingham the following week with no relocation expenses was held to be a breach of contract, because the employee was unable to comply.

Reps should also consider whether the effect of a mobility or flexibility clause is discriminatory (see Chapter 6).

Breach of contract

If the employee does not agree to proposed changes and the employer goes ahead and changes them unilaterally, this is generally a breach of contract. The employee can do a number of things in response:

◆ **accept** the change;

◆ **refuse to work** under the new terms — it is then up to the employer to decide what to do;

◆ **object** to the new terms but carry on working under them while they take legal action;

◆ carry on working but claim **unfair dismissal** (if there is a substantial difference in terms); or

◆ resign and claim **constructive dismissal** (if there is a fundamental breach).

Employees who **continue working** following a breach of contract may be taken to have accepted the change and therefore **waived** their right to pursue a breach of contract claim. If they wish to challenge the breach, it is important for them to **make it clear** that they do not accept the changes, and to **act quickly** in getting legal advice and in pursuing a claim. If they are not immediately aware that there has been a change, they should protest as soon as they become aware of it.

An employee cannot bring a breach of contract claim in an employment tribunal unless the employment has ended. In most cases (except those such as *Hogg* page 67, the only legal action an employee can take for a breach of contract while they are still employed is in the civil courts (County Court or High Court).

Employees may also choose to take this route rather than the tribunal route in other circumstances — for example, if their claim is worth more than £25,000; because legal aid may be available in some circumstances, or because they are past the tribunal time limit. The time limit for breach of contract claims in the civil courts is six years (as opposed to the three-month limit in employment tribunals).

A court has the power to order the employer to restore the contract to its original provisions, and to award damages (losses). The House of Lords upheld a High Court ruling in the case of *Rigby v Ferodo Ltd [1987] IRLR 516*, where the employer had imposed a pay reduction:

As a result of a financial crisis, the employer proposed a pay cut of around £30 per week. This was not agreed, but was introduced anyway. The employer's engineering workers continued to work but sued for breach of contract. The House of Lords upheld their claim and awarded damages for the difference in pay. They also refused to accept the employer's argument that damages should be limited to the 12-week notice period because this is how long it would have taken to lawfully end the contract and replace it with another on different terms. The Lords said it was clear that the employer had intended the contract to continue, albeit on different terms.

If the breach is fundamental to the contract, this can give the employee the right to resign and claim **constructive dismissal**. But it must be a fundamental breach, and the employee must be able to show that they resigned as a direct result of the breach and did not delay too long before doing so; delaying their resignation could be regarded as "waiving the breach".

To be able to claim constructive dismissal, an employee needs **one year's continuous service**. Even if a tribunal finds that there was a constructive dismissal, the dismissal can still be fair if the employer can show that it had a fair reason for the change and otherwise acted reasonably in implementing it (see Chapter 10).

Constructive dismissal claims are not limited to circumstances where the employer imposes a change to the employee's terms and conditions. They can arise in response to any fundamental breach of contract, and often result from an employer's breach of the implied term not to destroy mutual trust and confidence. The following have been found to amount to a fundamental breach of contract:

◆ issuing a final written warning without a proper investigation (*Thackeray v Acequip EAT/0396/03*);

◆ reducing pay and assigning additional duties — even though, due to a resulting stress-related illness, the employee did not immediately act on the breach (*Governing Body of St Edmund of Canterbury Catholic High School v Hines EAT/1138/02*);

◆ reducing working hours, even though in the past there had been agreement to change hours in similar situations (*International Packaging Corporation v Balfour [2003] IRLR 11*);

◆ giving an employee a final written warning for an offence which any employer acting reasonably would have regarded as minor (*Stanley Cole (Wainfleet) Ltd v Sheridan EAT/0824/01 ([2003] IRLR 52)*);

◆ transferring an employee to a higher graded post where the result was to deprive the employee of previous pay protection (*LB Camden v Collins & Clements EAT/1436/01*);

◆ unilaterally changing a fixed London allowance provided in the contract (*Security and Facilities Division v Hayes [2001] IRLR 81*);

◆ instructing an employee to change her hours in conflict with her domestic responsibilities (*Greenaway Harrison v Wiles [1994] IRLR 380*) — the employer argued that the employee had "jumped the gun" because the change had not yet been implemented, but the EAT ruled that there was a breach of contract;

◆ deciding to pay the national rate only, and ignoring the previous collectively agreed local rate which had already become incorporated within the individual's contract (*Gibbons v Associated British Ports [1985] IRLR 376*);

◆ replacing full-time work by part-time work (*Hogg v Dover College [1990] ICR 39*); and

◆ transferring employees to new work where there was nothing in their contract allowing for this (*Hughes v Southwark [1988] IRLR 55*).

If an employer fundamentally breaches the contract, the employee is no longer bound by the terms of that contract unless there is an express term that says otherwise — but it must be a fundamental breach that goes right to the root of the contract (*CRS Computers v McKenzie EAT/1259/01*).

If an employer **terminates the existing contract and offers new terms**, this is not a breach of contract as long as the employer gives adequate notice (either the statutory minimum or the amount stated in the contract, whichever is longer) (*Kerry Foods v Lynch EAT/0032/05 ([2005] IRLR 680*)).

However, employees can bring a claim for **unfair dismissal** as long as they have **a year's continuous service**. Whether the dismissal is fair will depend on whether the employer had a good business reason for introducing the change and acted reasonably in all the circumstances.

Employers will usually argue that the dismissal is fair for "some other substantial reason" (see Chapter 10).

When assessing whether the introduction of new terms was fair, a tribunal must take into account the employer's need for change and balance this against the injury done to the employee, although a change cannot be imposed for an "arbitrary reason" (*Catamaran Cruisers v Williams EAT/786/93 [1994] IRLR 386*). Any representations made by the union are also likely to be considered.

Some unilateral changes involve the termination of one contract and the offer of a new contract, even if the employer does not express it in this way. This can still amount to a dismissal, even if the employer says it is not. In the case of *GMB v Man Truck & Bus UK [2000] IRLR 636*, the dismissal of employees and their re-engagement on new terms amounted to a dismissal (which also gave rise to collective redundancy consultation rights).

If changes to the contract are substantial, the employee **may be able** to accept the new terms and still bring a claim of unfair dismissal without having to resign and claim constructive dismissal. This was found in the case of *Hogg v Dover College [1990] ICR 39*:

Teacher Mr Hogg was demoted from his post as head of department, put onto part-time hours and had his salary halved. The EAT held that he had been dismissed and re-employed on "wholly different terms" which amounted to an entirely different contract. Hogg was able to claim that he had been unfairly dismissed.

The same principle was applied in *Alcan Extrusions v Yates and others [1996] IRLR 327*, where the employer's fundamental change to the shift system resulted in different hours of work including working on weekends and bank holidays.

Other remedies

If the contractual change results in a loss of pay, a worker can bring a claim under Part II of the ERA 96 for their outstanding wages (see "Deductions and underpayments" in Chapter 4). The advantage of this is that the claim goes to an employment tribunal so the process is usually quicker, cheaper and less formal than the County or High Court. It may also be the preferred choice if there is a risk that the employer may bring a counterclaim against the employee.

An employee may be able to get an **injunction** (**interdict** in Scotland) to stop their employer from changing the contract before any breach occurs (see "Injunctions" in Chapter 10).

In the case of *Peace v City of Edinburgh Council [1999] IRLR 417*, the Court of Session in Scotland granted an interdict preventing the employer from adopting a new disciplinary procedure. The employee successfully argued that the established procedure was a term in his contract, and that an interdict was the appropriate legal action to deal with a breach of contract that had not yet happened but was anticipated.

Although an employee cannot claim compensation for **injury to feelings** in an unfair dismissal claim (see Chapter 10), they may be able to claim in certain circumstances for **damages** arising from the way they were treated prior to dismissal.

For example, in the case of *Malik and another v Bank of Credit and Commerce International [1997] UKHL 23 [1997] IRLR 462*, the claimants were awarded "stigma damages" because of the dishonest and corrupt way the bank had conducted itself prior to the dismissals.

But this is a complex area of law and was considered again in the cases of *Eastwood v Magnox Electric and McCabe v Cornwall County Council [2004] UKHL 35 ([2004] IRLR 733)*. Both concerned breaches of the implied term of trust and confidence prior to dismissal — one in respect of harassment and unjustified allegations, the other in respect of a long and unjustified suspension from work.

Considering the two cases together, the House of Lords ruled that a claimant can pursue damages for a breach of contract that occurred prior to dismissal — but not if the breach of contract occurred in the steps leading to dismissal. It may often prove difficult to establish when those steps began.

In the case of *Mennell v Newell and Wright [1997] EWCA Civ 2082 [1997] IRLR 519*, an employee was dismissed after his employer threatened a change to his contract and was able to bring a claim of automatically unfair dismissal because he had been dismissed for asserting a statutory right:

Mr Mennell was dismissed after refusing to accept a change to his contract that would result in a reduction in pay. He could not claim under ordinary unfair dismissal rules because he did not have the qualifying service (which was then two years). Instead he successfully claimed that he had been unfairly dismissed for asserting a statutory right, for which there is no qualifying period (see Chapter 10). The Court of Appeal upheld his claim.

The EAT has confirmed that a **failure to pay wages** on time is also a breach of a relevant statutory right for those purposes, as it is an unlawful deduction of wages (*Elizabeth Claire Care Management Ltd v Francis EAT/0147/05 ([2005] IRLR 858)*).

It is possible for employees also to be sued for breach of contract, although it is rare for an employer to take this course of action. In *Attorney General v Blake [2000] UKHL 45 [2001] IRLR 36*, the House of Lords held that employers can take account of any profits made by an employee as a result of their breach, and can claim damages based on these.

However, it can be difficult for an employer to establish the nature of the financial damage caused by an employee's breach. Indeed, in the case of *Giraud v Smith EAT/1105/99 [2000] IRLR 763*, the EAT held that an employer could not enforce a contractual clause saying that employees who left without giving proper notice had to pay the employer the equivalent of their notice.

More information: LRD booklet *Contracts of employment — a legal guide* (£4.70). *Workplace Report* has regular quarterly updates on contract law.

4. Rights to pay and conditions

National Minimum Wage

Under the *National Minimum Wage Act 1998*, UK workers have the right to a **minimum wage**, currently set at £5.80 an hour for those aged 22 or over (£5.93 from 1 October 2010 for those aged **21** and over). Young people aged 18 to 21 get a lower rate of £4.83 (£4.92 from 1 October 2010 for those aged 18 to **20**). Sixteen- and 17-year-olds have a lower rate of £3.57 an hour (£3.64 from 1 October 2010).

If an employer provides accommodation, they can count some of this towards minimum pay — currently up to £4.51 per day or £31.57 per week (£4.61 per day and £32.27 per week from 1 October 2010). The Department for Business, Innovation and Skills (BIS) has issued guidance explaining how the accommodation offset works which is available online at: www.berr.gov.uk/files/file38769.pdf.

Workers, including agency and homeworkers, are covered, as is anyone who works for another person, except those in the excluded sectors listed below. There are different methods of calculating the hourly rate of pay for the purposes of the national minimum wage, depending on whether the worker is paid a salary, paid according to hours worked, paid according to output (piece work) or does unmeasured work (involving specific tasks but no set times). BIS provides detailed information about calculating the minimum wage and also runs a minimum wage helpline (see "Further information" at the end of this booklet).

Hours when a worker is available for work but not actually working can still amount to **working time**. In the case of *Scottbridge Construction v Wright XA 104/01 [2003] IRLR 21*, the Court of Session in Scotland held that a night watchman had the right to be paid the national minimum wage for the whole of his night shift, even though he could read, watch television or sleep when not on patrol.

Similarly, in the case of *British Nursing Association v Inland Revenue [2002] EWCA Civ 494 ([2002] IRLR 480)*, the Court of Appeal ruled that workers **working in their own homes** during the night, answering telephone enquiries, had the right to be paid the national minimum wage. It did not matter that they could do other things when not answering the phone or that they might not get many calls.

But where workers do "unmeasured time" their employer is entitled to come to an agreement with them specifying the number of hours they will be paid, taking into account the duties performed, as long as this is a "realistic average".

In the case of *Walton v Independent Living Organisation Ltd [2003] EWCA Civ 199 ([2003] IRLR 469)*, the Court of Appeal held that a carer providing 24-hour cover did not have to be paid for all those hours. Although she had to be available, in practice she was only required to assist her client for around six-and-a-half hours a day and an agreement had been made accordingly. The court held that payment should be based on those hours.

The National Minimum Wage applies to all hourly rates of pay (i.e. lower rates can't be offset against higher rates in assessing whether the minimum wage has been paid).

In *Hamilton House Medical Ltd v Hillier UKEAT/0246/09* the individual worked as a care worker. Her basic pay rate was below the National Minimum Wage (NMW). However, she was entitled to time plus one-third for weekday nights and time plus two-thirds for weekend nights. As Ms Hillier almost always worked nights, her average hourly pay was above the NMW. Nevertheless as Ms Hillier's basic pay was below the NMW, the EAT ruled that regulation 31(1)(c)(i), *National Minimum Wage Regulations 1999* had been breached.

Similarly, following a successful union campaign, supported by some national newspapers, restaurant and bar employers are not able to meet part of the staff's NMW entitlement from customers' tips: Regulation 5, *National Minimum Wage 1999 (Amendment) Regulations 2009*.

Workers working at home and paid according to what they produce (piece workers) have the right to a minimum fair piece rate of 120% of the national minimum wage.

Those **excluded** from the right to the national minimum wage are: fishing vessel workers paid by share of catch; people working as volunteers in voluntary organisations; prisoners; apprentices under the age of 19 or who are under 26 but in the first 12 months of their apprenticeship; trainees on government-funded training; students on sandwich courses; trainee teachers; members of the armed forces; and schoolchildren. The EAT has ruled that a **child doing a newspaper round** was not covered by the minimum wage (*Addison v Ashby EAT/0851/01 [2003] IRLR 211*).

The **Inland Revenue** has the power to issue **compliance orders** against employers who are not paying the minimum wage. But if there is a dispute about how much is owed, it will be for the tribunal and not the Inland Revenue to calculate the amount. Enforcement officers can issue orders covering ex-employees as well as current employees, and can amend or withdraw enforcement and penalty notices where these are found to be incorrect (*National Minimum Wage (Enforcement) Act 2003*).

If an employer fails to pay the national minimum wage, a claim can be made to an employment tribunal, and it is up to the employer to prove that the minimum has been paid. You can also claim if your employer reduces your hours to keep your wages at what they were before the new minimum came into force. If an employer **increases the productivity target** to fund an increase in the national minimum wage and an employee unable or unwilling to meet the new target is dismissed as a result, the dismissal is automatically unfair (*Bopari v Grasshopper EAT/284/01*) (see "Automatically unfair dismissals" in Chapter 10). If an employer **reduces an existing bonus** or attendance payment to fund an increase in the national minimum wage, this can amount to an unlawful deduction (see "Deductions and underpayments" below).

Pay slips and pay intervals

Every employee must be given, by their first pay date, an itemised pay statement that lists **gross wages**, **deductions** and **net wages** (section 8, *Employment Rights Act 1996* (ERA 96)). If an employer fails to give a statement, an employee can go to a tribunal to get it.

If employees are currently **paid in cash**, this should remain as part of their contractual rights, and the usual rules for contract changes apply (see "Contract changes" in Chapter 3).

Employers must each year give every employee a **certificate (P60)** showing annual gross pay, take-home pay and total deductions.

Fixed deductions from pay do not need to be itemised separately on each pay statement as long as the total amount of fixed deductions is given and the employer has previously given the employee a statement detailing those deductions (section 9, ERA 96).

Deductions and underpayments

An employer is only entitled to make deductions from a worker's pay if:

◆ they have a **statutory duty or authority** to do so (for example, income tax and National Insurance contributions);

◆ a **term in the contract** allows them to do so and they have notified the worker in writing; or

◆ they have the **written consent** of the worker, which must have been given before the deduction is made (section 13, ERA 96).

A signed authorisation form for union subscriptions will amount to written consent, so this would be a lawful deduction.

If an employer deducts pay without consent, the worker can bring a claim for **unlawful deduction of wages** in an employment tribunal (unless it is an overpayment or other exception discussed below). This includes **shortfalls** in wages and **late payment**: if a worker does not receive the total amount of wages owed to them on any occasion, this amounts to an unlawful deduction.

However, if there is doubt about the worker's contractual entitlement, the Court of Appeal has recently held that the claim has to be taken to the County Court as a breach of contract claim (*Coors Brewers Ltd v Adcock & others [2007] EWCA Civ 19*).

If a payment is genuinely discretionary, you would need to be able to establish an entitlement to it first. But once an employer confirms that a discretionary bonus is due, it becomes contractual (*Farrell Matthews & Weir v Hansen EAT/0078/04 ([2005] IRLR 160)*). The courts have also confirmed that employers cannot exercise discretion in an irrational or perverse way (*Clark v Nomura International [2000] IRLR 766*).

The claim must be made **within three months** of the date the last payment should have been made (*Group 4 Nightspeed v Gilbert EAT/521/96 [1997] IRLR 398*) or, if there is a series of deductions, within three months of the last in the series.

Wages include fees, shift allowance, bonuses, commission, holiday pay, guarantee pay, sick pay and maternity pay. But notice pay cannot be claimed as an unlawful deduction:

Ms Delaney was dismissed without notice and given a cheque for pay in lieu of notice, which subsequently was stopped. She was also entitled to holiday pay and commission, neither of which was paid. She claimed payment on all three counts, arguing that the non-payment was a deduction under ERA 96. The House of Lords upheld her claim for holiday pay and commission, as these were wages, but not for pay in lieu of notice, which it classified as appropriate for a claim for damages for wrongful dismissal (*Delaney v Staples [1992] IRLR 191*).

A claim for statutory holiday pay must be brought under the *Working Time Regulations 1998* (WTR) and cannot be brought as an unlawful deduction of wages (*Commissioners of Inland Revenue v Ainsworth & others [2005] EWCA Civ 441 ([2005] IRLR 465)*).

Car allowances cannot be claimed as an unlawful deduction of wages. Claims over failure to pay these are based on a breach of contract and are pursued in the County or High Court. Under the *Attachment of Earnings Act 1971*, employers must make deductions from earnings where employees have had an **attachment of earnings order** made against them by the courts. Even where the employee has breached the employment contract (for example, by leaving without giving the appropriate notice), there is no automatic right to deduct pay. Any deductions made without authority from a final pay packet are unlawful.

Ms Chambers and others walked out without notice following a dispute. Their final pay packets had shortfalls said by the employer to offset claims for damages for breach of contract. The EAT stated that these amounted to deductions and were unlawful (*Chiltern House v Chambers [1990] IRLR 88*).

Deducting money from an employee's final pay packet because they have **taken more holiday** than they have accrued, amounts to an unlawful deduction unless there is a written agreement that allows the employer to do this. The law says a worker has the right to be paid wages properly due, and any shortfall is effectively a deduction unless it is an error of computation. But, as an EAT case (*Yemm v British Steel [1994]*

IRLR 117) makes clear, where employers make a conscious decision not to make a payment because they believe there is no contractual entitlement, they are not making an "error of computation".

If an employee has the right to a **fixed allowance** (for example, overnight expenses), the employer cannot unilaterally reduce the rate by arguing that the new rate is still more than the actual expenses incurred by the employee (*Security and Facilities Division v Hayes [2001] IRLR 81*).

Part II of the ERA 96 can be used to **challenge contract changes** that result in a reduction in pay. For example, in the case of *Kerr v Sweater Shop [1996] IRLR 424*, the EAT held that a change in the calculation of holiday pay, communicated to workers by way of a general notice only, did not comply with the law; the resulting pay reduction was therefore unlawful. In the case of *International Packaging Corporation v Balfour EAT/31/02 ([2003] IRLR 11)*, a reduction in working hours led to an unlawful deduction.

In the case of *Jowitt v Pioneer Technology [2003] EWCA Civ 411 ([2003] IRLR 356)*, the Court of Appeal reversed an earlier EAT ruling and held that an employer's failure to pay the employee his contractual permanent health insurance, because its insurers had decided that he could do some alternative work even though he could not do his own job, did not amount to a deduction. The insurance scheme only required a payment to be made when the employee was unable to do either his own job or any other paid work that he might realistically be expected to do.

In the case of *Bruce v Wiggins Teape [1994] IRLR 536*, the law was used to reinstate an **overtime rate** that the employer had scrapped unilaterally. And in the case of *Saavedra v Aceground [1995] IRLR 198*, the ERA 96 was used to reclaim a share of tips that the employer had unilaterally reduced.

However, in the case of *Nerva v UK [2002] IRLR 815*, the European Court of Justice (ECJ) confirmed that **tips added to a credit card** payment were not the property of the employees and that the employer's decision not to pay them to staff did not amount to an unlawful deduction.

Where the employer has a **contractual right** to impose a change, the resulting deduction will be lawful. In the case of *Hussman Manufacturing v Weir [1998] IRLR 288*, the employee's **shift was**

changed and as a result his pay was reduced. He claimed that this amounted to an unlawful deduction, but lost the case when the employer showed that there was a contract term giving it the right to make changes to shifts.

Deductions for other reasons, including dishonesty, poor work or misconduct, can also only be made if the worker has **agreed in advance in writing** to the deduction. But the agreement must be specific and clear and made before any incident giving rise to a deduction. An employee had signed a letter agreeing to repay **training** costs if he left employment but a tribunal said this did not constitute authority to deduct because it was not clear that this would be taken as a deduction from his wages (*Potter v Hunt Contracts [1992] IRLR 108*).

An employer who persuaded his employee to sign a form agreeing to future deductions in respect of previous stock shortfalls did not make a deduction lawful (*Discount Tobacco v Williamson [1993] IRLR 327*).

Overpayments and other exceptions

A worker cannot bring a claim for unlawful deduction of wages in the employment tribunal if the reason for the deduction is that their employer has overpaid them (section 14, ERA 96). This is the case even if the error is because the employer had wrongly calculated the amount due.

However, if there is a dispute and the worker believes they have not been overpaid, a tribunal can make a finding of fact as to whether or not there has been an overpayment — it just cannot decide whether any deduction was unlawful (see the *Gill* case below). Alternatively the worker could bring a claim in the civil courts.

But if the worker accepts that they have been overpaid once it is brought to their attention, their only route is the civil courts — where they may succeed if they can show that they had not realised there had been a mistake and had relied on the money thinking it was theirs, either by spending it or making provisions on the basis that they would be receiving that money (*Kleinwort Benson v Lincoln City [1998] 3 Weekly Law Reports 1095*).

In *Commerzbank v Price-Jones [2003] EWCA Civ 1663*, the Court of Appeal held that an overpayment which was clearly a mistake on the employer's part could be reclaimed, unless the employee could show that it would be inequitable for them to have to repay it.

SIP v Swinn [1994] IRLR 323 confirmed that the Act cannot be used to challenge such deductions, and that employees must pursue those claims in the County or High Courts.

Workers in **retail employment** have additional protection limiting deductions for cash shortages or stock deficiencies to a maximum of 10% of any one pay packet, except for the final one.

Deductions that are made because the worker has taken part in a **strike or other industrial action** short of a strike are also excluded by section 14 of the ERA 96, and cannot be pursued as an unlawful deduction of wages claim in an employment tribunal. However, the tribunal can consider whether there was industrial action, as in *Gill v Ford Motor Co EAT/0005/04 ([2004] IRLR 840)*. If the worker wants to challenge the amount of pay deducted, they must do so in the civil courts.

Guarantee pay

Employees **laid off** or on short time working should still receive their **normal pay** (*Miller v Hamworthy Engineering [1986] IRLR 461*), unless there is a clear contractual term or custom to the contrary. This is particularly the case for salaried employees whose pay is expressed as an annual sum.

A collective agreement said that short-time working could be introduced, but only where "approved as an alternative to redundancy" by the union. Introducing it without that consent gave employees the right to use Part II of the ERA 96 to claim their full wages, since their employer had made an unlawful deduction under the Act (*Davies v Hotpoint [1994] IRLR 538*).

If the employment contract specifically gives the employer the right to lay off employees without pay, they can claim **statutory guarantee pay** as long as they have been working for the employer for **at least a month**. The provisions for this are found in section 28 of the ERA 96. Although calculated on normal hourly earnings, guarantee pay is offset against contractual pay and limited to a maximum of five days' pay in any three-month period. The maximum paid for a day is £21.20 (2010-11) (section 31, ERA 96). Employees laid off because of industrial action taken by others employed by their employer cannot qualify for guarantee pay.

If employees are offered **suitable alternative work** for the days they are laid off, which they refuse, no guarantee pay is payable. If employees are denied guarantee pay in circumstances where they believe they have an entitlement, they can make a claim to a tribunal **within three months** of the day payment is claimed for (section 34, ERA 96). Employees with at least two years' service who are laid off for a period of **at least four consecutive weeks** (or six non-consecutive weeks in a 13-week period) may be able to claim a redundancy payment (section 148, ERA 96).

Medical suspension pay

Employees suspended by their employer on medical grounds because of a statutory requirement are entitled to medical suspension pay (section 64, ERA 96). This applies where there is a **potential danger to a worker's health** — for example, from lead, rubber, chemicals or radioactive substances.

The same requirements, exclusions and obligations to accept suitable alternative work apply as for guarantee pay (see above). However, payment is based on the week's pay calculation (see "Compensation" in Chapter 10) and is currently set at a maximum of £380 per week (2010-11). Contractual earnings are offset against this and the maximum period of entitlement is 26 weeks. Employees who have been refused medical suspension pay must lodge their claim with the tribunal within three months (section 70, ERA 96).

Working hours and breaks

The *Working Time Regulations 1998* (as amended) limit the length of the working day and the working week. The regulations cover "workers" and not just "employees" (see Chapter 2) and state that, in general, a worker should work no more than **48 hours in a week**, averaged over what is called a "reference period". This is normally 17 weeks, but is 26 weeks in the "special cases" listed in regulation 21 which include, for example, those working in security and surveillance, care services and at docks and airports. It can also be extended to 52 weeks by collective or workforce agreement only.

Employers cannot make workers do more than these hours (*Barber v RJB Mining [1999] IRLR 308*).

The regulations do not apply to **senior managers** and others whose **working time is not predetermined** and who can exercise control over it. But **transport sector** workers and **junior doctors**, who were initially excluded, are now covered by the regulations.

The regulations allow individuals to **opt out** of the 48-hour limit, but they can opt back in at any time by giving notice of not less than seven days and not more than three months, depending on what their contract says.

In the case of *Pfeiffer v Deutsches Rotes Kreuz C-397/01 to C-403/01 ([2005] IRLR 137)*, the ECJ held not only that emergency workers are covered by the Directive but also that opt-out provisions must be strictly defined and any worker who opts out must have done so freely and with full knowledge of the facts.

Working hours can include **time on call**, provided that the employee has to remain on the employer's premises even when they are not doing any work (*Sindicato de Medicos v Consumo de la Generalidad Valenciana C-303/98 ([2000] IRLR 845)*). This ECJ ruling was followed in the case of *Landeshauptstadt Kiel v Jaeger C-151/02 ([2003] IRLR 804)*:

The ECJ held that Norbert Jaeger, a doctor who had to stay at the hospital when on call but could sleep in a hospital room and rarely spent more than half his on-call time working, nevertheless should include all of that time within the definition of working time. This meant that Jaeger had the right to compensatory periods of time off immediately following the period he had been on call.

The principle was also applied in the UK in the case of *Anderson v Jarvis Hotels plc EAT/0062/05*, in which a hotel worker required to sleep over was found to be working for the whole of that time, even when he was asleep. The EAT said it was clear his employer required him to be there; he had been disciplined on one occasion for leaving the hotel for half an hour in the early hours of the morning.

However, where someone is on call but **not required on the premises**, the hours on call are not counted.

A proposal by the European Commission to amend certain aspects of the *Working Time Regulations* includes provisions to limit the maximum weekly hours for opted-out workers to 65, to extend the reference period from 17 weeks to a year and review the position relating to on-call time.

The proposal has been going through the negotiation process for some time and is currently stalled; the Commission is considering strategies to break the logjam.

There are additional rules covering **night workers** (those working at least three hours between 11pm and 6am). In general, these state that a worker should not do more than eight hours a night, when averaged over four months. Employers have to provide free health assessments for night workers.

Employers are also bound by an implied contractual duty not to require that employees work such long hours that could result in **damage to their health** (*Johnstone v Bloomsbury Health Authority [1991] IRLR 118*).

In the case of *Hone v Six Continents Retail Ltd [2005] EWCA Civ 922 ([2006] IRLR 49)*, the Court of Appeal found the fact a worker was working more than the 48-hour maximum was relevant evidence in a work-related stress claim:

Pub manager Mark Hone regularly worked 90 hours a week and was provided with only occasional help. He refused to sign an opt-out from the 48-hour limit and persistently complained about his hours and the lack of support. The Court of Appeal held that these factors were enough to show that the resulting injury Hone suffered was reasonably foreseeable, and his claim for stress-related injury succeeded.

The regulations also give workers the right to a **rest break of at least 20 minutes** if the working day is more than six hours (there is no statutory right to a second 20 minute break after twelve hours: (*The Corps of Commissionaires Management v Hughes UKEAT/0196/08/CEA*).

This break does not have to be paid. The regulations state that breaks can be deferred and compensated later where "the worker's activities involve the need for continuity of service".

The Court of Appeal, in the case of *Gallagher v Alpha Catering Services [2004] EWCA Civ 1559 ([2005] IRLR 102)*, held that the focus is on the worker's activities and not the employer's.

Employers cannot, for example, under-staff to avoid giving workers the right to breaks. In the case of seafarers, where there are separate regulations, short breaks are included within the definition of working hours (P&O Ferries (*Bermuda*) v *Spencer EAT/433/04*).

Workers are also entitled to a daily rest break of at least 11 hours and a weekly rest of not less than 24 hours, which can be averaged over two weeks. Young workers have additional protection (see "Young workers" in Chapter 2).

Under the *Sunday Trading Act 1994*, shopworkers who were in employment prior to 24 August 1994 and were not Sunday workers, or who have given their employers a written opted-out notice saying they do not wish to work on Sundays, are **"protected shopworkers"** and do not have to work on Sundays.

There may also be situations where a requirement to work at particular times is against the law on religion or belief grounds (see Chapter 6).

Holidays

All workers have the right to a minimum of **5.6 weeks' paid holiday** a year (equivalent to 28 days for someone who works a five-day week) under the *Working Time Regulations*, as amended. This entitlement was increased from 4 to 4.8 weeks in October 2007 and from 4.8 to 5.6 weeks in April 2009 as a result of union campaigning.

The Department for Business, Innovation and Skills (BIS) has produced guidance and a ready reckoner for calculating holiday entitlement at: www.direct.gov.uk/en/Employment/Employees/Timeoffandholidays/index.htm.

The right applies to all "workers" and not just "employees" (see Chapter 2), so can cover contractors. In the case of *Byrne Bros v Baird & others EAT 542/01 ([2002] IRLR 96)*, the EAT held that building workers whose contracts clearly required them to "personally perform services" were workers and therefore had the right to four weeks' paid holiday. Under the statutory scheme, holidays must be **taken in the year in which they accrue**. A worker cannot be paid in lieu of taking their holidays except where their employment has ended and they have not taken all the holidays they have accrued.

Pay during holidays is calculated in the same way as a **normal week's pay** in accordance with sections 221 to 224 of the ERA 96. A worker who is also entitled to commission will not automatically have this included in the calculation of normal earnings for holiday pay purposes (*Evans v Malley Organisation [2003] IRLR 156*).

Overtime pay will only be included in the calculation if the employer is contractually obliged to provide it (*Bamsey v Albon Engineering [2002] EWCA Civ 1834 ([2004] IRLR 457)*). Performance-related bonuses should be included (*May Gurney v Adshead & 95 others EAT/0150/06*).

Holiday rights are accrued on a monthly basis. In the first year, a worker gets entitlement to a twelfth of the statutory annual leave for every month worked. The amount of time that can be taken at any one time within the **first year of work** can be **rounded up by up to half a day**. Someone working five days a week who has worked for two months would be entitled to take three-and-a-third days, and so could take three-and-a-half days' leave.

Workers wanting to take leave need to **give notice** of at least twice the length of the holiday requested. The employer has the right to ask for the leave to be deferred, provided it tells the employee in advance, giving notice which is at least as long as the leave requested. However, where there is a "relevant agreement" the *Working Time Regulations* may permit shorter notice periods to be given.

In *Industry & Commerce Maintenance v Briffa UKEAT/0215/08/CEA*, Mr Briffa was given one weeks' notice of the termination of his employment. His employer required him to take four days holiday during his final week with the firm. Mr Briffa argued that his employer could not require him to take those four days as holiday as they had only given him four days notice rather than the eight required under the *Working Time Regulations*. However, the EAT agreed with the employer that a clause in the contract specifying that the employee could be required to be on holiday during their notice was a "relevant agreement" and therefore a permissible variation from the default position under the *Working Time Regulations*.

Mr Lyons, a security guard on a "zero hours" contract, had nine days' holiday to take before the new holiday year commenced on 1 April. As he had no further shifts scheduled during March, on 6 March he asked that his nine days' holiday be paid in lieu. He was not paid and, when challenged, the employer's stated reason was that Mr Lyons had not given sufficient notice. Although the contract specified that ordinarily four weeks' notice is required, it also set out that if less notice was given, a late holiday request would be considered on its merits and in light of staffing levels. Mr Lyons resigned and brought constructive unfair dismissal and breach of the *Working Time Regulations* (WTR) claims.

However, the Employment Appeal Tribunal (EAT) found that the employer did not have to allow an application for leave which did not comply with, or meet requirements permitted by, the WTR. The regulations specify that the default position that notice should be twice as long as the holiday, can be varied by the terms of an employment contract or collective agreement. Although the employer can make individuals jump through hoops detailed in an employment contract, the EAT did add that the way in which leave is authorised must not be unreasonable, arbitrary or capricious (*Lyons v Mitie Security UKEAT/0081/09*).

Following the ECJ's ruling in the combined cases of *Robinson-Steele v RD Retail Services Ltd, Clarke v Frank Staddon Ltd* and *Caulfield & others v Hanson Clay Products Ltd (formerly Marshalls Clay) C-131/04 and C257/04 ([2006] IRLR 386)*, it is unlawful to pay holiday pay as part of the hourly rate of pay. The ECJ said that the practice, known as **rolled-up holiday pay**, did not comply with the Working Time Directive which required that workers are paid for their holiday at the time that they take it.

If an employer **refuses to pay** statutory holidays, a worker can bring a claim in an employment tribunal. Since the House of Lords' decision in *HM Revenue and Customs v Stringer and others [2009] UKHL 31/ [2009] IRLR 677* (more below) it is possible to bring a claim in respect of statutory holiday entitlement as an unlawful deduction of wages. The advantage of this (over a Working Time Directive claim) is that a continuing series of deductions need only be the subject of one claim (rather than a claim for each time pay was docked).

The *Stringer* case also considered whether workers on **long-term sick leave** are entitled to take holiday during that sickness absence. This affects those whose contractual sick pay has expired and who would otherwise be entitled to full pay for days that they chose to take as holiday during that period. The case (which became known as *Schultz-Hoff v Deutsche Rentenversicherung Bund; HMRC v*

Stringer) made it to the ECJ. The Luxembourg court ruled that the four weeks (20 days a year for five day per week workers) of holiday guaranteed by the directive, should accrue during periods of long-term sickness.

Where a worker is ill during their holiday, they are entitled to take their leave again at a later date. In *Pereda v Madrid Movilidad SA (C-277/08) [2009] IRLR 959* an accident at work meant that the individual was ill for all but two days of his one month summer holiday. When his employer refused to let him re-book that holiday in November/December he sued.

The ECJ ruled that the purpose of sick leave (recovering from being ill) is different from annual leave (enjoying actual rest). A worker who is on sick leave during a period of previously scheduled annual leave is therefore entitled to take that leave some other time, if necessary during the next leave year. National rules may allow the worker to take paid annual leave during their sick leave instead, but only if the individual wants to.

The only circumstance in which a worker can be **paid in lieu** of statutory holidays is when the **contract ends** without the worker having taken all of the days due. The right to pay in lieu is absolute, and any clause in a contract that seeks to deny it, is void *(Witley & District Men's Club v Mackay EAT/151/00 [2001] IRLR 595)*.

In *Leisure Leagues v Maconnachie EAT/940/01 [2002] IRLR 600*, the EAT held that the amount of a day's holiday pay should be calculated by dividing the annual salary by the number of days actually worked (in that case, 233) rather than by 365, which was the previous practice. This was to take into account good industrial practice and the introduction of the *Working Time Regulations*, the court said. This was confirmed by the EAT in the case of *Yarrow v Edwards Chartered Accountants UKEAT/0116/07*.

Pay in lieu of contractual holidays (i.e. days in excess of the standard 5.6 weeks/28 days for those working five days a week) is only payable if the contract provides for it. There may even be circumstances where there is no express contractual term, but the court can imply a term (*Janes Solicitors v Lamb Simpson EAT/323/94*).

Bank holidays

There is **no statutory right** to bank holidays. Any entitlement to bank holidays is purely contractual — either through a specific term in the contract or through conduct or custom and practice. In the case of *Campbell & Smith Construction v Greenwood [2001] IRLR 588*, the EAT held that the government's announcement that there would an additional day's public holiday to mark the Millennium did not entitle employees to an extra day's paid holiday.

If employers do allow workers paid time off on bank holidays, they can count these as part of the minimum 4.8 weeks. As a result of union pressure, the government has increased the minimum holiday entitlement to make sure that workers benefit from additional paid bank holidays.

This took place in two stages: the first increase was in October 2007, the second was in April 2009. Although the change does not mean that everyone can take the extra days on designated bank holidays, it will mean that workers who previously had to take bank holidays out of their four weeks' holiday will get extra days to compensate.

Time off for public duties

Employees who hold certain **public offices** have the right to a "reasonable" amount of time off to perform their duties under section 50 of the ERA 96. This could include acting as a magistrate, local councillor or member of a tribunal, or serving on an NHS trust, school governing body, police authority, environmental agency or board of prison visitors.

In deciding what is **reasonable time off**, the employer can take account of the effect the time off will have on the business, how much time off is required and how much has already been taken.

In the case of *Riley-Williams v Argos EAT/811/02*, the EAT held that reasonable time off would be the amount needed to meet the requirements of the office. In that case, the employee had been appointed as a magistrate and her letter of appointment said that she would have to serve a minimum of 26 half-day sessions a year. The EAT said a reasonable employer would allow that amount.

An employee has the right not to be dismissed or to suffer any other detriment because they have been summoned or are absent from work on **jury service** (section 43M, ERA 96).

There is **no statutory right to be paid** for the time off, so it will be unpaid unless the employee's contract provides for payment. An employee who has been refused the right to time off in respect of any of the above functions can make a complaint to a tribunal within three months.

Time off for study or training

A new right to request time off for study or training has been introduced. As of 6 April 2010, individuals working in organisations with 250 employees or more, and as of 6 April 2010 all individuals irrespective of the size of the organisation for which they work, will have the statutory right to make such a request. Specifically, an employee will be eligible to make a request if they have worked for the employer continuously for six months and are over 18 (those aged 16–18 have a separate right to time off for study or training).

The procedure for the making and handling of a request for time off is governed by the *Employee Study and Training (Procedural Requirements) Regulations 2010*. Essentially the employee must write to the employer stating that s/he is applying under section 63D *Employment Rights Act 1996* to take time off to study or train; what the study or training is; where and when it will take place; who will provide or supervise it; what qualification it will lead to and how it will improve the employee's effectiveness at work and improve the performance of the employee's business.

Within 28 days of receiving the request, the employer must hold a meeting with the individual. (The employee has the right to bring a workplace companion, who is entitled to paid time off to attend). The employer must discuss the request with the individual and seriously consider his or her proposal. While the employer can ultimately decline the request, this may only be lawful if it is on one of a handful of specified grounds. If the employee is dissatisfied with the employer's decision (which s/he must receive within 14 days of the hearing) s/he can appeal. Again, the employer will have 14 days from the date of the appeal meeting to give its decision.

A successful tribunal claim about an employer's failure to comply with the regulations, can lead to an award of up to eight weeks' pay. (Pay is capped at a maximum, currently £380 a week.)

Other statutory rights to time off are explained in the following Chapters: trade union duties and activities and employee representatives — Chapter 5; antenatal care, family emergencies, parental and maternity leave — Chapter 8; alternative work in a redundancy situation — Chapter 11.

More information: LRD booklet *Working time*, £5.60, LRD's *Workplace Report* contains regular updates on pay and working time cases, as well as equal pay developments.

5. Union and collective organisation

Union and collective organisation rights are principally governed by the *Trade Union and Labour Relations (Consolidation) Act 1992* (TULRCA), which was amended by the *Employment Relations Act 1999* (ERA 99) and the *Employment Relations Act 2004* (ERA 04). In Northern Ireland these rights are found in the *Trade Union and Labour Relations (Northern Ireland) Order 1995* (TULRO), as amended.

These lay down the **status** of a union and its **duties** in respect of keeping accounts, submitting returns and the conduct of elections, as well as setting out rights of trade unions and members.

It is unlawful for unions to enforce 100% union organisation (a **"closed shop"**). Section 222 of TULRCA states that all industrial action to enforce 100% union membership agreements or to cause an employer to discriminate against a non-member is unlawful, leaving the union at risk of legal penalties. In addition, any dismissal of a non-union member to enforce 100% membership is automatically unfair.

It is unlawful under section 145A of TULRCA for an employer to offer a worker an **inducement** not to join a union or take part in union activities, or to join a union or any particular union(s).

It is also unlawful (section 145B of TULRCA) for an employer to offer a worker an inducement to stop, or prevent, their terms and conditions being negotiated by a union through a collective agreement (**"collective bargaining"**). In 2006, supermarket chain Asda was ordered to pay £850,000 for offering inducements to 340 members of the GMB general union to give up their collective bargaining rights. The workers at its distribution depot in Washington, Tyne & Wear, were offered a 10% pay rise in order to end collective bargaining at the site.

The amount of the award payable to a worker by an employer who has offered an inducement is £3,100 (2009-10).

The right to recognition

To gain access to many of the rights covered in this Chapter the union must be **recognised by the employer**. TULRCA provides a mechanism through which unions can gain statutory recognition, even where the employer is implacably opposed to it. However, the law does not apply to small employers — that is those with **20 or fewer workers**. The legislation extends to workers and not just employees. However, those who work freelance may be excluded from the calculation of the number of workers (*R v CAC [2003] IRLR 460*).

To apply for recognition under the statutory procedure, a union has to submit a request in writing to the employer. If it is unable to negotiate a recognition agreement, it makes a formal application in writing to the Central Arbitration Committee (CAC).

When making a formal application, the union has to **identify the "bargaining unit"** for which it is seeking recognition. This is the group of workers it wants to represent. It is important to choose the bargaining unit carefully, as the outcome of any eventual ballot can hang on who is, or is not, included in the unit. The law says that the CAC must examine whether a bargaining unit is "compatible with effective management".

The courts have interpreted this to mean that the union's bargaining unit will usually only be successfully challenged where the employer can show that it is not compatible with management. It does not have to be the most effective unit of organisation, as long as it is not an ineffective one. If the employer successfully challenges the union's preferred bargaining unit, the CAC can impose a different one. At this stage the union may choose to **withdraw the application**.

The ERA 04 obliges employers to provide the union and the CAC with an **up-to-date list of workers** in the bargaining unit. It also imposes a legal obligation on a union to provide the CAC with information about its membership. The Act also allows the CAC to intervene if the employer engages in "unfair practices" (section 10, ERA 04) to influence the result of a recognition ballot.

The procedure

The CAC has to first **accept the application** as valid. It will do this only if the union demonstrates that it already has **at least 10% of the bargaining unit** in membership and that a majority of the workers in the unit would be likely to favour recognition. The union has to produce evidence in support of these two requirements. This will usually consist of its own membership records and any letters, petitions and other evidence from the workforce showing that there is likely to be majority support for recognition. This information remains confidential — the employer is not given copies of any documents relating to workers' intentions regarding recognition or whether individuals are union members.

Normally only one union can apply for recognition for the bargaining unit at a time. Where **more than one union** wishes to gain recognition for the same group, they must apply together and show that they are capable of co-operation. If they cannot do this, both applications are invalid. A union cannot apply for statutory recognition where there is already a recognised union, even if the recognised union does not have the support of the majority of the workforce in the bargaining unit. An employer can even decide to recognise another union at any time until the CAC accepts the application as valid, which would block the first union from making a statutory claim.

However, the body with which the employer comes to a deal must be an independent union. Entertainment union BECTU challenged cinema group City Screen when it signed an agreement with a body whose membership consisted solely of four managers and which had no source of funds other than that provided by the company. The CAC held that this was not a union and therefore did not bar the BECTU claim for recognition (*BECTU v City Screen TUR1/309/2003*).

The aim of these restrictions is to avoid competition between unions for the same group of workers. It is not necessary for the recognition agreement to include a requirement to negotiate on pay, hours and holidays even though these are referred to in the legislation. In the case of *T&G v Asda TUR1/368 [2004] ([2004] IRLR 836)*, the CAC held that a "partnership agreement" which did not include pay bargaining was nevertheless a recognition agreement and thus barred another union from making a statutory claim for recognition. However, it means that there will be situations where a union has the majority of members but cannot gain recognition because the employer has reached a voluntary recognition agreement with another union, which could include non-TUC unions, even if this is not what most of the workers want. This occurred in the case of *NUJ v CAC [2004] EWHC 2612 ([2005] IRLR 28)*:

The NUJ journalists' union sought recognition in a unit where it had a significant number of members. But the employer — part of the Mirror Group — recognised the British Association of Journalists (BAJ) instead, which had at the most one member. The High Court rejected the NUJ's application. Although recognising the result as a "loophole", it said that a recognition agreement was in force from the moment it is signed and a union can act "on behalf of" workers without having their consent.

If the union has recruited **more than half the workers** in the bargaining unit, the CAC may be able to award recognition without the need for a ballot. Only a minority of unions have achieved statutory recognition this way. Generally the claim goes through a series of procedures and is most likely to be concluded by means of a secret ballot of workers.

The ballot can either be held by post sent to the individual's nominated address, or at the workplace, or a combination of the two. It is up to the CAC to decide. Regardless of the employer's attitude to the union, they have a **legal duty to co-operate** generally with the union and with the person appointed to conduct the ballot and to provide the CAC with a list of workers' names and addresses. The CAC can order a ballot to be re-run if not all the workers entitled to vote had been given that opportunity (R (on the application of *Ultraframe (UK)) v CAC [2005] EWCA Civ 560 ([2005] IRLR 641)*).

Unions must be given reasonable **access to the workforce**. The Department of Trade and Industry (now BIS) introduced a **Code of Practice** on recognition and derecognition which came into effect on 1 October 2005, *Access and unfair practices during recognition and derecognition ballots*. This replaces the 2000 Code and can be found on the BIS website at: www.berr.gov.uk/files/file14418.pdf.

The Code gives advice to employers and unions on what arrangements should be made so that the union gets the opportunity to put its case to workers in the bargaining unit. It suggests a mass meeting lasting at least 30 minutes every 10 days of the access period and, where appropriate, for "surgeries" to be held during working hours where workers can meet with the union individually or in small groups. The union should be allowed to display material in a prominent place and, where appropriate, workers should have access to information on the internet and by email. The Code also explains the unfair practices that are prohibited during the balloting process, which include offers of money, threats or coercion intending to influence the outcome of the ballot. In addition it contains a guide to fair campaigning.

The *Employment Relations Act 2004* introduced postal voting rights to workers who are absent from work on the date of the recognition ballot.

Whatever the methods agreed, the union should have the **same access** to the workforce as the employer. If the employer puts out a circular with arguments against recognition, the union should be allowed to circulate its arguments in favour.

To win a recognition ballot it is not enough simply to get a majority of the votes cast (50% plus one). **At least 40%** of the entire bargaining unit must also vote in favour of recognition. In effect, abstentions count as votes against the union.

If the ballot goes in the union's favour, or if the CAC declares that there should be recognition without a ballot because the union already has more than 50% of the workforce in membership, the employer and union have to try to **negotiate a collective bargaining procedure**. With a statutory recognition award the union is limited to an agreement to negotiate over pay, hours and holidays. **"Pay"** had been defined widely by the CAC to include pension rights. The ERA 04 reverses this position, making it clear that pensions are excluded from the definition of pay.

If employers and unions cannot reach an agreement on procedures, the CAC will impose one. This will normally involve setting up a joint negotiating body and a six-stage bargaining procedure, with each stage having a specified timetable.

Although the law on recognition appears extremely complicated, unions have had significant successes since its introduction. It has led to both statutory awards for recognition and to a significant increase in voluntary recognition, as employers realise that they could secure a more acceptable agreement through co-operation.

The legislation also sets out the circumstances where the employer or workers can apply to the CAC to have a union with statutory recognition derecognised. In general, these provisions are not operative unless statutory recognition was granted more than three years earlier. However, in one of the first cases on the issue, the CAC issued a derecognition award at the employer's request because evidence was offered to show that the bargaining unit was no longer in existence.

Protection of union members

Under section 137 of TULRCA, there is a statutory right not to be **refused work** on the grounds of membership or non-membership of a union or because of a refusal to leave or join a union. The EAT has held that a refusal to hire a known trade union activist, because he was believed to be "uncooperative and anti-management", came within the definition of discriminatory action on the grounds of union membership (*Harrison v Kent CC [1995] ICR 434*).

It may be difficult to prove an allegation of refusal to hire because of an individual's trade union membership. If a prospective employer is known to systematically exclude trade union members; refuses to process an application or makes the claimant withdraw; refuses employment or makes a spurious offer of employment; and the grounds are believed to be because the individual is (or is not) a trade union member, that person can complain to a tribunal. Complaints can also be made over advertisements or against employment agencies that seek similarly to exclude claimants (section 138, TULRCA). Compensation can include a sum for injury to feelings.

Also, since 2 March 2010 anti-union blacklists have been outlawed under the *Employment Relations Act 1999 (Blacklists) Regulations 2010*. Specifically, the regulations prohibit the compiling, supplying, selling or using of lists of trade union activists and members, with the purpose of discriminating against those individuals. (There are some limited exceptions — for example, where the list is in the hands of a whistleblower/journalist.)

The regulations also make it unlawful for employers to make decisions about recruiting or dismissing anyone on the basis of an anti-union list, and unlawful for agencies to decline to assist someone because they are on such a list. Anyone who finds that they are on a blacklist (as well as the relevant unions) will have the right to bring a claim. Also, even if some of the individuals were not union activists or members (e.g. were on the list simply because they were viewed as troublesome by the employer) they too will have a claim.

As usual, the complaint must normally be lodged at a tribunal within three months of the date of the relevant incident. Fortunately, a reverse burden of proof operates — for example, where an individual can show that he was on a blacklist, and despite being qualified for a post had his application turned down, it will be for the employer to show that there was a lawful reason for the individual's treatment.

Damages will reflect both the individual's loss of earnings and injury to feelings — the tribunal award being not less than £5,000 (other than in Scotland). However, the award is subject to reductions for contributory fault (e.g. if the individual was on the list because of violent conduct).

In addition to ordering the employer to pay compensation, tribunals can recommend that employers take steps to remedy the situation. Furthermore, it is possible to apply for an injunction to prevent a blacklist being used, or to seek an order that a blacklist be destroyed. Finally, complaints involving blacklists should also be directed to the Information Commissioner, who will have the power to investigate and issue a fine.

The European Convention on Human Rights (through the *Human Rights Act 1998*) (see "Civil liberties and employment law" in the Introduction) guarantees the right to **peaceful assembly** and freedom of association. Unions may be able to pursue a claim under the Act where there have been attempts by an employer to restrict their freedom to associate (see for example the case of *ASLEF v UK* on page 98 which confirmed unions' right to exclude BNP members).

Victimisation

Individual members of unions have protection against victimisation by their employer. They have the right not to have **action short of dismissal** (for example, suspension) taken against them, together with the right **not to be dismissed** because of membership of a trade union (see "Automatically unfair dismissals" in Chapter 10) and the right **not to be selected for redundancy** for that reason (see "Selection for redundancy" in Chapter 11).

Mr Williams was selected for redundancy on the grounds of the manner in which he carried out his union duties. The EAT held that provided that the behaviour to which the employer objected was carried out as a trade union activity and not just a reflection of Williams' own personality, his redundancy selection amounted to unlawful discrimination on trade union grounds. *Krupp Camford Pressings v Williams EAT/397/01*

In an important ruling in 1991, the Court of Appeal said that dismissal because an employee had been an active union member in a previous job was unfair and fell within the protection afforded by section 152 of TULRCA (*Fitzpatrick v British Railways Board [1991] IRLR 376*). The key issue is **why** the employer dismissed the employee.

Ms Lindsay was dismissed shortly after joining a union. Her employer denied the dismissal was anything to do with her union membership, claiming it was because of her timekeeping. Lindsay successfully argued that it was only after she had joined the union that her employer started complaining about her timekeeping. The EAT agreed that this amounted to a dismissal for trade union reasons. *Lindsay v General Contracting EAT/1126/00 .*

In the case of *MANCAT v Smith & others UKEAT/0460/06*, evidence of the college principal's hostility to the claimants allowed a tribunal to conclude that he was motivated by animosity towards them because of their trade union activities.

Section 146 of TULRCA protects trade unionists from action short of dismissal by employers where this involves either preventing or deterring them from joining or taking part in union activities. If an employer decides to **no longer recognise a shop steward** who has been accredited by the union, this amounts to action short of dismissal for the purpose of deterring the individual from taking part in union activities (*Farnsworth v McCoid [1999] EWCA Civ 1064 ([1999] IRLR 626)*).

An employee carrying out his/her trade union duties at an appropriate time, who is **disciplined** on account of those activities, is unlawfully victimised (*LB Islington v Hutchings EAT/34/01*).

However, according to the Court of Appeal in the case of *Gallacher v Department of Transport [1994] IRLR 231*, an employer's **refusal to promote** someone on the grounds that their trade union duties had prevented the individual from acquiring relevant experience does not fall within the protection.

The Court of Appeal held that **withholding a pay rise** from an employee until such time as she agreed to give up her union duties amounted to unlawful victimisation. The employers argued that they had not taken action against her, but that they had merely "omitted" to take action in her favour, but the court rejected this explanation (*LB Southwark v Whillier [2001] ICR 1016*).

Victimisation claims must go to the tribunal **within three months** of the date when the action complained of occurred, and if the claim is upheld the tribunal will order the employer to pay compensation that is "just and equitable". There is no length of service requirement to pursue the claim. If the victimisation results in a dismissal, a minimum of £4,700 (2009-10) basic compensation will be awarded. In addition the tribunal can make a compensatory award of up to £65,300 (2010-11), which could include damages for injury to feelings. The EAT, in the case of *LB Hackney v Adams EAT/1318/01 ([2003] IRLR 402)*, held that damages for injury to feelings are as relevant in trade union cases as in any other field of discrimination law.

If an employee is dismissed on grounds of their union activities they are entitled to claim **interim relief** at an employment tribunal. Interim relief is a remedy available in cases of unfair dismissal that are automatically unfair on grounds of trade union activities or certain health and safety activities. The application must be supported by the union in the form of a written certificate. A tribunal can make an order for interim relief if it considers that the employee is likely to succeed in their unfair dismissal claim. The effect of the order is to continue the contract of employment until the full claim has been heard, which means the employee will continue to be paid by the employer. The employee and union must act quickly — a claim for interim relief must be brought **within seven days** of the effective date of termination.

Disciplinary action against union representatives should not be dealt with under the organisation's normal disciplinary procedure but should be covered by a special procedure. Acas advises that: "Disciplinary action against a trade union official can lead to a serious dispute if it is seen as an attack on the union's functions". For this reason, while normal disciplinary standards should apply, no action beyond an oral warning should be taken until the case is discussed with a senior trade union representative or full-time official.

Rights to time off

Union lay officials, including shop stewards, staff reps and branch secretaries of recognised unions, have the right to **time off with pay** (based on average hourly earnings) to carry out trade union duties (section 168, TULRCA).

If an employer refuses a right to time off in circumstances where it would have been reasonable to provide the right, the union representative can take a claim to an employment tribunal. The tribunal can award financial compensation, even in cases where the representative has not incurred any financial loss (*Skiggs v SW Trains EAT/0763/03 ([2005] IRLR 459)*).

Trade union duties are those concerned with negotiation with the employer over what are termed **"section 178(2)"** matters (terms and conditions, recruitment, suspension, dismissal, work allocation, discipline, union membership, time off facilities and procedures). Alternatively, with the employer's agreement, they can be for functions related to these matters but which are not within the scope of negotiations. To benefit from the time-off rights, the union must be recognised by the employer for the section 178(2) matter for which the time off is required.

Trade union officers have the right to **time off for training**, again if related to section 178(2) matters. This right is qualified by the words "reasonable in all the circumstances". The Acas Code of Practice on *Time off for trade union duties and activities* gives, as examples of "reasonableness", the employer's need for safety and security at all times, the size of the organisation, the production process and the need to maintain a service to the public. There is no service qualification for this right.

Employee representatives appointed or elected for consultation on redundancy and business transfers (see Chapters 11 and 12) similarly have the right to time off for training in their duties. An employer who persistently refuses time off, arguing that there are **staff shortages**, is likely to be in breach of the law where no efforts are made to overcome the shortages.

The EAT has held that time off is not rigidly limited to the section 178(2) matters since an employer acting reasonably has to take account of factors such as the history, timing and agenda of the meeting in question (*London Ambulance Service v Charlton [1992] IRLR 510*).

Trade union representatives on the management committees of their company pension schemes have the right to paid time off for training on pensions, even where the pension scheme itself is not negotiable, according to the EAT.

Part-time workers should be paid for the same number of hours as a full-time employee when attending union training. A ruling of the European Court in the case of *Arbeiterwohlfahrt der Stadt Berlin v Botel Case C-360/90 ([1992] IRLR 423)* held that an employee whose working day is shorter than that of other employees, but who takes part in a course with hours in excess of the employee's contractual hours, should be paid for the hours on the course at the same level as the full-time workers. This interpretation was also adopted by the ECJ in the case of *Kuratorium v Lewark C457/93 ([1996] IRLR 637*.

All members of recognised unions, not just representatives, have the right to reasonable **time off without pay** to take part in trade union activities, except for industrial action (section 170, TULRCA). These would include shiftworkers attending trades council and union branch meetings. Circumstances where the time off rights have been held to apply to workplace union representatives include attendance at trade union meetings and at a conference dealing with new laws on working conditions. However, the EAT ruled, in the case of *Luce v LB Bexley [1990] IRLR 422*, that there is no right to time off to attend a **lobby of parliament** to protest over legislation not significantly specific to the workers concerned.

An employee can bring a claim relating to time off to a tribunal, but only if a specific request for time off has been denied (*Ryford v Drinkwater [1996] IRLR 16*). The claim must be presented to a tribunal **within three months** (section 171, TULRCA). If the claim is successful, the tribunal will make a declaration of the employee's rights and may award "just and equitable" compensation.

Employee representatives in workplaces with no recognised union who are elected for consultation on redundancy and business transfers (see

Chapters 11 and 12) have rights to time off with pay for their duties.

Union learning representatives also have the right to a reasonable amount of paid time off to carry out their duties. These would include addressing learning or training needs, providing information and advice and promoting the value of learning. They also have the right to time off for training to understand the different methods for identifying learning needs, drawing up learning plans and working with employers to promote the value of learning.

Rights to information

Section 181 of TULRCA says that, **for the purpose of collective bargaining**, employers have a duty to disclose, to representatives of independent recognised unions, information:

◆ without which representatives would be impeded in carrying out collective bargaining; or

◆ which, in accordance with good industrial relations practice, should be disclosed.

This can include an order to an employer to give the union information on the distribution of percentage pay awards across certain staff groups and information about the amount and distribution of overtime.

The Acas Code of Practice *Disclosure of information to trade unions* for collective bargaining purposes states that information that should be disclosed includes:

◆ **pay and benefits** — structure of the payment system, earnings analysed by work group, details of fringe benefits;

◆ **employee numbers** — numbers employed by age and sex, turnover, absenteeism;

◆ **performance** — productivity and efficiency data, sales; and

◆ **financial** — profit, assets, liabilities, loans, sales.

The right to disclosure is **restricted** on limited grounds by section 182 of TULRCA. This states that an employer can decline to give the information on the grounds: of national security; that the information has been obtained in confidence; that it relates specifically to an individual; or that it would cause "substantial injury" to the employer's undertaking.

The Acas Code of Practice gives examples of information that could lead to "substantial injury", which includes cost information on individual products and marketing and pricing details.

Complaints over an employer's failure to disclose must be presented in writing to the Central Arbitration Committee (CAC), which will attempt first to mediate to resolve the matter. Failing this it may, if it finds the claim justified, make a ruling (section 183, TULRCA). Claims under section 183 are presented by the union, not by individuals.

Employee reps and European works councils

In companies with operations in two or more European Union states employing more than 1,000 employees in total, a European works council (EWC) must, if requested, be established to provide a forum for informing and consulting employees.

EWC members need not be trade union representatives, although in practice in most large workplaces where there are recognised unions they will nominate candidates for election. The rules for setting up an EWC are laid down in the *Transnational Information and Consultation of Employees Regulations 1999*.

Companies have to supply information about their structures and organisation where requested. The ECJ, in the case of *Betriebsrat v Bofrost C-62/99 ([2001] IRLR 403)*, held that this is a **legal requirement** even if it has not, at that stage, been possible to establish whether the company itself is the controlling undertaking. The court held that information on company structure is essential to the opening of negotiations on the establishment of an EWC. Where the company headquarters are located outside the EU, the largest employer based in an EU state in the group has to assume responsibility for the provision of information to assist the establishment of the EWC (*Gesamtbetriebsrat der Kuhne & Nagel v Kuhne & Nagel C-440/00 ([2004] IRLR 332)*).

Where the central management is based in an EU state, a company must supply other undertakings in the same group with information needed for the establishment of an EWC (*Betriebsrat der Firma ADS Anker Gmbj v ADS Anker GmbH C-349/01*).

In May 2004, the European Commission launched a formal process that could lead to a revision of the EU Directive upon which the 1999 regulations are based. The review covered the process of initiating the establishment of an EWC, the effectiveness of information and consultation, facilities for EWC members and trade union involvement in EWCs.

An EU Directive obliges employers to **consult employee representatives at national level**. The *Employment Relations Act 2004* transposes these requirements into UK law. Under the *Information and Consultation of Employees Regulations 2004* which came into effect on 6 April 2005, UK employers have to establish consultation bodies for the information and consultation of employees (known as ICE) if 10% of the workforce requests it. Once in place the terms of reference of the ICE body can only be changed if 40% of the workforce votes in favour.

The ICE body is the body through which the employer should consult with reps on the situation, structure and probable development of employment and on future job plans.

Initially, the law only applied in firms where there are 150 or more employees. In March 2007 it was extended to workplaces with 100 to 150 workers and from April 2008 included those with 50 to 100 workers. Part-time workers are counted, although those working fewer than 75 hours per month can each be counted as half an employee if the employer so wishes. The legislation additionally excludes casual and agency staff from the calculation of the number of employees.

In a successful claim brought by general union Amicus (now part of the Unite union), publishing firm Macmillan became the first employer fined for a breach of its duty to consult under the ICE regulations. Noting that the company's responses to the Central Arbitration Committee (which has responsibility for decisions under ICE) were "vague" and "fudged", the EAT fined Macmillan £55,000 (*Amicus v Macmillan Publishers Ltd UKEAT/0185/07*).

Internal union matters

A number of internal union procedures are also regulated by legislation. The main areas covered by the law are bars on membership, internal union elections, ballots on political funds and discipline of members.

Union members also have rights as defined by the **union's rulebook**. These can lay down the circumstances under which a member can expect support or representation from the union. The rulebook defines the **contractual relationship** between the member and the union.

Under section 174 of TULRCA a union can exclude or expel someone from union membership if s/he does not meet the membership requirements or because of their conduct. In 2004, this was amended to specify that "conduct" can include activities carried out as a member of a political party, but not membership of a political party itself. This meant that unions were unable to expel members who were in far-right political parties such as the BNP even though their values were completely opposed to those of the union.

However, in February 2007 unions won the **right to expel members of the BNP** at the European Court of Human Rights. In the following case the court held that the right to freedom of assembly and association under the European Convention on Human Rights entitles unions to refuse membership to individuals whose political views are fundamentally opposed to their own.

Train drivers' union ASLEF expelled a member after it became aware that he had been accused of harassing Anti-Nazi League campaigners and had written racist and fascist material for the BNP's Spearhead magazine. The member, Mr Lee, brought a claim in an employment tribunal under section 174 of TULRCA.

The ruling by the Employment Appeal Tribunal that a union could expel a member for their conduct when carrying out the activities of a political party and not just because they were a member of a party resulted in the change to the law and the union was expected to win its case. But a second tribunal found in favour of Lee, saying that his membership of the BNP was the reason for his expulsion, and not his activities. The union was forced to re-admit him and would have been liable to pay him compensation of up to £60,600 had the decision stood.

ASLEF, with financial help from 18 other unions, took the case to the European Court of Human Rights which ruled in their favour, saying that there was a violation of the union's rights as Lee's values and ideals fundamentally clashed with its own. *ASLEF v UK (application 11002/05)*

As a result of this case, section 174 was amended (by the *Employment Act 2008*) to allow unions to expel members of far right organisations such as the BNP. Sections 24-61 of TULRCA lay down the procedures to be adopted by unions in relation to:

◆ maintaining **a register of members' names and addresses**;

◆ submitting **annual returns**; and

◆ conducting **union elections**.

When conducting elections unions must ensure that:

◆ all members of a union's national executive body, including its president and general secretary, are elected at least every five years (section 46);

◆ elections must be by **secret postal ballot** (section 1);

◆ elections must be supervised by **independent scrutineers** who are responsible for inspecting the membership register and producing a report on the election (section 49);

◆ an **"independent person"** must undertake the administration of the vote (this person may also serve as scrutineer); and

◆ **members must be told** who the scrutineers are to be and their names must be included on the ballot paper (section 51).

Section 65 says that a union may not **"unjustifiably discipline"** a member and defines this as where the reason for the discipline is that the member:

◆ fails to **participate in or support industrial action**;

◆ seeks to take **legal action against the union**;

◆ **fails to agree to check-off** arrangements; or

◆ **works with non-union members** or non-union employers.

Political fund ballots must be conducted every 10 years and are subject to the same general rules. There is a right of complaint to the Certification Officer or the courts if any member believes the ballot has not been conducted according to the rules.

The government-appointed Certification Officer has prime responsibility for checking the finances and independence of unions and for assisting individuals with complaints against their unions.

A complaint has to be submitted to the tribunal **within three months** of the action complained of.

> **More information:** See the LRD booklets *Time off for trade union duties and activities* (£4.25); *Learning and training* (£4.20); *Worker representation in Europe* (£10.95); *Information and consultation* (£5.15).

6. Discrimination

The last few decades have seen the introduction of laws designed to prevent discrimination in employment. At different times, and using different tests, the following have been outlawed: discrimination on the grounds of **sex** and **transsexuality**, **race** and **nationality**, **disability**, **sexual orientation**, **religion** or **belief** and **age**. Discrimination in pay on grounds of sex is covered by **equal pay** legislation.

The *Equality Act 2010* (which is expected to largely come into force in October 2010) includes measures to consolidate and harmonise existing discrimination legislation. However, even before the consolidating provisions of the *Equality Act 2010* come into force, there are significant similarities in the way that the law deals with discrimination. This means that, where the wording of the legislation is the same, case law concerning discrimination on one ground can also apply to discrimination on another ground. For example, case law on sex discrimination is readily applied to cases of race discrimination.

This Chapter sets out the different grounds for unlawful discrimination, and explains how the law relating to different forms of discrimination — direct, indirect, harassment and victimisation — operates. There are important differences in the law relating to disability and age discrimination and these are dealt with under separate headings.

Grounds for unlawful discrimination

Sex

Currently it is the *Sex Discrimination Act 1975* (SDA) which prohibits discrimination on the grounds of sex, gender reassignment or because someone is married or is a civil partner. The SDA has been amended on several occasions — including by the *Sex Discrimination Act 1975 (Amendment) Regulations 2008* (which revised the definition of sexual harassment and extend employers' liability to harassment carried out by third parties). In Northern Ireland the equivalent legislation is the *Sex Discrimination (Northern Ireland) Order 1976*. (It is expected that from October 2010 the *Equality Act 2010* (which expressly outlaws discrimination on the grounds of marriage/civil partnership as well as civil pregnancy/maternity) will replace the SDA).

Race

Under the *Race Relations Act 1976* (RRA), discrimination is outlawed "on racial grounds", which means on grounds of "colour, race, nationality or ethnic or national origins". However, the newer definition of indirect discrimination (see "Types of discrimination" below), brought in by the *Race Relations Act 1976 (Amendment) Regulations 2003*, applies only on grounds of "race or ethnic or national origins". In Northern Ireland the equivalent legislation is the *Race Relations (Northern Ireland) Order 1997*.

It is expected that from October 2010, the *Equality Act 2010* will replace the RRA. The Act largely just harmonises the tests that have developed for establishing whether discrimination has occurred (see below). However, under section 9(5), *Equality Act 2010*, the secretary of state will acquire the power to outlaw discrimination on the grounds of caste (i.e. the class system often observed amongst groups originally from the Indian sub-continent).

Sexual orientation

The *Employment Equality (Sexual Orientation) Regulations 2003* (EE(SO)R), outlaws discrimination on the grounds of sexual orientation, defined as an orientation towards:

◆ persons of the same sex;

◆ persons of the opposite sex; or

◆ persons of the same sex and the opposite sex.

The regulations cover discrimination based on a person's perceived as well as actual sexual orientation (and this is expressly stated to be the case for all forms of discrimination under the *Equality Act 2010*). So if an employer discriminates against a worker because s/he is thought to be gay, s/he has the right to pursue a claim even if s/he is not gay.

In *English v Thomas Sanderson Ltd [2008] EWCA Civ 1421*, a heterosexual man was subjected to homophobic insults at work, even though his colleagues knew that he was not gay. Mr English was entitled to privacy and did not have to declare his sexuality in order to be able to bring a claim. The Court of Appeal found that the verbal abuse (on grounds of sexual orientation) that Mr English suffered was an insult to his dignity and he was, accordingly, entitled to damages under the 2003 regulations.

The *Equality Act 2010* is expected to replace the EE(SO)R. The Act largely just harmonises the tests that have developed for establishing whether discrimination has occurred (see below). However, the government's proposal of a more restrictive interpretation (contained within an earlier version of the *Equality Act*) of when religious establishments can lawfully not employ homosexual people was rejected by the House of Lords. This is not the end of the matter however, as the European Commission is expected to pursue this further.

Gender reassignment

Transsexuals are protected from direct discrimination under the SDA, as amended by the *Sex Discrimination (Gender Reassignment) Regulations 1999*. Gender reassignment is defined as "a process, which is undertaken under medical supervision, for the purposes of reassigning a person's sex by changing physiological or other characteristics of sex, and includes any part of such a process".

The Act prohibits less favourable treatment of a person because they intend to undergo or have undergone gender reassignment (section 2A SDA).

In a landmark ruling in 2002, the European Court of Human Rights held that post-operative transsexuals must have all the rights available to their new sex, including the right to marry a person of the opposite sex. The ruling also means that post-operative transsexuals have the right to state benefits appropriate to their new sex (*Goodwin v UK [2002] IRLR 664*).

In another key ruling in 2003, the European Court of Justice (ECJ) held that pension fund rules must be interpreted so as to ensure that the **survivor of a partnership** where one is a post-operative transsexual has the right to a pension if it would have been available had they been married (*KB v The NHS Pensions Agency C-117/01 ([2004] IRLR 240)*).

A post-operative transsexual police constable was refused a job where she would be required to undertake searches of female prisoners. The House of Lords ruled that she should be recognised as female and was therefore able to carry out the work. The refusal to offer her work was discrimination. *A v Chief Constable of the West Yorkshire Police [2004] UKHL 21 ([2004] IRLR 573).*

The *Gender Recognition Act 2004* gives legal recognition to those who can demonstrate that they have taken decisive steps towards living permanently and fully in their acquired gender. It provides that applications for legal recognition in the acquired gender are considered by a Gender Recognition Panel. If the panel issues a Gender Recognition Certificate, a new birth certificate is issued.

Where an individual is going through the process of gender reassignment, s/he has to undergo a "real life test"; this involves having to live as a member of their chosen sex.

Employers need to consider whether any adjustments should be made during that period, and the question of appropriate toilet facilities may arise.

In the case of *Croft v Royal Mail [2003] EWCA Civ 1045*, the Court of Appeal held that it was appropriate for the employer to suggest the use of disabled toilet facilities for an interim period only, until the gender reassignment was concluded.

The Equality and Human Rights Commission (EHRC) provides a summary of cases relating to the treatment of transsexual people at www.equalityhumanrights.com/en/yourrights.

It is ecpected that from October 2010, the *Equality Act 2010* will the SDA. The Act largely just harmonises the tests that have developed for establishing whether discrimination has occurred (see below). However, the *Equality Act 2010* will introduce a new concept of indirect discrimination on the grounds of gender reassignment. It is also expected that from October 2010 under section 7, *Equality Act 2010,* the requirement that a transsexual person be under medical supervision in order to be able to bring a claim, will be removed.

Religion or belief

The *Employment Equality (Religion or Belief) Regulations 2003* (EE(RB)R) cover cases where a person is discriminated against on the grounds of their religion or belief (defined as "any religion, religious belief, or similar philosophical belief") or of their perceived religion or belief. For example, if people are discriminated against because they are thought to be Muslim, they can use the law even if in fact they are not of that (or any) faith.

In *Eweida v British Airways [2010] EWCA Civ 80*, an employee was refused the right to wear a crucifix outside her clothing. This decision was in accordance with the agreed dress code, as the wearing of a crucifix is not a scriptural requirement,. However, exceptions had been made in similar situations (specifically, in relation to head coverings). In order to establish that indirect discrimination had occurred, Ms Eweida needed to show that she was part of a group of people suffering a disadvantage. In other words, she needed to show that she was one of an identifiable group of people working at BA who (as a result of their religion) were disadvantaged in their ability to comply with BA's dress code.

The Court of Appeal noted that none of BA's other 30,000 employees had complained about this issue. Accordingly, the Court of Appeal was not satisfied that a sufficient number of people other than Ms Eweida were, by being refused permission to visibly wear a crucifix put at a particular disadvantage. The fact that the wearing of a crucifix is not a doctrinal requirement of Christian faith, was important. In any event, even if these hurdles had been cleared, the court decided that the fact that the dress code banned the visible wearing of necklaces outside uniforms, was justified (i.e. the rule was a proportionate means of achieving a legitimate aim).

In the case of *Saini v All Saints Haque Centre UKEAT/0227/08*, Mr Saini and his colleague Mr Chandel (both of whom were Hindus) worked at an advice centre where the directors were of the Ravidass faith. When the directors sought Mr Saini's assistance in unlawfully terminating Mr Chandel's employment, both workers brought religious discrimination claims. The EAT agreed that Mr Saini's claim should succeed as the term in the legislation "on the grounds of religion or belief" does not require the discriminatory conduct to be on the grounds of the claimant's own beliefs. It was sufficient that his colleague Mr Chandel had been discriminated against on the grounds of his beliefs.

The case of *Grainger PLC & others v Nicholson UKEAT/0219/09; [2010] IRLR 4 EAT* concerned a claim by an individual who asserted that he had been selected for redundancy on the basis of his beliefs about green issues. Mr Grainger's argument that his position on climate change and the environment amounted to a protected philosophical belief under the *Employment Equality (Religion and*

Belief) Regulations 2003 was resisted by the employer. The tribunal, noting Mr Grainger's assertion that his beliefs affected how he lived his life (e.g. his choice of home, method of travel, and items he purchased) found that they were capable of being protected under regulation 2(1) of the 2003 regulations.

On appeal the EAT upheld the tribunal's judgment in favour of Mr Grainger. The EAT set the following tests for establishing whether an individual's beliefs amount to protected philosophical beliefs:

(i) The belief must be genuinely held; (ii) It must be a belief and not simply an opinion based on the present state of information available; (iii) It must be a belief as to a weighty and substantial aspect of human life and behaviour; (iv) It must attain a certain level of cogency, seriousness, cohesion and importance; (v) It must be worthy of respect in a democratic society, be not incompatible with human dignity and not conflict with the rights of others.

Subject to this, a protected "belief" need not be a full-fledged system of thought. Pacifism, vegetarianism, Darwinism would probably all be covered. Support of a political party would be excluded, but the EAT did not rule out belief in a political philosophy, such as socialism being protected.

In *Chondol v Liverpool City Council UKEAT/0298/08*, a Christian mental health worker was accused of seeking to promote God and church attendance to vulnerable adults. Mr Chondol, who admitted giving out copies of the Bible to his clients and visiting them outside of work unaccompanied (both of which were prohibited), was dismissed. He, unsuccessfully, brought a religious discrimination claim. The EAT decided that dismissing someone for proselytising (provided that was the real reason for termination) was not unlawful.

In *Ladele v London Borough Islington UKEAT/0453/08/RN*, a Christian births, marriages and deaths registrar refused to perform civil partnerships. Having been disciplined and threatened with dismissal, Ms Ladele claimed that she had suffered religious discrimination.

The Court of Appeal found that there was no direct discrimination or harassment because the reason the Council had treated Ms Ladele as it did, was not because she was a Christian but because she was refusing to carry out civil partnership ceremonies. As to indirect discrimination, the policy of requiring all registrars to perform civil partnerships did put Ms Ladele, who believed that civil partnerships were contrary to the will of God, at a disadvantage when compared with others. The question was whether the Council could justify its policy as a proportionate means of meeting a legitimate aim.

The Council aimed to provide an efficient civil partnership service and maintain its commitment to promote equal opportunities. The CA decided that the Council's requirement of Ms Ladele was therefore proportionate and in pursuit of a legitimate aim. Ms Ladele was working in a secular job and was being asked not to discriminate against gay people in the course of that job. It did not stop her worshipping the way she wished. The CA said that Ms Ladele's religious views should not be permitted to override the Council's wish that all its registrars manifest equal respect for the homosexual and heterosexual community.

The *Equality Act 2010* is expected to replace the EE(RB)R from October 2010. The Act largely just harmonises the tests that have developed for establishing whether discrimination has occurred (see below). However, the government's proposed more restrictive interpretation (contained within an earlier version of the *Equality Act*) of when religious establishments can lawfully not employ homosexual people was rejected by the House of Lords. This is not the end of the matter however, as the European Commission is expected to pursue this further.

Northern Ireland has had anti-religious discrimination for longer than the rest of the UK under the *Fair Employment and Treatment (Northern Ireland) Order 1998 (FTO)*, which also outlaws discrimination on grounds of political belief. FETO obliges employers to register with the Equality Commission for Northern Ireland and file annual monitoring returns. Employers are also required to regularly review their employment practices and to assess whether affirmative (positive) action policies are necessary.

The Northern Ireland Court of Appeal held that an employer was guilty of discrimination when he accepted the resignation of a Catholic bar worker who feared for his safety when working in a public house in a Protestant area. It was no excuse for the employer to allege that he would have responded similarly had he employed a Protestant in a public house in a Catholic area (*Smyth v Croft Inns [1996] IRLR 84*). Under the Northern Irish legislation, political discrimination is not limited to sectarian political opinions but covers all discrimination on political grounds, according to the Court of Appeal case of *McKay v NIPSA [1995] IRLR 146.*

Types of discrimination

There are four types of discrimination specified by law, which are looked at in more detail below:

◆ **direct discrimination** is treating someone less favourably than someone else;

◆ **indirect discrimination** is imposing the same conditions on all workers, but with the result that they adversely affect one group more than another;

◆ **victimisation** is subjecting someone to a detriment because of something they have done in connection with a complaint of discrimination (either their own or someone else's); and

◆ **harassment** is behaviour that violates someone's dignity or creates an intimidating, hostile, degrading, humiliating or offensive environment for them.

Discrimination law applies to workers as well as employees (see Chapter 2 for definitions), as long as there is an employment relationship. In the case of *Mingeley v Pennock and Ivory t/a Amber Cars [2004] EWCA Civ 328 ([2004] IRLR 373)*, the Court of Appeal rejected a discrimination claim taken by a private hire taxi driver against the company that allocated work to him, because his contract did not meet the definition of an employment relationship.

There is **no qualifying period of employment** before a worker is protected by discrimination law. Job applicants are also protected, as are former employees.

Direct discrimination

Direct discrimination in employment occurs when someone is **treated less favourably** than someone of a different sex, race, sexual orientation, religion or belief or age, or who is not transsexual, because of that characteristic.

Subjecting someone to a **detriment** amounts to less favourable treatment, even if the action does not result in loss of pay or grading. This was the ruling of the House of Lords in the case of *Shamoon v Chief Constable of the RUC [2003] UKHL 11 ([2003] IRLR 285)*, where a female officer had some of her responsibilities removed in circumstances where a male officer would not. Dismissing or refusing to hire a woman because she is **pregnant** comes within the definition of direct discrimination, as does having a workplace **retirement policy** where women retire earlier than men.

It is unlawful to discriminate against a Scottish person in favour of an English person, or vice versa. This is because, even though they are both British citizens, they are of different nationality.

To succeed in a claim of direct discrimination, the claimant will need to compare their treatment with that of a person in a similar position, but who is of a different sex, race, sexual orientation, religion or belief or age or is not transsexual. This person is called the **comparator**. If there is no actual comparator, the claimant can show that a hypothetical comparator would have been treated differently. In cases of pregnancy discrimination (see page 174), there is no need for a comparator; it is enough to show that the reason for the treatment was that the worker was pregnant or on maternity leave.

The claimant must show that there was "less favourable treatment". This can include:

◆ setting different questions at interview;
◆ asking only women about their domestic commitments;
◆ asking intrusive questions only of workers believed to be gay;
◆ making assumptions of how individuals will behave, based on their perceived religion or belief;
◆ instructing employees to discriminate;
◆ paying different redundancy pay to women or black workers; and
◆ presuming that some work is unsuited to women or black workers.

The fact that the alleged **perpetrator** of a discriminatory act may be of the **same** sex, race and so on, is irrelevant.

The following have been held to amount to direct discrimination:

◆ the offer of a "disturbance payment" to mostly male shift workers to encourage them to accept changes to their terms, when no offer had been made to shifts made up of mostly female workers (*MFI UK v Bradley and others EAT/1125/02*);

◆ treating a black employee more harshly than a white colleague for a less serious offence (*Wandsworth BC v Warner EAT/0671/04*);

◆ dismissing a female employee after allegations of an affair with a more senior male colleague who was not dismissed (*Chamberlin Solicitors v Emokpae EAT/0989/03 ([2004] IRLR 592)*);

◆ refusing to promote someone to the post of area inspector because her husband was the divisional commander (*Chief Constable of the Bedfordshire Constabulary v Graham EAT/1061/00 ([2002] IRLR 239)*); and

◆ failing to follow a disciplinary procedure for an Asian employee when a white employee would have been treated differently (*Aziz v Crown Prosecution Service [2006] EWCA Civ 1136*).

There may be circumstances where a dress code imposed only on one sex could amount to discrimination. In a test case brought by public services union PCS on behalf of around 8,000 members who worked for JobCentre Plus, the Employment Appeal Tribunal (EAT) held that a requirement for men to wear ties could (but did not necessarily) amount to discrimination. JobCentre Plus had a "smartness code" stipulating that men (but not women) must wear ties. The EAT said the tribunal should have asked whether or not the men could only achieve the required level of smartness by wearing ties. As a result of the decision, PCS settled the claim and the JobCentre Plus collar and tie rule was abolished (*Department for Work and Pensions v Thompson EAT/0254/03 ([2004] IRLR 348)*).

Refusing to appoint someone on discriminatory grounds is unlawful. In the case of *Cardiff Women's Aid v Hartup [1994] IRLR 390*, the EAT confirmed that no complaint can be pursued unless the individual has actually applied for the job. Following the decision of the ECJ in *Centrum voor gelijkheid van kansen en voor racismebestrijding v Firma Feryn C 54/07 ([2008] IRLR 732)*, individuals, as well as the EHRC, can bring claims about discriminatory adverts.

Exemptions exist if the employer can show that a **genuine occupational qualification** (GOQ) is needed for a job to be carried out by someone from a specified group. For example, advertising a job as suitable for an "Afro Caribbean worker" to maintain a racial balance in a daycare centre comes within the GOQ requirements (*Tottenham Green Under Fives v Marshall [1991] IRLR 162*).

In *Amnesty International v Ahmed UKEAT/0447/08* an individual of Sudanese ethnic origin was turned down for the post of researcher for Sudan. Amnesty decided that as Ms Ahmed was from one of the two ethnic groups engaged in the conflict in Sudan, she would be seen as biased (which would undermine the organisation's reputation for neutrality and put her safety at risk). Ms Ahmed's claims for direct and indirect discrimination were upheld. The EAT found that the decision to turn down Ms Ahmed was on the basis of her ethnic origin, and the fact that Amnesty's motive was good or benign was irrelevant. Also, Amnesty had not proved that not promoting Ms Ahmed was reasonably necessary under the *Health and Safety at Work Act 1974*, and in any event this defence did not apply to a case of discrimination on grounds of race or national or ethnic origin. However, the outcome might have been different if Amnesty had used the genuine occupational requirement/qualification defence.

Indirect discrimination

Prior to the coming into force of the relevant provisions of the *Equality Act 2010* (expected to be in October 2010) there are two definitions of indirect discrimination. The first applies only to discrimination under the SDA and the RRA, while the second applies to all the grounds for discrimination listed above.

This is because the recent regulations outlawing discrimination on grounds of religion or belief and sexual orientation were brought in to comply with the European Employment Directive, and adopted its definition of indirect discrimination. But the Directive required all discrimination legislation to comply, so the SDA and RRA were amended by simply adding the new definition alongside the existing definition. This was particularly confusing for race discrimination, because the grounds on which it is outlawed under the Directive also differ; the result is that the first form of indirect race discrimination applies to discrimination on grounds of "colour, race, nationality or ethnic or national origins" and the second on grounds of "race or ethnic or national origins".

As a result, unions and individuals dealing with tribunal claims must take care that they are relying on the right provision. Under the first definition (which applies under the SDA and the RRA only), indirect discrimination occurs where the employer applies a **"requirement or condition"** which is:

◆ to the detriment of a **considerably larger proportion** of one group;
◆ **not justified**; and
◆ to the **detriment** of the person making the complaint.

It is necessary to establish whether statistically more people of one sex or race are adversely affected by the requirement.

The second definition (which applies under the SDA, the RRA, the EE(SO)R and the EE(RB)R, as well as the age regulations, is that indirect discrimination occurs where the employer applies a **"provision, criterion or practice"** which:

◆ puts people of that group at a **particular disadvantage** compared with other people;
◆ puts the **individual claimant** at a disadvantage; and
◆ cannot be shown by the employer to be a **proportionate means of achieving a legitimate aim**.

This definition does not require statistical comparisons.

Whatever the nature of the indirect discrimination, claimants also have to show that they have suffered a detriment — in other words, that they have lost out in some way as a result of the imposition of the provisions or requirements.

In one case, an investigation into fraud which lasted longer than it would have done if the employee had been white, was held to amount to a detriment even though the employee did not lose out financially (*Garry v LB Ealing [2001] IRLR 681*).

The law allows indirect discrimination (but not direct discrimination — except on grounds of age) to be objectively **justified** if the employer can show a reason why it needed to apply the requirement or provision. In the case of *Hardys & Hansons plc v Lax [2005] EWCA Civ 846 ([2005] IRLR 726)*, the Court of Appeal held that this test goes beyond the "band of reasonable responses" test required in a claim of unfair dismissal:

Lisa Lax asked to do her job on a part-time or job-share basis when she returned from maternity leave, but her employer refused. She brought a claim for indirect sex discrimination on the grounds that the requirement to work full-time disadvantaged more women than men. The court held that the employer's refusal to offer a job share did amount to indirect discrimination and could not be justified. It said that a tribunal must carry out a detailed, critical evaluation of the reasons put forward by the employer and assess whether the employer's proposal (in this case, the insistence on working full-time) was "reasonably necessary".

A tribunal must balance the needs of the business against the rights of the individual when assessing whether a requirement is justified, as confirmed by the EAT in the case of *Loke v Governing Body of Calthorpe School EAT/0594/04*:

Mr Loke was a temporary special needs assistant at a school for children with learning difficulties, and was recruited to work with a child requiring constant one-to-one care. As a practising Muslim, Loke needed time off on Fridays to attend prayers for half an hour between 1.30pm and 4.00pm. On one occasion he left work at 1.30pm without consent, and the school said it could not employ him in the role unless he could be with the pupil throughout school hours.

The EAT found that the school's requirement was indirectly discriminatory, and that the tribunal hearing the claim had not properly considered whether it was justified. The tribunal should have set out all the factors it needed to take into account — including Loke's need to pray at particular times, the school's concern for its pupils' welfare and the pupil's history of behavioural problems involving assaults on staff and pupils. The reasonable needs of the school had to be weighed against the discriminatory treatment of the claimant. Loke's case was sent to a different tribunal to be heard again.

Under section 19, *Equality Act 2010* the second definition will be adopted as the test for all types of discrimination.

Harassment

Harassment is established through case law as a form of direct discrimination. It is **defined** as conduct on discriminatory grounds (sex, race, and so on) that:

◆ violates another's dignity; or

◆ creates an intimidating, hostile, degrading, humiliating or offensive environment for the other.

Harassment occurs if its **effect**, rather than just its purpose, is to violate dignity. This means there is no need to show that the harassment was **intentional**.

However, as a result of a successful case brought by the Equal Opportunities Commission (EOC) in February 2007, the definition of harassment in the SDA has been changed to conduct **"related to"** instead of **"on grounds of"** sex (*Equal Opportunities Commission v Secretary of State for Trade and Industry [2007] EWCH 483*). Although the review related only to the SDA, the government will have to amend the other equality legislation in the same way, as it all has to comply with the same Directive.

When deciding whether behaviour amounts to harassment, a tribunal must take into account the **perception of the person** on the receiving end. It can still be harassment if that individual perceives it to be so, even if another individual would not (although with the proviso that it must "reasonably" be considered as such). If the worker makes it clear at the time that the behaviour is unacceptable and unwelcome, a tribunal may be more likely to find that it amounted to harassment. But workers who do not complain at the time can still pursue a claim later.

In the case of *Moonsar v Fiveways Express Transport EAT/0476/04 ([2005] IRLR 9)*, the EAT held that Rea Moonsar had been discriminated against when colleagues in the same office downloaded pornographic material, even though she did not complain until she was later selected for redundancy. The EAT agreed that her colleagues' behaviour could be regarded as degrading and offensive, and was obviously less favourable treatment.

A case can be successful even if there has only been a **single act** of harassment as in *Bracebridge Engineering v Darby [1990] IRLR 3*:

Two male employees subjected Ms Darby to a serious sexual assault. Despite her complaints, the matter was not properly investigated. She resigned, claiming unfair dismissal. The EAT upheld the claim, saying that the employer's failure to act was a breach of contract.

The following case of sexual harassment failed because the offensive remarks were addressed to a mixed audience:

Ms Brumfitt, an acting corporal in the RAF military police, brought a claim of sex discrimination after attending a training course at which her male supervisor made a number of offensive and obscene remarks directed at both men and women. The EAT held that this was not sex discrimination: it had not been directed specifically at Brumfitt, and she could not show that she had been treated less favourably than a male comparator. *Brumfitt v MOD EAT/1004/03 [2005] IRLR 4*

However, it is likely that the above claim would succeed under the current definition of harassment.

The employer is responsible for harassment carried out by its employees. A tribunal will look at what steps the employer took to prevent the discrimination and will consider whether it could have done more (*Canniffe v E Riding of Yorkshire Council EAT/1035/98*

[2000] IRLR 555). It is not enough to show that the employee concerned was initially disciplined, if the harassment continued without any further action from the employer.

As a result of the EOC's successful challenge in the High Court employers are also now liable for acts of sexual harassment by **third parties** if the harassment has occurred more than once (whether by the same person or not) and the employer has known about it but has done nothing to prevent it. Third parties are anyone other than the employer or a fellow employee, so could include customers in a restaurant or hotel. The SDA has been amended to reflect this. Although the other discrimination acts have not yet been changed, the same principle applies because the legislation all has to comply with the same European Directive which the High Court found had not been properly implemented in the EOC case.

In most cases of harassment the appropriate response from an employer would be to **suspend** the alleged harasser pending an investigation, but there may be rare cases where this could amount to a breach of the implied term of mutual trust and confidence (see "Implied terms" in Chapter 3). In the case of *Gogay v Hertfordshire CC [2000] IRLR 703*, the immediate suspension of a female employee over what proved to be a completely unsubstantiated allegation of sexual abuse, leading her to suffer clinical depression, amounted to a breach of contract.

Under section 11 of the *Employment Tribunals Act 1996*, tribunals have discretion to **protect the identity** of the parties or witnesses in sexual misconduct cases — but, except in serious cases of indecent assault, this protection applies only until the tribunal decision is given. The media can attend the hearing, but cannot report it while the order is in force; the Act does not, however, give an automatic right of protection to the employer.

If the harassment has left the employee feeling that they have no option but to resign, they may, if they have a year's service, have a separate claim for **constructive dismissal** (see Chapter 10).

The rules on **time limits** in cases of continuing harassment are the same as those for continuing discrimination (see "Bringing a discrimination claim" page 138).

Someone who has been subjected to harassment can also bring a **civil claim** for negligence against their employer. The House of Lords has held that, if an employer knows or ought to know that harassment is taking place but takes no action, it can be liable in negligence for any physical or psychiatric injury caused by that harassment (*Waters v Commissioner of Police of the Metropolis [2000] UKHL 50 [2000] IRLR 720*).

Harassment at work can also be dealt with under the *Protection from Harassment Act 1997*. This Act was initiated in an attempt to curb stalking, but the House of Lords has held that it can apply to employment situations (*Majrowski v Guy's & St Thomas' NHS Trust [2006] UKHL 34*). It covers both criminal and civil harassment, and is not limited to harassment on discriminatory grounds. In fact, it may be more likely to be used in serious cases of bullying and harassment which are not protected by any of the discrimination laws, as there are few legal remedies in those cases.

To succeed, the employee must show that there was a course of oppressive conduct directed at them, which was deliberately intended to cause alarm or distress.

In *Conn v Council of City of Sunderland [2007] EWCA Civ 1492*, an employee refused to inform on colleagues whom the manager suspected of finishing work early. In response, the manager behaved aggressively and (on one occasion) threatened violence. The Court of Appeal noted that if the *Protection from Harassment Act 1997* were to be activated, the acts complained of would need to be considered sufficiently serious as to warrant a criminal sanction. The Court of Appeal decided that while the acts complained of in this case were unattractive they did not cross the boundary into being oppressive as multiple acts were needed for this definition to apply.

Victimisation

"Victimisation" is a particular form of discrimination. It means the less favourable treatment of a worker **because they have made a complaint** of discrimination (whether or not they have brought legal proceedings) or because they have given evidence or information in relation to someone else's complaint or claim. This means that a worker can bring a claim under one of the discrimination acts for supporting a colleague, even if they would not otherwise be eligible for protection under that act. A claim for victimisation resulting from an equal pay claim (see "Equal pay" below) is brought under the SDA and not the *Equal Pay Act*.

Calling an employee to a performance review meeting after they had made allegations of race discrimination could amount to victimisation (*London Metropolitan University v Henry EAT/0344/04*).

In the case of St *Helens MBC v Derbyshire and others [2007] UKHL 16*, the House of Lords, overturning the Court of Appeal, held that a local council had victimised its catering staff by writing to them that the cost of contesting their equal pay claims would result in more expensive school meals and lead to a loss of jobs.

A refusal to provide a reference for either an existing or a former employee because they had brought a discrimination claim can amount to victimisation. However, this will not apply if the reason for the refusal is to protect the employer's position in legal proceedings (*Chief Constable of West Yorkshire Police v Khan [2001] UKHL 48 ([2001] IRLR 830*) — see also "References and employer checks" in Chapter 3).

A refusal to pay to an individual, compensation awarded by a tribunal following a successful discrimination claim, can also amount to victimisation. In *Rank Nemo Ltd v Coutinho [2009] EWCA Civ 454* the Court of Appeal upheld the individual's claim, finding that non-payment of the award was connected with Mr Coutinho's employment, and was brought as a separate claim rather than to enforce a tribunal award.

Former employees are protected by victimisation legislation if the action complained about (for example, the refusal to provide a reference) is sufficiently closely connected to the employment relationship.

A victimisation claim will only succeed if the claimant can show that the employer acted in the way it did because of the complaint. If the alleged treatment is carried out by someone who did not know that the claimant had made such a complaint, there can be no victimisation.

In the case of *TNT Express v Brown [2000] ICR 182*, the Court of Appeal ruled that an employer who refused an employee time off to see an adviser about a race discrimination claim, but who would have given staff time off for domestic reasons, victimised the employee.

Victimisation can be unconsciously motivated. In the case of *Nagararajan v LRT [1999] IRLR 572*, the House of Lords held that, where an individual had been refused a job, the fact that his previous discrimination complaints may have subconsciously influenced the interviewing panel was enough to uphold a claim.

Proving and inferring discrimination

It is often difficult to prove discrimination by pointing to evidence that clearly shows a worker has been subjected to less favourable treatment on discriminatory grounds. Because of this, tribunals are entitled to draw an inference of discrimination from the facts presented to them. They are entitled to consider events that occurred throughout the claimant's employment history, even if these do not relate directly to the subject of the claim itself.

This was confirmed in the case of *Anya v University of Oxford [2001] EWCA Civ 405 ([2001] IRLR 377)*, which concerned a black employee who was rejected for a new post in favour of a white candidate. The Court of Appeal, which pointed out that "very little direct discrimination today is overt or even deliberate", said that a tribunal is entitled to take into account indicators from before the decision was made — and also noted that the tribunal had failed to draw any conclusions from the fact that the person specification was not drawn up until moments before the interview.

The burden of proof in discrimination cases is normally switched to the employer. Specifically, if the worker proves facts from which the tribunal could conclude that there has been less favourable treatment, then "in the absence of an adequate explanation" the complaint will be upheld. This reversal of the burden of proof does not apply to cases of victimisation following the Court of Appeal's decision in *Oyarce v Cheshire County Council 2008 ICR 1179*.

The worker must first demonstrate that there is a potential case of discrimination, as the case of *Glasgow City Council v Dhesi EAT/0027/04* shows:

Kuldip Dhesi claimed that he had been treated unequally, and that it was for his employer to prove that the treatment was not on grounds of his race. The EAT held that a tribunal could not infer race discrimination solely on the basis that there was unfair treatment and that Dhesi was Indian: it had to find evidence that the unequal treatment was on the grounds of race, so that there was at least a prima facie (on the face of it) case of racial bias, before it could infer discrimination. Since the tribunal had not found any such evidence, there could be no shift in the burden of proof from the employee to the employer. However, Dhesi's claim for victimisation under the RRA succeeded, as his employer had refused to hear his grievance because he had issued a claim.

The application of this principle was considered by the Court of Appeal in the cases of *Igen Ltd & others v Wong; Webster v Brunel University; Emezie v Emokpae [2005] EWCA 142 ([2005] IRLR 258)*, in which it also held that the employer must show the treatment to have been "in no sense whatsoever" on discriminatory grounds in order to defeat a claim. If the treatment is influenced at all by discrimination, the claim will succeed.

If discrimination is alleged on more than one ground, for example sex and race discrimination, each must be separately proven.

There is a **statutory questionnaire** procedure for all types of unlawful discrimination. Claimants can send a questionnaire to their employer asking for information, and this can be used as evidence in a tribunal. Although there is no legal obligation to complete the questionnaire, a tribunal is entitled to draw an adverse inference if the employer fails to complete it or provides inadequate details.

The questionnaire can be obtained from: **Equal pay**: www.equalities. gov.uk/Docs/Equalpayquestionnaire.doc; **Sex discrimination**: www. equalities.gov.uk/Docs/Equalpayquestionnaire.doc; **Race discrimination**: www.equalityhumanrights.com/Documents/CRE/ PDF/rr65.pdf; **Religious discrimination** or **sexual orientation discrimination**, can be found in Schedule 2 of the EE(RB)R or EE(SO)R; **Age discrimination** (see page 148), can be found in Schedule 3 of the EE(A)R; the **disability** questionnaire is in Schedules 1 and 2 of the *Disability Discrimination (Questions and Replies) Order 2004 (SI 2004/1168)*.

Positive action

While employers have a legal obligation not to discriminate **against** an individual, they also (until the *Equality Act 2010* comes into force in October 2010) have an equal obligation not to discriminate **in favour** of anyone. However, in some circumstances, "positive action" is permitted — this is where a measure, often of a temporary nature, is adopted to re-establish equality of opportunity by removing the effects of discrimination.

The SDA (section 48) and RRA (sections 37 and 38) allow employers to provide training for under-represented groups and to encourage individuals from those groups to apply for jobs. However, an employer cannot select candidates for jobs or training because of their sex and race (unless there is a **genuine occupational requirement**).

There is nothing to prevent positive action under the DDA as this Act only prevents discrimination against disabled people. In addition an employer has a duty to make adjustments to remove a disadvantage faced by a disabled person in a particular situation and this places a requirement for a certain amount of positive action in relation to disabled employees and job applicants.

The ECJ has held that a scheme giving preference to women candidates as part of an equality policy to address existing imbalances between the sexes was lawful (*Badeck and others C-158/97 ([2000] IRLR 432)*). However, an appointments system that automatically favours a female candidate when there are more highly qualified male candidates, is contrary to equal treatment law (*Abrahamsson v Fogelqvist C-407/98 ([2000] IRLR 732)*). In the case of *EFTA Surveillance Authority v Kingdom of Norway E-1/02 ([2003] IRLR 318)*, the court held that, by not even allowing male candidates to be assessed as suitable, the employer had breached European law.

The legislation on **religion or belief, sexual orientation and age** (regulations 25, 26 and 29 respectively) has similar provisions for training and encouragement to take advantage of work opportunities. The main difference is that the test is whether, in the employer's view, the training "prevents or compensates for disadvantages" linked to the specific form of discrimination.

Under section 159, *Equality Act 2010* positive discrimination (i.e. acting in favour of disadvantaged groups) will be potentially lawful. Specifically, where equally qualified candidates are applying for a job (including a promotion), the employer will have the option to appoint a candidate on the basis that they are from a disadvantaged group (provided that to do so would be proportionate).

According to Paragraph 7.21 of the Equality and Human Rights Commissions's *Employment Statutory Code of Practice* (currently in draft form): "Candidates do not have to be identical in all ways before a preference can be shown. For example, candidates may have different strengths and weaknesses in different areas but both can be deemed to be 'as qualified' for the post."

Public Sector Equality Duty

The RRA (amended by the *Race Relations (Amendment) Act 2000*) places a duty on public authorities, such as local authorities and the prison service, to **promote race equality**; they must consider how each of their policies affects race equality, and must publish Race Equality Schemes to explain how they will meet their legal duties. Those employing more than 150 staff must also monitor grievances, disciplinaries, appraisals, training and dismissals for discrimination.

The **disability equality duty** was brought in under the *Disability Discrimination Act 2005*, which substantially amended the DDA95. The duty is similar to the duty to promote race equality under the RRA, but also covers services that have been contracted out to the private sector. It also requires employers to involve disabled people in its development.

In April 2007, the **gender equality duty** was introduced by the *Equality Act 2006* which made similar changes to the SDA. Like the disability duty, this also applies to private companies carrying out public functions. Equality duty Codes of practice are available from the "Publications and resources" section of the EHRC website at www.equalityhumanrights.com.

It is expected that from October 2010, the *Equality Act 2010* will consolidate and develop existing legislation by:

◆ harmonising the existing public sector equality duties of tackling discrimination and promoting equality for race, gender and disability so that the requirements do not vary between groups — known as the Equality Duty; and

◆ extending the harmonised Equality Duty to include gender reassignment, age, sexual orientation and religion or belief so that all groups can rely on the same treatment.

The duty to publish monitoring data will be used to assess the success of equal opportunity legislation in closing pay gaps and to monitor employment rates for various groups.

Equal pay

It is unlawful for an employer to discriminate on the grounds of sex, which includes paying people of one sex less than the other for comparable work. Discrimination in pay and conditions is covered by the *Equal Pay Act 1970* (EPA), whereas the SDA prohibits other forms of unequal treatment on grounds of sex.

The EPA states that an equality clause is presumed to operate in every employment contract, giving women the right to equal pay with men and vice versa. Either a man or a woman can bring a claim under the EPA; to bring a claim with someone of the opposite sex whose job is comparable to yours, you have to show that there is an appreciable difference in pay between the two jobs and that the reason for this difference is the sex of the workers.

In the past, many people didn't realise that they were being unlawfully underpaid relative to their colleagues of the opposite gender. This was partly because some employers routinely sought to impose a blanket ban on employees discussing how much they earned. However, under section 77, *Equality Act 2010* (which is expected to come into force in October 2010) employees cannot be prevented from disclosing details of their pay to either colleagues or trade union representatives.

Also, under section 78, *Equality Act 2010* (expected to come into force October 2010) public sector organisations employing 250 or more individuals, will be required to publish information on the gender pay gap amongst their employees. (The government will have the power to extend this requirement to private sector employers if there is insufficient progress towards equal pay for men and women.)

In the case of *MOD v Armstrong EAT/551/03 ([2004] IRLR 672)*, the EAT made it clear that the "fundamental question is whether there is a causative link between the applicant's sex and the fact that she is paid less than the true value of her job as reflected in the pay of her named comparator". You have to establish that there is a case of pay discrimination

based on a sex difference: just pointing to the fact that someone earns more than you is not enough (*Parliamentary Commissioner for Administration v Fernandez EAT/0137/03 ([2004] IRLR 22)*).

Employees who think they may have grounds for an equal pay claim can use a questionnaire procedure to get information from their employer about pay and grading in the workplace. But they must ensure that they do not ask for information that goes beyond finding out about their comparators: in one case, where an employee asked for information about the pay of everyone on her pay band, the EAT held that employees on the same pay band or grade are not necessarily doing like work or work of equal value (*Villalba v Merrill Lynch EAT/461/04*). If the employer refuses to respond to the questionnaire, a tribunal can infer that there is unequal pay.

The Acas Code of Practice on equal pay provides practical guidance and suggests good practice. In particular, it recommends that employers carry out equal pay reviews, meaning that employers who fail to do so can have this fact used against them at a tribunal. Public authority employers have a duty to promote equal pay under the gender equality duty (see above). Besides basic pay, the EPA also covers other **contractual terms and conditions** such as sick pay, holiday pay, special retirement privileges (such as travel concessions, pensions and redundancy pay) and any "fringe" benefits that can be defined as pay, including discretionary bonuses.

In the case of *Hoyland v Asda Stores [2006] CSIH 21 ([2006] IRLR 468)*, the Court of Session held that a bonus scheme that was "discretionary" (and therefore not an automatic contractual right) still amounted to pay that was "regulated" by the contract of employment — meaning that a claim relating to discriminatory application of the scheme had to be brought under the EPA and not the SDA. Each term in the employment contract stands separately, so an employer cannot justify one unequal term by saying that the employee benefited under another, different term (*Jamstalldhetsombudsmannen v Orebro C-236/98 ([2000] IRLR 421)*).

Some pay systems have been found to be justified under European law, even though they are indirectly discriminatory, because they have an equality objective:

Mr Lommers was denied a place for his child at a work-subsidised nursery, whose places were mainly offered to female employees as a way of encouraging their participation in the labour market. However, since male single parents might also be offered places, the ECJ held that the practice was not contrary to the Equal Treatment Directive. *Lommers v Minister Van Landbouw C-476/99 ([2002] IRLR 430.*

In another case, the ECJ upheld the legality of a scheme which paid an extra allowance to women who had been made redundant, to take account of evidence that they were more likely to remain out of work following redundancy (*Hlozek v Roche Austria Case C-19/02*).

The EPA applies equally to **part-time workers**. The ECJ case of *Bilka Kaufhaus v Weber von Hartz [1986] IRLR 317* established that refusing part-time workers access to a company pension scheme infringed the law on equal pay. And **pieceworkers** can also use the Act. According to the ECJ in the case of *Specialarbejderforbundet i Danmark v Dansk Industri C-400/93 ([1995] IRLR 648)*, if there is an appreciable difference in pay between pieceworkers of different sexes, it is for the employer to prove that there is no sex-based discrimination.

Even if there are **some men employed** doing the same work as women, this does not bar the women from bringing an equal value claim by comparing their jobs with those of other male workers (*Pickstone v Freemans [1988] IRLR 357*). In the case of *Home Office v Bailey and others [2005] EWCA Civ 327 ([2005] IRLR 369)*), the Court of Appeal held that female support officers could bring an equal pay claim using male governors as comparators, even though about 50% of support officers were male.

Equally, men engaged in lower-paid work predominantly carried out by women can bring "piggyback" claims (i.e. claims contingent upon their female colleagues' equal pay claims succeeding). In this way when female colleagues receive back pay from a tribunal, their male colleagues will be able to secure the same amounts reimbursed: *Hartlepool Borough Council v Llewellyn and others; Middlesbrough Borough Council v Matthews and others; South Tyneside Borough Council v McAvoy and others; Middlesbrough Borough Council v Ashcroft and others UKEAT/0006/08; 0057-58/08; 0168/08; 0276/08.*

A woman does not need to have worked for a particular length of time before claiming equal pay. She can claim at any time while she is in the job, or **within six months** of leaving that job. (Even if she stays with the same employer, if she changes jobs she must bring the claim within six months of leaving the job that her equal pay claim relates to).

If a worker has been employed on a **series of contracts** with the same employer, this can amount to a stable employment relationship for the purposes of the EPA, and the time limit for bringing a claim will run from the end of the last contract.

Comparing jobs

Section 1 of the EPA says that women have the right to equal treatment in pay where they carry out:

◆ **like work** to that of a man;
◆ work **rated as equivalent** to a man's; or
◆ work of **equal value**, in terms of, for example, effort, skill and decision-making, to a man's.

Like work is defined as work that is "the same or broadly similar" to the comparator (see below); the differences, if any, are not of practical importance. Tribunals will look at how work is carried out in practice to determine this. Where there are differences in the work, they will examine the frequency with which these occur.

Work **rated as equivalent** refers to work rated under a **job evaluation scheme**. The existence of a job evaluation scheme may act as a bar to workers taking equal value claims to a tribunal, but only if it was applied specifically to the group of workers — a job evaluation of health workers in Britain did not bar a claim by workers in Northern Ireland, for example (*McAuley v Eastern Health & Social Services [1991] IRLR 467*).

To bar a claim, a scheme must be "thorough in analysis" and "capable of impartial application" (*Diageo v Thomson EAT/0064/03*). If the scheme itself is **discriminatory** (for example, if factors generally seen as favourable to women have been excluded or wrongly weighted), it can be challenged, and a tribunal can reject a scheme where there is a "reasonable suspicion" that it is discriminatory.

To claim **equal value**, a woman (or man) must show that her/his job is of equal value to that of a more highly-paid male (or female) employee (the comparator), as measured by criteria such as skill and decision-making. For there to be a valid equal pay claim, there must be evidence that the reason for the difference in pay is the sex of the workers:

In the case of *Glasgow City Council v Marshall [2000] UKHL 5 [2000] IRLR 272*, the House of Lords held that school instructors doing almost identical work to schoolteachers could not claim equal pay. The pay differences were for historical reasons, but there was no evidence to show that these were in any way linked to differences based on sex.

The claim will not succeed if the employer can show a **material difference** between the jobs or a **genuine material factor** (see "Bringing an equal pay claim" below), other than the workers' sex, that accounts for the difference in pay. For example, it may be lawful to pay workers different rates to reflect their **different qualifications,** even though in practice they appear to perform similar work. They can also be paid differently on account of their **job performance**, as long as it is their actual work and not their work potential that is assessed (*Brunnhofer v Bank der Österreichischen Postsparkasse C-381/99 ([2001] IRLR 571)*).

Different or additional tasks can also justify pay differences. In the case of *Christie and others v John E Haith EAT/793/02 ([2003] IRLR 670)*, the EAT held that a requirement for male employees to **lift heavy loads** was lawful grounds for a pay difference.

A pay difference resulting from pay protection after a TUPE transfer (see Chapter 12) is also justifiable under equal pay law. Different pay rates based on length of service may also be justifiable. In the long-running case of *Cadman v HSE C-17/05*, the ECJ held that, as a general rule, length of service is enough to objectively justify a difference in pay as long service goes "hand in hand" with experience, which generally enables a worker to perform his or her duties better.

However, the ECJ did recognise that there were cases in which this general rule would not apply. It said this would be where the worker provides evidence giving rise to "serious doubts" that length of service goes hand in hand with experience and/or that experience enables the worker to perform his or her duties better.

In *Wilson v Health and Safety Executive and EHRC (intervener) [2009] EWCA Civ 1074; [2010] IRLR 59* the employee challenged the lawfulness of a pay scale which by a series of fixed pay increases, rewarded up to 10 years' service. The tribunal agreed that a 10-year period was not justified and that a five-year period would have been appropriate. On appeal, the Court of Appeal said the effect of the earlier decision in *Cadman* is that an employer can be required to provide objective justification for its use of a length of service criterion as well as its adoption in the first place. The "serious doubts" test is not an additional hurdle for the claimant to cross. It is a low test and simply operates as a preliminary filter to see whether the claimant is likely to be able to prove that in a particular case, justification may be required. The tribunal's decision was correct.

Women **transferred to alternative work** for health reasons during pregnancy cannot pursue an equal pay claim in respect of the alternative work. Equally, men do not have the right to claim equality in respect of any additional lump sum or loyalty bonuses paid to women on maternity leave (*Abdoulaye v Renault [1999] IRLR 811*).

Comparable worker

To win an equal pay claim, the claimant must be able to show that there is a worker of the opposite sex — the **comparator** — who is being paid more. Normally, the comparator will be in the same establishment (workplace). It is helpful to choose a comparator (or comparators, as more than one can be chosen) whose **circumstances are most similar to the worker**, to reduce the chances that the difference in pay can be explained by factors other than the sex of the worker.

In *Somerset County Council and Secretary of State for Children, Schools and Families v Pike [2009] EWCA Civ 808*, a teacher who had taken early retirement came back to work on a part-time basis. Only teachers in receipt of a pension who restarted work on a full-time basis, were permitted to rejoin the pension scheme. Ms Pike argued that this policy indirectly discriminated against her and 73 colleagues on the basis of their gender. The Court of Appeal decided that the correct pool for comparison was not all teachers, but teachers who returned post-retirement. On this basis the policy had a statistically and legally significant adverse impact on the claimants.

A claimant can choose a comparator in **another workplace** owned by the same employer, if they work under the same terms and conditions (*British Coal v Smith [1994] IRLR 342*). Some workers, such as those in NHS trusts and local councils, may be able to compare their pay with that of workers in other trusts or councils.

In the case of *Scullard v Southern Region Council for Education [1996] IRLR 344*, an employee was able to claim equal pay with those employed by other regional councils. All were funded by the Department for Education and Employment, and the fact that the employers were different did not bar the claim.

However, the Court of Appeal ruled in the case of *Robertson v Department for Environment, Food and Rural Affairs [2005] EWCA Civ 138 ([2005] IRLR 363)* that civil servants working for different civil service departments could not compare their jobs under equal pay law as there was no single source for their rate of pay — each department set its own terms and conditions.

In *Dumfries and Galloway Council v North and others UKEATS/0047/08* the EAT considered the equal pay claims brought by female classroom assistants, support for learning assistants and nursery nurses. These school-based staff sought to compare their pay with male manual workers employed elsewhere (depots and a swimming pool). The EAT noted that the *Equal Pay Act* permits a comparison between male and female workers employed at different establishments. However, there was no evidence that any of the male workers would ever be employed in schools, and furthermore the men and women were also employed on different sets of terms and conditions (Green and Blue Books respectively). Accordingly the claim failed.

In the case of *Allonby v Accrington & Rossendale College C-256/01 ([2004] IRLR 224)*, the ECJ ruled that agency worker Debra Allonby could not compare her rate of pay with that of a directly employed male worker, even though both worked at the "same establishment". They had different employers and there was no common controlling entity regulating their pay.

Additionally, in the case of *Walton Centre for Neurology v Bewley UKEAT/0564/07/MAA ([2008] IRLR 588)*, the EAT was asked by a health care assistant to compare the salary that she had been paid with that of the man that took on her post. The EAT decided that the *Equal Pay Act* does not permit such a comparison. Specifically, contrary to the EAT's 1996 ruling in *Diocese of Hallam Trustee v*

Connaughton, the claimant's comparator must be or have been contemporaneously employed and not a successor bringing an equal pay claim.

Under section 64, *Equality Act 2010* (which comes into force in October 2010) it is expressly possible for an individual bringing an equal pay claim, to name as a comparator someone who previously carried out that role (e.g. for a claimant to use someone who has since left the organisation, as a comparator).

Bringing an equal pay claim

Before issuing a tribunal claim, the claimant must first **issue a grievance** to comply with the Acas code. The time limit for a claim under the EPA is **six months** from the end of the employment.

If there is a **business transfer**, the employment will transfer under the TUPE regulations (see Chapter 12) and the new employer will still be liable for any equal pay claim — except if the claim relates to pensions. In the case of *Powerhouse Retail Ltd & others v Burroughs & others [2006] UKHL 13 ([2006] IRLR 381)*, the House of Lords held that, because occupational pension rights do not transfer under TUPE, any equal pay claim in relation to those rights must be brought against the old employer within six months of the date that the employment transferred.

There are special procedures for taking **equal value claims** to tribunals. These include a provision for the appointment of an **independent expert**, instructed by the tribunal to evaluate the jobs being compared. The expert examines the jobs and presents the resulting report as evidence. A tribunal can decide on a claim without using an expert, but must first give the parties the opportunity to appoint their own experts before giving its ruling on the claim (*William Ball v Wood EAT/89/01*).

The employer has a defence against equal pay claims if there is:

◆ a **"material difference"** justifying the pay gap (in like work cases); or
◆ a **"material factor"** justifying the pay gap (in equal value cases).

A **material difference** can include such aspects as merit pay, longer hours and so on. But the employer has to show that the difference is genuine and accounts for the whole of the pay disparity.

If a measure has been introduced for budgetary savings, the fact that it has not achieved the gains anticipated will not, in itself, cancel out the employer's defence. An ECJ ruling, however, suggests that budgeting constraints can never be used to justify sex discrimination unless there is a legitimate social policy behind them (*Jorgensen v Foreningen C-226/98 ([2000] IRLR 726)*).

The case of *Redcar & Cleveland Borough Council v Bainbridge; Surtees v Middlesbrough Borough Council [2008] EWCA Civ 885 [(2008] IRLR 690)*, concerned steps taken by local authority employers in response to complaints of unequal pay patterns. The Court of Appeal found that a programme of phased changes to pay designed to shield male employees from more rapid drops in pay could amount, in itself, to unlawful discrimination. The relevant test remains whether the employer's actions were objectively justified (i.e. a proportionate means of achieving a legitimate aim).

Material factors include matters such as skill shortages or an employee's special role in giving advice and training. Once the employer has shown genuine reasons, unconnected with sex, for the pay difference, it is under no further obligation to justify the difference (*Villalba v Merrill Lynch & Co Inc & others EAT/0223/05*).

In one case, bonus schemes purportedly designed to encourage productivity were attached to jobs which were predominantly carried out by men (such as joiners and painters rather than care assistants and office cleaners, for example). A tribunal found that the bonus payments were in fact additional payments for completing the work that individuals were already paid to do and were a sham. Accordingly, the employer's defence that the bonus payments were genuinely intended to encourage productivity failed (*Dolphin v Hartlepool Borough Council and Housing Hartlepool Ltd UKEAT/0007/08/CEA*).

In *Chief Constable of West Midlands Police v Blackburn & Manley EWCA Civ 1208*, two WPCs (with childcare responsibilities) complained that a shift bonus scheme for officers who worked at least four hours at night indirectly discriminated against them. The EAT disagreed with the tribunal and found that the payment of the bonus was to reward those who worked night shifts. Having found that this was a legitimate aim and was not related to any discrimination based on sex, the EAT decided that the tribunal should have gone on to conclude that it was justified.

In the case of *Barber v NCR [1993] IRLR 95*, a reduction in hours of work for male workers gave them a higher hourly rate than that of women whose work was equally evaluated. The women won the right to the higher hourly rate.

In some situations, pay rates may be set by two or more different collective processes. However, the ECJ has held (*Enderby v Frenchay HA [1993] IRLR 591*) that this does not provide an "objective justification" as a defence to an equal pay claim — even if the processes, considered separately, have no discriminatory effect. It accepted that market forces could be an objective justification, but said that the claimants were entitled to any proportion of the difference that could not be objectively justified; this meant that speech therapists could successfully compare themselves with clinical psychologists, enabling them to negotiate a compensation deal worth around £50,000 on average for each employee.

The case of *Allen v GMB [2008] EWCA Civ 810 [2008]IRLR690* concerned complaints by female union members about the settlement of their equal pay claims. In an effort to save jobs by not making a very large claim against the employer for compensation, the union had not sought full back-pay for female members who had been, relative to male comparators, underpaid. Instead it focused on serving the interests of all its members (including through pay protection for male members). The Court of Appeal stated that the employer's assertion that job cuts would have to follow if the settlement package was any larger, should have been more closely scrutinised by the union. The court also recommended that information given to members be more complete and balanced (i.e. not strongly recommending a particular course of action without more clearly pointing out the disadvantages to the members concerned). Although the union was pursuing a legitimate aim, the effort taken to persuade the female members to sign up to the deal, was not found to be a proportionate means of achieving that aim (i.e. the female members were indirectly discriminated against).

In the case of *Ratcliffe v N. Yorkshire CC [1995] IRLR 439*, the House of Lords said that reducing the pay of school meals workers to win an in-house contract was contrary to equal pay laws. The women's work had been evaluated as equal to that of male workers who did not face a wage cut.

Back pay of up to six years can be recovered, plus interest from the halfway point. It is also possible for a claim to go back further than six years in two particular circumstances (section 2ZB, EPA):

♦ in a "concealment case" where the employer deliberately concealed relevant facts from the claimant; or

♦ in a disability case where the claimant is a minor (under-18 in England, Wales and Northern Ireland; under-16 in Scotland) or suffering from a mental disability (defined as someone who "lacks capacity" under the *Mental Capacity Act 2005* in England and Wales or is "incapable" under the *Adults with Incapacity (Scotland) Act 2000* and the *Mental Health (Northern Ireland) Order 1986*). Note that this is entirely different from the definition of a disability under the DDA.

Disability discrimination

Discrimination against a disabled person is prohibited by the *Disability Discrimination Act 1995* (DDA) — soon to be replaced by the *Equality Act 2010* which is expected to come into force in October 2010. The law covers recruitment, selection and promotion and applies to contract workers as well as directly employed workers. It also applies to dismissal, including constructive dismissal. Individuals are also protected from discrimination on grounds of a past disability (section 2, DDA).

Definition of a disability

To gain protection under the DDA, an individual must normally have a disability (unless they are bringing a claim of victimisation after they, for example, gave evidence in someone else's claim). This means that someone who is treated less favourably because an employer thought they had a disability will not be covered (*Hart v Bolton Hospitals NHS Trust EAT/0909/04*).

However, in *Coleman v Attridge Law C-303/06*, the ECJ considered a complaint of discrimination by association — specifically, an able-bodied female employee who as the principal carer of her disabled son, believed she had suffered less favourable treatment. Ms Coleman alleged that her employer was less flexible in its approach to her hours than with female employees caring for non-disabled children or relatives. The ECJ agreed that the Equal Treatment

Framework Directive prohibits associative direct discrimination (or harassment) on the grounds of disability.

Following the case being remitted to the UK domestic courts, consequential amendments were made to the *Employment Equality (Age) Regulations 2006* (soon to be covered by section 13, *Equality Act 2010* in October 2010). In *EBR Attridge Law LLP and another v Coleman (No.2) UKEAT/0071/09; [2010] IRLR 10 EAT* the EAT added the following new sub-section to section 3A, *Disability Discrimination Act 1995*:

A person also directly discriminates against a person if he treats him less favourably than he treats or would treat another person by reason of the disability of another person

Under the *Equality Act 2010* protection from discrimination on the basis of being associated with someone from a protected group (on any of the protected grounds) is expressly stated to be unlawful.

It has been quite common for employers to state that a job offer is subject to receipt of a satisfactorily completed health questionnaire. However, under section 60, *Equality Act 2010* (coming into force in October 2010) it will be unlawful for employers to continue this practice. Specifically, employers won't be able to ask job applicants disability or health-related questions (except in certain circumstances). The Equality and Human Rights Commission is responsible for enforcement.

Often the effect of an individual's disability is not apparent in the workplace. Conditions that can amount to disabilities but may not always be recognised as such include sensory impairments, fibromyalgia, depression, epilepsy, asthma, autistic spectrum disorders, dyslexia, learning difficulties, eating disorders, obsessive compulsive disorders and some personality disorders.

For the purposes of the DDA, an individual is defined as having a disability if s/he has **"a physical or mental impairment which has a substantial and long-term adverse effect on her/his ability to carry out normal day-to-day activities."**

It is up to the claimant to provide evidence to establish that s/he has a disability. It is not the duty of the tribunal to present evidence (*McNicol v Balfour Beatty Rail Maintenance [2002] EWCA Civ 1074 ([2002] IRLR 711)*).

Guidance on matters to be taken into account in determining questions relating to the definition of disability, issued by the secretary of state for work and pensions, came into force on 1 May 2006 and provides explanations and examples of how the definition is applied. Although the DWP guidance at: www.direct.gov.uk/en/ DisabledPeople/RightsAndObligations/DisabilityRights/DG_ 4001069 — is not legally binding itself, section 3(3) of the DDA says that tribunals must take it into account in their decisions.

An **impairment for the purposes of the DDA** is only taken into account if it affects the person in respect of one or more of the following:

◆ mobility;
◆ manual dexterity;
◆ physical co-ordination;
◆ continence;
◆ ability to lift, carry or otherwise move everyday objects;
◆ speech, hearing or eyesight;
◆ memory or ability to concentrate, learn or understand; and/or
◆ perception of the risk of physical danger.

All of these criteria should be applied to both physical and mental impairments. There is no longer a requirement for a mental impairment to be "clinically well recognised", and it does not matter whether an impairment has a physical or a mental cause (*Millar v Inland Revenue Commissioners [2005] CSIH 71 ([2006] IRLR 112)*).

There is no definitive list of what constitutes a physical or mental impairment.

Since the Act was amended in 2005, a person who has cancer, HIV infection or multiple sclerosis is deemed to have a disability from the **point of diagnosis**; they will not need to go on to show its effect. Anyone who is certified or registered as blind or partially sighted is also automatically covered.

In other cases, a claimant will have to show that the impairment has a substantial, long-term adverse effect on their ability to carry out day-to-day activities in order to establish that they have a disability. **Long-term** means an effect that has lasted or is likely to last for a year or more. However, an individual does not have to be disabled for as long as a year to claim, provided that the disability is likely to last that long or is recurring (*Greenwood v BA [1999] IRLR 600*). The effect of any **medication or other treatment is ignored** when assessing the effects of an impairment.

If an impairment is **recurring**, it will be regarded as "long-term" if the substantial adverse affect is likely to recur. For example, someone with rheumatoid arthritis may have adverse effects for a few weeks; if the effects then stop but are likely to recur more than 12 months after the first occurrence, they are long-term. The focus is on whether the substantial adverse affect, rather than the impairment itself, is likely to recur (*Swift v Chief Constable of Wiltshire Constabulary EAT/484/03 ([2004] IRLR 540)*).

In *SCA Packaging Ltd v Boyle and Equality and Human Rights Commission (Intervener) [2009] IRLR 746* the House of Lords considered the meaning of "likely" in disability discrimination law. In 1975 Ms Boyle started suffering from hoarseness and vocal nodes. Despite undergoing surgery in 1975, the condition recurred in 1981 and 1992 (at which point further surgery took place). By following a voice management regime, the problem did not return. The issue was whether, by 2000, Ms Boyle counted as disabled. Specifically, was she suffering from an impairment that was "likely to recur"? The House of Lords decided that, in a disability context, the term "likely" means "could well happen" (and not the harder-to-meet threshold of "more probable than not").

Progressive conditions (other than those classed as a disability from the point of diagnosis) amount to a disability if medical or statistical evidence indicates that they are more likely than not to have a substantial adverse effect at some stage (*Mowat-Brown v University of Surrey EAT/462/00 ([2002] IRLR 235)*).

There are some conditions explicitly **excluded** from the legal definition of a disability; these include **alcohol and drug addiction**. However, if these give rise to a condition that does come within the definition of a disability, the individual will be classed as disabled. For example, depression arising from addiction could be classified as a disability.

Annette Power was off work through depression and alcoholism, and was dismissed as a result. She claimed protection under the DDA. The EAT noted that her depression had a long-term adverse affect on her ability to carry out normal day-to-day activities, and ruled that the fact that it may have arisen due to her addiction was not relevant to the question of whether she was disabled. *Power v Panasonic EAT/747/01 ([2003] IRLR 151)*.

In the case of *Hewett v Motorola EAT/0526/01*, the EAT held that an inability to interact socially, caused by the employee's suffering from autism, amounts to a mental impairment. Learning difficulties can amount to a disability without the claimant's having to show a specific medical condition; evidence from a suitably qualified educational psychologist will be sufficient (*Dunham v Ashford Windows EAT/0915/04 ([2005] IRLR 608)*).

If the substantial adverse effect is only triggered by a particular environment, the worker can still be disabled. For example, a worker whose asthma attacks were brought on because he was working with fumes was disabled while he was working in that environment (*Cruickshank v VAW Motorcast [2002] IRLR 24*).

Normal day-to-day activities are things that people do on a regular or daily basis and include shopping, reading and writing, having a conversation or using the telephone, watching television, getting washed and dressed, preparing and eating food, carrying out household tasks, walking and travelling by various forms of transport, and taking part in social activities.

But they must be normal activities for a large group of people, not just for that individual. Putting on make-up is regarded as a normal day-to-day activity, even though it is almost exclusively done by one sex only and therefore cannot be said to be done by most people. Work activities are not included, because there is no particular form of work that is normal for most people, and work may be highly specialised. The same applies to other specialist activities such as playing a musical instrument to a high standard or playing a sport to a high level of ability.

In *Chief Constable of Dumfries and Galloway Constabulary v Adams UKEAT/0046/08* a police constable suffered from ME. He struggled to complete night shifts (he walked slowly, needed to be driven home and have help undressing), so his employer allowed him to finish his shifts a little early. This didn't help much and he still sometimes suffered difficulties — the employer therefore decided to dismiss him. Mr Adams brought a claim of disability discrimination. The EAT was asked to consider whether Mr Adams was disabled — did the activities that he struggled to do (climbing stairs, etc) amount to "normal day-to-day activities" given that he was trying to do them at night. The EAT considered that they did, on the basis that night shift working is common in the UK, and the tasks were non-specialist. Mr Adams' case could therefore proceed in the tribunal.

If normal day-to-day activities can only be carried out in pain or with difficulty, this can still amount to a substantial adverse effect — it is not necessary to show that they cannot be done at all.

Section 212, *Equality Act 2010* (which comes into force in October 2010) expressly states that the requirement for the impairment to be substantial, means something which is not minor or trivial.

Types of disability discrimination

Under the amended DDA, there are five forms of disability discrimination in the employment field:

◆ direct discrimination;
◆ disability-related discrimination;
◆ failure to make reasonable adjustments;
◆ harassment; and
◆ victimisation.

(The *Equality Act 2010* will introduce a new concept of indirect discrimination on the grounds of disability).

Direct discrimination

Under section 3A(5) of the DDA, direct discrimination occurs if someone treats a disabled person **less favourably** than they treat or would treat a person without a disability in similar circumstances.

As with direct discrimination on other prohibited grounds such as sex or race (see earlier in this Chapter), the individual must point to a **comparator** — someone without a disability who was treated differently. If there is no actual comparator, a hypothetical comparator can be used.

Dismissing a disabled employee because s/he had been absent on sick leave with a disability-related illness would amount to direct discrimination, if the employer had not dismissed a non-disabled employee who had been absent on sick leave for other reasons. Direct discrimination **cannot be justified** by the employer (see below).

Disability-related discrimination

Section 3A(1) of the DDA states that disability-related discrimination occurs if a disabled person is treated less favourably, for a reason related to their disability, than someone else to whom that reason does not apply.

So, if a disabled employee is dismissed because s/he has been absent on sick leave for six months with a disability-related illness, and the employer has a policy to dismiss any employee who is absent for six months (meaning that disabled and non-disabled employees are treated the same), even though the dismissal does not amount to direct discrimination, could that termination/policy amount to disability-related discrimination? On the basis of *London Borough of Lewisham v Malcolm [2008] UKHL 43 ([2008] IRLR 700)*, quite possibly not:

In this case, the House of Lords considered a claim by a schizophrenic man who sublet his council house for a year. Mr Malcolm resisted the local authority's attempt to take possession, arguing that he would not have sublet the premises had it not been for his schizophrenia. Although the House of Lords accepted he would not have done so but for his condition, it found that the local authority had sought possession of the property for housing management purposes and that the decision had nothing to do with Mr Malcolm's disability.

The House of Lords considered that the correct comparator for Mr Malcolm was someone who was not disabled but who had been absent from their council property for 12 months. Such an individual would have been treated in the same way: the court found that no discrimination had occurred and noted that in order for a person or an organisation to be liable for an act of disability discrimination, they must know that the individual concerned is disabled.

This decision made it considerably harder for disabled individuals to challenge potentially discriminatory acts. However, the impact of this decision will be moderated by the *Equality Act 2010* which brings the test for establishing whether disability-related discrimination has occurred, into line with other types of discrimination.

Specifically, it is expected that from October 2010 disability discrimination occurs where someone treats an individual unfavourably because of something arising in consequence of that individual's disability, and the perpetrator cannot show that their treatment of the individual is a proportionate means of achieving a legitimate aim: section 15, *Equality Act 2010*.

In any event, the current concept of disability-related discrimination **can be justified** by the employer, as long as it has complied with its duty to make reasonable adjustments, or if reasonable adjustments would have made no difference (section 3A(6), DDA).

Failure to make reasonable adjustments

If a disabled worker is placed at a **substantial disadvantage** by any **provision**, **criterion or practice** applied by the employer, or by any **physical feature** of the employer's premises, the employer has a legal duty to make **reasonable adjustments** to remove the disadvantage (section 4A, DDA). A failure to make adjustments may well amount to disability discrimination.

However, in *Eastern & Coastal Kent PCT v Grey UKEAT/0454/08/RN*, the EAT considered the defence that employers have, to a claim for failure to make reasonable adjustments. The EAT decided that an employer needs to satisfy all four of the following tests:

◆ that it didn't know that the individual had a disability;
◆ that it didn't know that the individual was likely to be at a substantial disadvantage compared with people who are not disabled;
◆ that it couldn't reasonably be expected to know that the individual had a disability; and
◆ that it couldn't reasonably be expected to know that the individual was likely to be placed at a substantial disadvantage compared to non-disabled people.

The adjustments that should be made will depend on the **individual circumstances**. However, section 18B of the DDA sets out the following examples of steps that may need to be taken:

◆ making adjustments to premises;
◆ allocating some of the worker's duties to another person;
◆ transferring the worker to fill an existing vacancy;
◆ altering the worker's hours;
◆ providing an alternative place of work;
◆ allowing time off for rehabilitation, assessment or treatment;
◆ arranging training or mentoring;
◆ acquiring or modifying equipment;
◆ modifying instructions or reference manuals;
◆ modifying procedures for testing or assessment;
◆ providing a reader or interpreter; and
◆ providing supervision or other support.

Note that these are examples only; it is important that the employer considers what adjustments are needed for the individual worker. In the case of *Archibald v Fife Council [2004] UKHL 32 ([2004] IRLR 651)*, the House of Lords held that on occasions the duty to make reasonable adjustments can require an employer to treat a disabled worker **more favourably** than other staff:

Following complications arising from surgery, road sweeper Susan Archibald was no longer able to walk. She retrained and applied for more than 100 posts with her employer, but was dismissed for capability reasons after failing to secure any of the jobs. She lost her claims in the lower courts, but appealed (with the help of the Disability Rights Commission) to the House of Lords. It ruled in her favour, holding that there was a duty on her employer to consider transferring her to one of the posts she had applied for, even if this meant treating her more favourably.

A tribunal will look at the nature of the adjustments proposed by the employer, and the extent to which they might have overcome the disadvantage faced by the employee.

In the case of *BT v Pelling EAT/0093/03*, the EAT held that a reasonable adjustment would have been to allow an agoraphobic employee to work from home, since homeworking was already permitted for some employees.

There is no general obligation to create a new post for a disabled worker who becomes unable to do his/her existing work. However, in the case of *Southampton City College v Randall EAT/0372/05*, the EAT ruled that the employer should have done so — it was carrying out a restructuring, and creating a new post would have been reasonable in those circumstances.

Leo Randall, a lecturer for 26 years at the same college, was diagnosed with dysphonia — a disability that caused his voice to break down. While he was off sick, the college told him there would be a restructuring process; he was later identified as the only employee whose job was at risk, and was given the option of taking ill-health retirement or "redundancy".

The EAT upheld a tribunal's findings that the college's process was "grotesquely unfair" and was intended to put Randall at a disadvantage because of his disability. It found that Randall's manager had been given a "blank sheet of paper" for the restructuring, so could have devised a job specifically for him which took account of his disability. The college admitted in its evidence that it had never considered making adjustments.

Where retirement is a cost-effective and desired alternative, an employer may in some unusual circumstances or specific sectors be able to lawfully avoid transferring an employee.

In *Chief Constable of Lincolnshire Police v Weaver UKEAT/0622/07/DM*, a police officer with 30 years' service wanted to take advantage of a scheme that allowed him to carry on working and simultaneously receive his pension. Accordingly, Mr Weaver applied for a speed camera offences post suitable for someone on restricted duties. However, following a review of the force's financial position and operational requirements, he was turned down.

The EAT overturned a tribunal's finding that Mr Weaver had suffered discrimination. The EAT noted that the Disability Rights Commission's Code of Practice states that it may be relevant to take account of other employees, adjustments made for other disabled employees and overall cost when considering reasonable adjustments. The EAT agreed that if Mr Weaver were to retire (which he had expressed a desire to do) he would free up a restricted duties post for someone else and enable an able-bodied officer to be recruited.

There is also no obligation for the employer to find work on the same grade or to "red circle" a disabled employee's post to maintain their previous earnings in their new job, but it is something that could be seen as a reasonable adjustment in appropriate circumstances.

In the case of *Nottinghamshire CC v Meikle [2004] EWCA Civ 859 ([2004] IRLR 703)*, the Court of Appeal ruled that an employer's refusal to extend sick pay for a disabled employee amounted to a failure to make reasonable adjustments. But in *O'Hanlon v Commissioners for HM Revenue & Customs EAT/0109/06*, the EAT held that it is "very rare" for an employer to be required to extend sick pay. It said that the particular circumstances of Meikle's case explained the court's decision; these were that the employer had failed to make adjustments to Meikle's work that would enable her to do it, and this was the only reason she was still off sick. This decision was confirmed by the Court of Appeal.

Where an employer fails to make a reasonable adjustment for a disabled person, the time limit for bringing a claim starts to run from the end of the period during which the employer might reasonably have been expected to have made the adjustment (*Matuszowicz v Kingston Upon Hull City Council [2009] EWCA Civ 22*).

Employers cannot ignore **health and safety legislation** in order to accommodate a disabled employee. For example, if a risk assessment reveals a need to wear protective clothing which is unsuited to a disabled employee, the employer can lawfully dismiss as long as no reasonable alternatives exist. If an employer includes disability-related absences when applying a sickness absence procedure or even dismissing an employee on grounds of capability, this may be regarded as disability-related discrimination and the employer will have to justify it:

Mrs Dunsby (who worked as a nurse) had a disability based on gynaecological problems, migraines and depression. She was dismissed because of her high levels of sickness absence, but pointed out that two of her absences had been recorded as headaches when they were for migraine; if these had been discounted because they were a result of her disability, she would not have triggered the final stage of the employer's absence procedure and would not have been dismissed.

The EAT said that it is rare for disability-related absences to be disregarded, and an employer can take these absences into account as long as any resulting less favourable treatment is justifiable. In Mrs Dunsby's case, the EAT said it was not necessarily unreasonable to include the two migraine absences, particularly when they were the only absences for that reason in the entire absence record. *Royal Liverpool Children's NHS Trust v Dunsby EAT/0426/05 ([2006] IRLR 351.*

A failure to consult an employee before dismissing him was held to be a failure to make reasonable adjustments in the case of *Rothwell v Pelikan Hardcopy Scotland Ltd EAT/0008/05 ([2006] IRLR 24)*. The employer based its decision on an occupational health report; although it held a meeting with the employee, it had already made up its mind to dismiss him by that stage.

In *Tarbuck v Sainsbury Supermarkets Ltd UKEAT/0136/06 ([2006] IRLR 664)*, the EAT said it is the need to consider reasonable adjustments rather than consultation itself which is the legal duty, which would mean that a lack of consultation with the employee is not itself unfair.

However, it is good practice to consult the employee, and in many cases it can be argued that an employer will not be able to properly consider what adjustments are reasonable without consulting the employee.

Some aspects of reasonable adjustments are also dealt with in the *Equality Act 2010* (expected to come into force in October 2010). In particular, section 20(7), *Equality Act 2010* will make it expressly unlawful for employers to pass on the cost of making reasonable adjustments to the individual concerned (unless there is a specific contractual provision allowing this).

Also, section 20(6), *Equality Act 2010* seeks to tackle the situation where a disabled person is put at a substantial disadvantage (compared with a non-disabled person) because information that they need is not available in an accessible format. Employers will have a duty to provide such information in accessible formats.

Justification

Disability-related discrimination is the only form of discrimination that can be justified by the employer under the DDA. The employer must show that the reason for the treatment is both **material to the circumstances** of the particular case and **substantial**.

If an employer fails to make reasonable adjustments, it cannot justify the treatment unless it can also show that making reasonable adjustments would have made no difference because the nature of the employee's disability meant that s/he would still have been unable to work. In the case of *Murphy v Slough BC and Governing Body of Langley Wood School [2005] EWCA Civ 122 ([2005] IRLR 382)*, the Court of Appeal held that a school could use its "precarious financial position" to justify the refusal of paid leave to a disabled employee who was about to receive her surrogate child. But in the case of *Smith v Churchills Stairlifts plc [2005] EWCA Civ 1220 ([2006] IRLR 41)*, the employer had not made reasonable adjustments and therefore could not justify its less favourable treatment:

Mr Smith was offered a job selling radiator cabinets if he completed a training course. He was told that he would have to carry samples, the size of which was to be decided; the company later decided that they would be full-sized cabinets. Smith has lumbar spondylosis, meaning that he has difficulty walking and cannot lift heavy objects. Deciding that he could not carry the samples, the company withdrew the offer of the course and failed to consider other selling methods. The Court of Appeal held that the requirement to carry a full-sized radiator cabinet was a relevant "arrangement" that put Smith at a disadvantage. The failure to consider other sales methods was a failure to make reasonable adjustments, and the withdrawal of the training could not be justified. Both amounted to disability discrimination.

Harassment and victimisation

In common with other discrimination legislation, the DDA (in sections 3B and 55 respectively) now specifically includes harassment and victimisation, which are defined in the same way as in the other acts.

Age discrimination

The *Employment Equality (Age) Regulations 2006* (EE(A)R) were introduced on 1 October 2006 to bring into effect the European

Employment Directive. These make it unlawful to discriminate against individuals in employment and vocational training on grounds of their age. Definitions of direct and indirect discrimination, harassment, victimisation and instructions to discriminate on grounds of age are defined in the same way as for other types of discrimination.

The general **justification** defence is the same as for the religion or belief and sexual orientation regulations: the employer must show their conduct to be "a proportionate means of achieving a legitimate aim". The age regulations have also affected some other areas of law — for example, age limits in unfair dismissal claims and age- and service-related criteria in the calculation of redundancy pay and unfair dismissal compensation. These are explained in the relevant Chapters.

In *Chief Constable of West Yorkshire Police v Homer UKEAT/0191/08*, the employer, in an effort to attract and retain more highly qualified staff, introduced a new grading scheme designed to reward staff with a law degree. Mr Homer claimed that this discriminated against him as a 61 year old because he would not be able to obtain a law degree prior to retiring.

The EAT decided that Mr Homer had been treated in the same way as everyone else and that age was no impediment to obtaining a degree. The EAT found that the reason that Mr Homer could not materially benefit from a law degree was that an individual's working life is limited rather than because of age itself. The EAT did, however, comment that if Mr Homer had established that indirect age discrimination had occurred, it would have found that the new grading scheme was a disproportionate means of recruiting and retaining appropriately qualified staff. The regulations include provisions relating to length-of-service benefits and retirement.

Length-of-service benefits

Any employment benefits based on a worker's age or length of service are potentially discriminatory. Age-related benefits will have to be justified under the general objective justification defence. But there are different criteria for justifying length-of-service benefits:

◆ if the length of service required for a particular benefit is **five years or less**, the benefit is not unlawful because there is an automatic exemption; but

◆ if the benefit relates to length of service of **more than five years** it will be justified (and therefore lawful) if it "reasonably appears" to the employer that the benefit "fulfils a business need ... for example, by encouraging the loyalty or motivation, or rewarding the experience, of" its workers.

A common example of a length-of-service benefit is additional holiday after a certain number of years' employment.

Retirement

One of the most disappointing aspects of the age equality laws is that the retirement of employees aged 65 and over has been **exempted** from their scope. At the moment, an employer can force an employee to retire at the age of 65 and this will not amount to age discrimination according to the law unless the employer fails to follow some basic procedures. These are explained in Chapter 10.

The membership organisation Heyday, which was formed by the charity Age Concern, has brought a legal challenge to the UK government's introduction of the default retirement age, saying it does not comply with European law. The issue was referred to the ECJ (*Incorporated Trustees of the National Council on Ageing v Secretary of State for Trade and Industry C-388/07*) which gave judgment in March 2009.

The ECJ decided that a mandatory retirement age is capable of being justified (i.e. if in pursuit of certain social objectives, such as tackling youth unemployment). The issue of whether having a mandatory age in the UK, is a proportionate means of achieving a legitimate aim was referred back to the High Court.

The High Court found the introduction of a retirement age (in 2006) to be justified on the grounds of maintaining confidence in the labour market, the need for workforce planning and to avoid an adverse impact on the provision of pensions and workplace benefits. The High Court was less certain about the justifiability of imposing a default retirement age of 65 rather than 70. It said that, had it been adopted for the first time in 2009, or had the government not committed to an imminent review of the appropriate retirement age, it would have found that the selection of the age of 65 was not proportionate: *R (on the application of Age UK) v Secretary of State for Business, Innovation & Skills (Equality and Human Rights Commission — intervenor) [2009] EWHC 2336 (Admin).*

However, it is unlikely that the mandatory retirement age will remain lawful for very much longer. There is strong cross-party support for its withdrawal, and the government has already committed to a review in 2010.

Combined discrimination

Under section 14, *Equality Act 2010* (expected to come into force in October 2010) discrimination based on two of an individual's protected characteristics will be unlawful. Specifically, if on the basis of two characteristics — out of age, disability, gender reassignment, race, religion or belief, sex and sexual orientation — an individual suffers less favourable treatment than someone who does not have either of those characteristics, s/he will have a claim.

Ms DeBique, a Foreign and Commonwealth soldier fell pregnant (and subsequently gave birth) while serving in the Army. Ms DeBique was strongly criticised for missing training (due to her child's illness), missing parade (due to childcare problems) and being unavailable for deployment on a 24/7 basis. Ms DeBique proposed solving her childcare needs by bringing her half-sister from St Vincent to stay with her at Chelsea Barracks. The MoD rejected this on the basis that the half-sister's immigration status meant that she would only have visitor status and her stay would have been limited to six months.

Facing disciplinary action and anticipating dismissal, Ms DeBique resigned and brought a claim in the tribunal. Her indirect sex and race discrimination claims were upheld by the employment tribunal — however, the employer appealed. The EAT noted that as the Crown was Ms DeBique's employer it was responsible for both her terms and conditions, and immigration policy.

The EAT agreed with the tribunal that the immigration provision, criterion or practice (PCP) put people of Ms DeBique's national origin at a greater disadvantage than single parents of British national origin. Logically the extended families of those of Vincentian national origin (from which Vincentians can find family members to be childcarers) are more likely to be foreign nationals subject to immigration control. Although the immigration PCP pursued a legitimate aim, it was not a proportionate means of achieving that aim, and the MoD should have sought a concession for Ms DeBique from the UK Border Agency. Also, although the tribunal had conflated the sex and race PCPs, there had been no error of law and the tribunal's approach reflected the twin disadvantages that Ms DeBique suffered. *Ministry of Defence v Ms DeBique UKEAT/0048/09/MAA.*

Bringing a discrimination claim

Before submitting a claim to the employment tribunal, an employee must first (in order to comply with the Acas code) raise a written grievance. An individual can bring a claim for both direct and indirect discrimination, but should specify this on the claim form (*Ali v Office of National Statistics [2004] EWCA Civ 1363 ([2005] IRLR 201)*).

The time limit for all discrimination cases is **three months** from the date of the discriminatory act. If the individual is subject to continuing discrimination, the time limit runs from the end of that period of **continuing discrimination** — this would be the case if the employer operated a discriminatory policy, for example, rather than committing one-off acts of discrimination.

If an employee can show that for the whole of their career they have been held back on discriminatory grounds, this could amount to a continuing discrimination claim (*Fearon v Chief Constable of Derbyshire EAT/0445/02*).

If a woman claims discriminatory treatment, the fact that she does not suffer this treatment while away from work on maternity leave does not break the continuity of discrimination (*Spencer v HM Prison Service EAT/0812/02*).

In a disability case, discrimination was found to continue during the employee's absence on sick leave (*Hendricks v Commissioner of Police of the Metropolis [2002] EWCA Civ 1686 ([2003] IRLR 96)*).

Where an employer promises but fails to take remedial steps to improve the working environment and prevent a recurrence of discrimination, this falls within the definition of continuing discrimination (*Littlewoods v Traynor [1993] IRLR 154*). So too does a case where an employer has more than once rejected an employee for promotion on discriminatory grounds (*Owusu v London Fire and Civil Defence Authority [1995] IRLR 574*).

Where the claim is based on an employer's discriminatory recruitment policies, the three months run from the date of the last refusal of employment.

There is a difference between the continuing existence of a discriminatory rule or policy and its single or occasional application to a complainant — a claim based on refusal of a job because of a discriminatory policy must be brought within three months of the refusal (*Tyagi v BBC World Service [2001] IRLR 465*).

An employment tribunal has discretion to **extend the time limit** for bringing a discrimination claim if it is just and equitable to do so, although there must be a very good reason for this; a claimant should never rely on time being extended, but should not be put off bringing a claim outside the normal time limit if there is a specific reason why s/he could not bring it in time.

A worker's right to bring a discrimination claim does not depend on their length of service.

Discrimination laws apply to workers at an establishment in Great Britain (or Northern Ireland). However, a worker can still be covered if part of their work is done outside the UK, or if their employer has a place of business there and the employee has lived in the UK either when s/he applied for or was offered the job, or at any time during the employment.

Claims of discrimination can be taken against **bodies other than employers**. Partnerships, trade unions, qualifying bodies, vocational training bodies, employment agencies and statutory bodies are all covered under the legislation.

Claims can also be taken against work colleagues who have discriminated against or harassed other colleagues. In the case of *Miles v Gilbank [2006] EWCA Civ 543*, the Court of Appeal held that a claim could be brought against an individual manager as well as the company:

Miss Gilbank was subjected to a campaign of bullying and harassment by her manager, Ms Miles, and others, after she told Miles she was pregnant. The Court of Appeal said that Miles had knowingly fostered and encouraged the bullying and discrimination, which was targeted and deliberate, and found her, as well as the company to be liable. It also upheld the EAT's finding that £25,000 for injury to Gilbank's feelings was not too high, particularly as the EAT had noted that the figures given in the *Vento* case (see below) had been devalued slightly by inflation.

Tribunals have the power to **make an order** declaring the rights of the parties, **award compensation** to the employee discriminated against, and **recommend action** for the employer to take within a specific period.

Under section 124, *Equality Act 2010*, where an employer is found to have discriminated, the tribunal will have the power to make recommendations covering the whole workforce (e.g. that employees undergo equality training). Although a tribunal's recommendation won't be binding, failure to follow its recommendations, will be taken into account in any future discrimination cases involving the employer. Specifically, if in a subsequent case an employer is found to have ignored a tribunal's recommendations, the tribunal will be able to increase the amount of damages awarded to the claimant.

Compensation

There is **no upper limit** for compensation in discrimination claims, and compensation can be claimed under a number of different headings.

If the claimant has left their job as a result of discrimination, compensation for loss of earnings will include any actual financial loss sustained plus an estimate of future loss — assessed by taking the sum they would have earned at work, deducting what might have been earned elsewhere and then reducing this by a percentage to reflect the possibility that they might have left the employer at some stage anyway (*MoD v Wheeler [1998] IRLR 23*). The fact that the employer "unintentionally" discriminated is not a defence.

Claimants can also claim damages for **injury to feelings**. The size of this award can reflect the length of time that the employer took to resolve the employee's grievance (*BT v Reid, [2003] EWCA Civ 1675 ([2004] IRLR 327)*), and will also be affected by the seniority of the person who has discriminated and how persistent the discrimination has been.

The Court of Appeal established (in the case of *Vento v Chief Constable of West Yorkshire Police [2002] EWCA Civ 1675 ([2003] IRLR 102)*) three bands within which injury to feelings awards should be made. Those bands have since been uplifted (following the case of *Da'Bell v NSPCC UKEAT/0227/09*) in order to take inflation into account.

There is a top band of between £18,000 and £30,000 for the most serious cases (e.g. where there has been a lengthy campaign of discriminatory harassment); a middle band of between £6,000 and £18,000 for serious cases which do not merit an award in the highest band; and a lower band of between £500 and £6,000 for less serious cases (e.g. where the act of discrimination is an isolated or one-off occurrence). Awards above or below these limits should only be made in exceptional circumstances.

Injury to feelings awards are not "grossed up" to take account of any tax liability the claimant might have (*Orthet v Vince-Cain EAT/0801/03 ([2004] IRLR 857)*).

In the case of *Essa v Laing [2004] EWCA Civ 02 ([2004] IRLR 313)*, the Court of Appeal held that an employer was still liable to pay compensation for injury to feelings even though it could not have been foreseen that the discrimination would have affected the employee's health so badly. The court held that there was a strict obligation on employers to pay compensation where health was damaged.

Tribunals can also award **aggravated damages** for the manner of the discrimination — for example, where the discriminatory conduct was high-handed, malicious, insulting or oppressive. In one case this led to an award of £7,500.

There may be circumstances in which tribunals will award additional compensation for **psychiatric injury**, and in the case of *MoD v Cannock [1994] IRLR 509*, the EAT held that compensation could also be claimed for hurt caused by loss of a chosen career. Separate claims for personal injury (physical or mental) can be pursued in the civil courts (*Sheriff v Klyne Tugs [1999] IRLR 481*). Exceptionally, tribunals may also award **exemplary damages** — that is, damages that are punitive (rather than compensatory) where a public authority has behaved in an oppressive, arbitrary or unconstitutional way.

The case of *Ministry of Defence v Fletcher UKEAT/0044/09 [2010] IRLR 25, EAT* concerned an individual who was subjected to sexual harassment by the Army — followed by disciplinary action when she tried to complain. She won her tribunal case for direct discrimination and harassment under the *Sex Discrimination Act 1975* and victimisation under the *Employment Equality (Sexual Orientation) Regulations 2003*. On appeal the EAT awarded Ms Fletcher £30,000 for injury to feelings, £8,000 aggravated damages (a sum to take into account the way that the MoD had conducted its defence in the tribunal, but less than the tribunal awarded so as not to overlap with her injury to feelings claim) as well as £10,000 costs.

The EAT overturned the award of exemplary damages. It commented that exemplary damages could be awarded in principle, but not on the basis that they were awarded by the tribunal (failure to provide a mechanism for redress of Ms Fletcher's complaints). Also, if the EAT had allowed the award of exemplary damages (e.g. for use of disciplinary action to victimise the claimant) an award of £7,500 would have been appropriate.

If an individual who has made a discrimination claim dies, the claim for compensation can be continued by **relatives or beneficiaries** (*Executors of Soutar v James Murray [2002] IRLR 22*).

In determining compensation in **harassment** cases, tribunals will take account of the impact of harassment and how the employer responded to it. They may also take account of factors such as the victim's age (for example, if s/he was a young person, if s/he was particularly vulnerable), whether the employer's attitudes had encouraged the harassment, and whether complaints were ignored. It cannot take into account the size of the employer's organisation or resources (*Corus Hotels v Woodward EAT/0536/05*).

The Equality and Human Rights Commission

The **Equality and Human Rights Commission** (EHRC) began work on 1 October 2007, taking over the functions of the former Equal Opportunities Commission (EOC), Commission for Racial Equality (CRE) and Disability Rights Commission (DRC) as well as having responsibility for equality on grounds of religion or belief, sexual orientation and age together with human rights.

The EHRC was established under the *Equality Act 2006* and exists to "reduce inequality, eliminate discrimination, strengthen good relations between people, and promote and protect human rights."

The Commission gives advice and guidance to businesses, the voluntary and public sectors, and also to individuals.

However, while the Commission has the power to take legal action on behalf of an individual, this is normally limited to particularly complex cases or those where a question of legal principle is involved. It also has powers to enforce the equalities duties of organisations and authorities, including instituting official inquiries and formal investigations. Northern Ireland already has a single **Equality Commission Northern Ireland**, which covers all forms of unlawful discrimination

Codes of practice

The Commission has the power to issue Codes of practice, which contain practical guidance and information on the interpretation of discrimination law. The Codes are not legally enforceable themselves, but must be taken into account by tribunals when deciding discrimination claims; if employers ignore a Code's recommendations, this can be used against them at a tribunal.

Codes of practice on sex discrimination and equal pay, racial equality and disability issued by the previous commissions (the EOC, CRE and DRC) which are still valid are available at the "Publications and resources" section of the EHRC website on www.equalityhumanrights.com

More information: See the LRD booklets *Discrimination at work* (£4.50), *Lesbian and gay workers' rights* (£4.00), *Black and minority ethnic workers — tackling discrimination* (£6.00), *Age discrimination — a guide to the new regulations* (£4.70), *Promoting equality for disabled workers — a guide to the law and best practice* (£5.70). LRD's *Workplace Report* contains quarterly updates on discrimination law.

7. Sick pay and sickness absence

Statutory sick pay

An employer must provide his/her employees with details of their sick pay entitlement as part of the written statement of employment particulars (see "The employment contract" in Chapter 3). Many employers provide an occupational sick pay scheme more generous than the **statutory sick pay** (SSP) scheme. Employees who do not benefit from such a scheme but who meet the qualifying criteria are entitled to SSP of **£79.15** a week (unchanged from 2009), for a **maximum of 28 weeks**. To be entitled to SSP an employee must be **earning an average of at least £97 a week**. SSP is paid by the employer in the same way they would normally pay wages but reclaimed from the state.

Agency workers on contracts of three months or less are not entitled to SSP but become entitled to SSP if their contracts are extended beyond that time (*HMRC v Thorn Baker Ltd & others [2007] EWCA Civ 626*). Workers or employees who do not qualify for SSP may be entitled to Employment and Support Allowance (ESA).

Pregnant women can claim, and will only be excluded from SSP if sick for a pregnancy-related reason from four weeks before the baby's expected week of birth, in which case they will start getting Statutory Maternity Pay (SMP) or Maternity Allowance (MA) (see "Maternity pay" in Chapter 8). Women in receipt of SMP cannot claim SSP at the same time.

Ms Sutcliffe's maternity leave was due to start on 1 August 2006. However, from June 2006 onwards she was off sick. She was paid sick pay before her maternity leave, but only maternity allowance thereafter. She lodged an unlawful deduction from wages claim for the difference between sick pay and maternity allowance. The EAT noted that regulation 71(5), *Employment Rights Act 1996* preserves all a woman's terms and conditions during Ordinary Maternity Leave — other than, crucially, remuneration. As remuneration includes sick pay and Ms Sutcliffe had no contractual right to sick pay while on maternity leave, her claim failed. *Department of Work and Pensions v Sutcliffe UKEAT/0319/07*.

To claim SSP an employee has to be ill for at least **four days in a row** (including weekends and bank holidays). SSP is only paid for the days the employee normally works. These are called "qualifying days". However, it is not paid for the first three qualifying days, which are called "waiting days". So an employee who works Monday to Friday and who falls ill on a Saturday cannot claim SSP until the Thursday — if the illness lasts that long. If the employee is ill again within eight weeks, and each period of illness lasts at least four days, the two are linked together in one claim and the employee does not have to serve the waiting days again.

To claim SSP the employee **must notify** his/her employer. Since 6 April 2010 a new sick note system has been in operation: *Social Security (Medical Evidence) and Statutory Sick Pay (Medical Evidence) (Amendment) Regulations 2010*. GPs signing individuals off from their normal duties, are now invited to state what steps can be taken to help an employee return to work, as well as whether the person may be fit for some work. Specifically, a GP can comment on the impact of the individual's illness and recommend a phased return to work, altered hours, amended duties or adaptations to the workplace.

While the employer may have its own notification procedure, they cannot insist that the employee notifies them in person nor can they insist on a doctor's certificate for the first seven days' absence. **Claims for non-payment** of SSP can be pursued against the employer as unlawful deductions through the employment tribunals, but if there is a dispute about whether the employee is entitled to SSP this must be resolved by HM Revenue and Customs (HMRC).

Occupational sick pay

An employer may provide an **occupational sick pay scheme**, which must pay at least the SSP rate. But as this is a **contractual entitlement** the employer can set its own rules. In the case of *Stirling & Mair v Meikle EAT/27/02*, an employee's refusal to be **examined by the company doctor** made it lawful for the employer to stop her occupational sick pay.

However, if the employer does not follow its own rules, this may be a breach of contract and an employee can bring a claim for unlawful deduction of wages (see Chapter 4).

Most occupational sick pay schemes will set out a period of

entitlement to pay. A typical scheme might pay three or six months' full pay followed by three or six months' half pay. However, in some cases entitlement may be **discretionary**.

If the employer does have discretion over whether to pay sick pay it must not exercise it arbitrarily and must make sure that it acts in accordance with the implied term of trust and confidence, as the EAT pointed out in the following case:

Ian Guthrie was off sick after an accident at work. There was a contractual sick pay policy that said sickness absence would be paid if it was genuine. The company's occupational health adviser (OHA) disagreed with Guthrie's GP over the date he would be fit to return and Scottish Courage refused to pay him beyond the date given by OHA. The EAT held they were wrong to do so. There had been no suggestion that his illness was not genuine and the employer had an obligation to pay for any genuine sickness absence. Guthrie had a reasonable expectation based on past practice that he would be paid. *Scottish Courage Ltd v Guthrie EAT/0788/03.*

But an employer does not have an obligation to consider an employee's financial position before exercising its discretion:

Mr King worked for the fire service. He was off on long-term sick leave, suffering from depression. Unfortunately, his wife was also off sick and as a consequence their family income was reduced. King argued that his employer should have exercised its discretion to extend his period of full pay given that his illness was work-related and his financial situation was poor. The EAT held there was no such requirement. *West Yorkshire Fire and Civil Defence Authority v King EAT/0961/03*

If there is no written term and the contractual entitlement is in dispute, a tribunal can look at what has happened in the past and what the parties' understanding was to establish the contractual position.

In the case of *Secession Ltd t/a Freud v Bellingham EAT/0069/05*, the employee had always received full sick pay during her 15 years of employment, with no indication that it was discretionary. Her employer then refused to pay her when she was signed off work for a month. The EAT found that she had a contractual entitlement to full sick pay and her employer's failure to pay it was a breach of contract entitling her to resign and claim constructive dismissal.

If the employee's doctor says that they are fit to return to work, but the employer wants further medical checks, the employee should be paid full wages while waiting for the checks to take place. A person **willing and able to work** has a common law right to be paid (*Beveridge v KLM EAT/1044/99 ([2000] IRLR 765)*).

There is generally no requirement to extend the sick pay provisions for **disabled employees** (*O'Hanlon v Commissioners for HM Revenue & Customs [2007] EWCA Civ 283*). However, in exceptional cases where the reason the employee is still off sick is because their employer has failed to make adjustments, failure to extend sick pay can amount to disability discrimination (*Nottinghamshire CC v Meikle [2004] EWCA Civ 859*) (see page 146).

In the following case the ECJ ruled that an employer can treat **pregnancy-related sickness** absences in the same way as any other sickness absence and this does not amount to discrimination:

Ms McKenna was off sick while pregnant, and had to use up much of her occupational sick pay entitlement. The ECJ ruled that while dismissing a woman because she is pregnant obviously amounts to unlawful sex discrimination, reducing a woman's pay because she is absent with a pregnancy-related illness does not. In particular, an employer is entitled to calculate a pregnant employee's sick pay in the same way as it would for a man who is absent for any kind of illness. *North Western Health Board v McKenna Case C-191/03 ([2005] IRLR 895).*

There is no general right for an employee to reclaim holiday if they have been **sick during a holiday**. It is therefore a good idea for unions to negotiate terms that cover that situation.

However, the SSP rules under the *Social Security Contributions and Benefits Act 1992* say that sickness during a holiday (unless the employee falls ill outside the European Union) qualifies for SSP as long as the employee has the required medical certificate. An employee who is off sick during their notice period is entitled to their normal full pay during that period even if they have used up all their sick pay entitlement unless, by a quirk of the legislation, they are entitled to contractual notice of at least a week more than the statutory minimum (section 87, ERA 96).

Dismissal while sick

Dismissal for long-term or frequent sickness absence can amount to a potentially fair reason for dismissal. Most commonly this will be on grounds of "capability" but in the case of *Wilson v Post Office [2000] IRLR 834*, the Court of Appeal held that an employee could be fairly dismissed for "some other substantial reason" when his attendance was below the level required by the agreed attendance procedure (see "Fair reasons for dismissal" in Chapter 10).

An employee can be dismissed even if s/he has a **current medical certificate** and is still receiving sick pay. The reason for the sickness absence does not necessarily matter. If an employee is off sick after an accident, or after having been a victim of a crime, or even following a work-related injury, this does not mean that they cannot be dismissed as a result of their sickness absence. However, in the case of *Frewin v Consignia EAT/0981/02*, the EAT held that this is not the same as suggesting that the cause of the illness be completely disregarded. And an employer should "go the extra mile" in looking for an alternative to dismissal if the employee is absent as a result of a work-related injury (*McAdie v Royal Bank of Scotland [2007] EWCA Civ 806*).

Where an employee is entitled to an enhanced pension for **early retirement** on grounds of ill-health the employer must consider this first as an alternative to dismissing them (*First West Yorkshire Ltd t/a First Leeds v Haigh UKEAT/0246/07 ([2008] IRLR 182)*).

In all cases dismissal must be "reasonable in all the circumstances". Tribunals will take into account matters such as the size of the firm, difficulties in arranging for short-term replacements, the employee's length of service, the nature of the illness and whether, taking all things into account, the employer's decision to dismiss was one a "reasonable" employer would have taken.

The steps an employer must take before dismissal will depend on the individual circumstances but should normally include:

◆ **investigating** the reasons for the sickness absence (which might include consulting a doctor, with the employee's consent);

◆ **consulting the employee**;

◆ looking at **alternative work**;

◆ **warning** the employee that continued or further absence may result in dismissal.

In the following case, dismissing an employee without consultation made the dismissal unfair.

Mr Daubney suffered stress/depression-related ill-health following a problem at work. Having been absent through illness for a considerable period, his employers commissioned a medical report. The report recommended that Mr Daubney be retired, which he was and the dismissal took place without any consultation. The EAT found that Mr Daubney had been unfairly dismissed. *East Lindsey District Council v Daubney [1977] IRLR 181.*

Where there is a **sickness absence policy** providing guidance on how absences should be dealt with, the employer should follow it. If the policy is contractual any departure from it could give rise to a claim: for example, in the case of *Robertson v Rockware Glass EAT/107/01*, an attempt to stop the employee's sick pay entitlement was unlawful. If the sickness policy does not form part of the employee's contract, the employer can change it unilaterally (*Wandsworth BC v D'Silva [1998] IRLR 193*). However, an employer who has failed to follow its own existing procedure may be found to have acted unreasonably, making the dismissal unfair.

Many sickness absence procedures set down rules for **keeping in touch** during sickness absence. They may require employees to contact their employer at regular, even pre-set, intervals, but should not be exercised in a manner which would be regarded as unreasonable.

Some procedures give the employer the right to make contact, which may be intrusive if the employer turns up unexpectedly or telephones too frequently or at inappropriate times of the day. In more extreme situations, employees in the public sector may be able to use the *Human Rights Act 1998* to argue that the employer's intrusion breaches their right to a private life (see "Civil liberties and employment law" in the Introduction). However, the case would probably have to be a serious one to succeed.

Mr Ridge complained that the employer had made a secret video of him while he was off sick and had used the video at a disciplinary hearing, resulting in his dismissal. He argued that his human rights had been breached. The EAT held that the employer had the right to video an employee who it suspected was not genuinely sick. *Pendragon Motor Co v Ridge EAT/962/00.*

Although an employer is obliged to take steps to discover the true medical position before dismissing, the overriding principle is one of **"reasonableness"**, so that a failure to consult with the employee's GP is not an absolute guarantee that the resulting dismissal is unfair. But at the same time, there is no corresponding obligation on the employee to inform the employer of the prospects of recovery (*Mitchell v Arkwood Plastics [1993] ICR 471*).

Ms Slaughter was dismissed because she was unable to lift heavy loads due to a back injury. A tribunal tried to reduce her compensation on the grounds that she had an obligation to inform her employer of her medical condition. The EAT rejected this view and said that while she had an obligation to co-operate with her employer's medical enquiries, she was under no obligation to instigate them. *Slaughter v Brewer & Sons [1990] IRLR 426.*

In cases of **intermittent absences** due to ill health, the employer may not have the same obligation to obtain medical evidence. The EAT has said that the employer has to have regard to the whole history of the employment and to take account of a range of factors including the nature of the illness and the likelihood of its recurrence, the length of absences compared with the intervals of good health, the employer's need for that particular employee, the impact of absences on the rest of the workforce and the extent to which the employee was made aware of the position (*Lynock v Cereal Packaging [1988] IRLR 510*).

The tribunal will still be able to look at whether the dismissal was reasonable in cases of intermittent but genuine sickness absence.

The case of *Leeson v Makita Manufacturing Europe EAT/0911/00* held the dismissal of an employee who had frequent absences for genuine reasons to be unreasonable. It had more to do with the employer's wish to make an example of the employee to deter others, than dealing with the employee's genuine sickness.

The dismissal of **disabled employees** for disability-related absences could amount to disability discrimination (see "Disability discrimination" in Chapter 6).

A growing number of employers provide **permanent healthcare insurance** (PHI), which insures them against the financial costs of long-term illness while providing a financial safety net for employees. The High Court has held, in the case of *Aspden v Webbs Poultry [1996] IRLR 521*, that there is an implied term in a contract that an employee will not be dismissed, except for redundancy, if a PHI scheme requires the individual to remain an employee to receive the benefit.

In the case of *Villella v MFI Furniture [1999] IRLR 468*, the employer paid into a PHI scheme. The insurers investigated the employee's illness and decided they would no longer pay out on the policy. The EAT held that the fact that the insurers were no longer paying did not alter the employer's contractual obligation to pay wages, since the employee's rights under the PHI scheme were not dependent on how the scheme viewed the employee's state of health.

However, an employee may lose their protection from dismissal under a PHI scheme if they fundamentally breach their contract. This happened in the case of *Briscoe v Lubrizol [2002] EWCA Civ 508 ([2002] IRLR 607)*, in which the Court of Appeal held that an employee's **refusal to attend a meeting** with management was a fundamental breach of contract and that, even if it had not been, would have amounted to gross misconduct justifying dismissal.

Where there is a PHI scheme, the fact that an employee may be doing **some** work does not necessarily negate the contractual right to make a PHI claim (*Brompton v AOC [1997] IRLR 639*).

For example, in the case of *Walton v Airtours plc & another [2002] EWCA Civ 1659 ([2003] IRLR 161)*, the Court of Appeal held that where an employee's medical condition allowed him to try an alternative job this did not deny him the right to PHI, since there was no evidence that he could permanently follow the new occupation.

Workers **sick before the beginning of a strike** are not viewed as taking part in it. Workers who are off sick have no obligation to supply their labour and therefore cannot be said to be withdrawing it. This would not apply, however, where the sick employee was somehow actively participating in the strike.

Mr Smith was off sick for the whole period of a strike. Every week he would go to work to hand in his doctor's certificate and would stop to chat to the pickets on the gate. The EAT had to determine whether he was taking part in the strike, and on the facts they held that merely talking to pickets did not amount to taking part in a strike. *Hindle Gears Ltd v McGinty [1984] IRLR 477.*

However, if the **sickness begins after the strike begins**, the worker is usually considered to be taking part in it.

Employers can use sickness as a method of **selecting for redundancies** (see "Selection for redundancy" in Chapter 11). However, reasonable adjustments to the selection criteria should be considered in relation to disabled employees (see Chapter 6 — "Disability discrimination").

Any award of compensation made by a tribunal in an unfair dismissal claim can be reduced to take account of SSP or Employment and Support Allowance received (*Morgans v Alpha Plus Security EAT/0436/04 ([2005] IRLR 234*).

Frustration of contract

A contract of employment will automatically come to an end in the event that it becomes impossible for an employee to perform their duties. This is called a *frustration of contract*. Once a contract has been frustrated all rights under it cease and there will have been no dismissal, which means the employee will not be able to bring a claim of unfair dismissal.

It is possible for a contract to become frustrated through illness, in which case the following factors are likely to be taken into account:

◆ the duration of the illness;
◆ the nature of the employment;
◆ the terms of the contract;
◆ the employer's need for the work to be done and the need for a replacement;
◆ whether the employee is still being paid; and
◆ whether a reasonable employer could be expected to wait longer.

However, because an employee is left with no legal right to challenge the termination of their employment and employers have the ability to dismiss an employee on grounds of incapacity under the ERA, courts will be reluctant to find that a contract has been frustrated in these circumstances.

For example, in the case of *Thorold v Martell Press EAT/343/01*, the EAT commented that the operation of the law of frustration in cases where employment is lost through incapacity could lead to injustice. In cases such as this it said that the employee should look at what rights they have under the *Disability Discrimination Act 1995* which may require the employer to offer alternative work under the existing contract.

Medical reports

The *Access to Medical Reports Act 1988* gives employees (and prospective employees) the right to see medical reports prepared by their own GP, or any other medical practitioner responsible for their care, in connection with their employment. The Act says that the employer must obtain the individual's consent before seeking a report from her/his doctor; that the individual has the legal right to have a copy of the report before it is forwarded to the employer; that the individual can query items in it; and that, if the doctor refuses to accept it, the individual's objection may be appended to the report.

Individuals who want to see records relating to them but which are not prepared by someone responsible for their care (for example, an occupational health consultant) can make a request under the *Data Protection Act 1998*.

More information: See the LRD booklets *State benefits and tax credits 2009* (£6.40), and *Sickness absence and sick pay* (£4.15). LRD's *Workplace Report* has monthly updates which highlight any relevant new cases on sickness.

8. Leave for working parents

The *Work and Families Act 2006* introduced a number of new rights for parents and carers from April 2007. These included an increase in paid maternity and adoption leave from six to nine months; the introduction of "keeping in touch" days for employees on maternity or adoption leave, and the extension of the right to request flexible working to carers.

The Act also includes provision for paid maternity leave to be extended to a year and for additional paternity leave to be paid if the mother returns to work earlier.

The changes to maternity and adoption leave can be found in the *Maternity and Parental Leave etc* and the *Paternity and Adoption Leave (Amendment) Regulations 2006*, and the changes to flexible working in the *Flexible Working (Eligibility, Complaints and Remedies) (Amendment) Regulations 2006*.

Antenatal care

Pregnant employees have the right to **paid time off** to attend appointments for antenatal care under section 55 of the *Employment Rights Act 1996* (ERA 96). For this right to apply the appointment must have been made on the advice of a registered medical practitioner, midwife or nurse and, except for the first appointment, the employee must, if she is asked by her employer, provide a copy of a certificate showing she is pregnant and written **proof of the antenatal appointment**.

If an employer unreasonably refuses time off or does not pay the employee the amount she is entitled to she can bring a claim in an employment tribunal, which must normally be done **within three months** of the appointment. If the claim is upheld, the tribunal can order the employer to pay her at the appropriate rate. She is entitled to this even if the employer's refusal to allow time off meant she worked, and was paid, during the time when the appointment would have occurred.

Maternity leave

Every woman in work has the right to maternity leave (although not necessarily paid — see the next section for rights to maternity pay).

There are three types of leave:

◆ **ordinary** maternity leave (OML) — 26 weeks.
◆ **compulsory** maternity leave — two weeks within the period of OML (four weeks in the case of factory workers) immediately following the birth, which must be taken; and
◆ **additional** maternity leave (AML) — a further 26 weeks.

Any woman who qualifies for OML also qualifies for AML — the additional qualifying conditions having been removed. To get OML a woman must still be in work into the **15th week** before the baby is due. By the 15th week she has to have given her employer **notice** of her pregnancy and of the date when she intends to begin her maternity leave.

A woman can **change her mind** about this date but has to give her employer at least 28 days' notice of the new start date. If her employer requests it, she also has to provide a copy of a doctor's or midwife's notice that she is pregnant. She can begin the leave any time after the 11th week before the baby is due, up to the week it is born. She must, as a minimum, be off for the whole of the compulsory leave period.

During her maternity leave a woman can, if she wants to, carry out work or training of up to **10 days** for her employer without losing her right to Statutory Maternity Pay (see below) and without bringing her maternity leave to an end. This is for the purpose of **"keeping in touch"** with the workplace.

While on maternity leave a woman has the right to all **non-wage contractual benefits**. She has the right to be given the opportunity for **assessment**, wherever the pay system is performance based. In the case of *Boyle v EOC [1998] IRLR 717, the European Court of Justice (ECJ)* confirmed that where the pension provision is entirely funded by the employer, all of a woman's statutory maternity leave, including any unpaid leave, is to be taken into account in calculating length of service for pension purposes.

Although women on additional maternity leave used to retain less comprehensive contractual rights, this was part of the EOC's challenge to the UK legislation and they successfully argued that women should not have fewer rights when they take additional leave

(*EOC v Secretary of State for Trade and Industry [2007] EWHC 483*). These changes have now been incorporated into the *Sex Discrimination Act 1975*.

As far as **statutory holiday rights** are concerned, a woman who is on maternity leave must be able to exercise those rights even if that means taking her holidays at a time that does not coincide with when her colleagues take leave.

She also has the right to be **told of any jobs** that become available while she is on maternity leave, for which she might be interested in applying. A failure to give this information amounts to a breach of trust and confidence, according to the EAT in the case of *Visa International Service Association v Paul [2004] IRLR 42*. And she has the right to be consulted about any changes to her job or reorganisation. If she has been serving a probationary period and, due to her maternity leave, has had less time in the job the employer must **extend her period of probation** if the alternative is dismissal for failing her probation (*Haines Lee v Relate Berkshire EAT/1458/01*).

Additional leave starts at the end of the period of ordinary leave and lasts for another 26 weeks. In total, a woman can have up to a year's maternity leave (although not all of it is paid under the statutory scheme — see below).

Also, where the expected week of childbirth begins on or after 3 April 2011, a mother will be able to transfer up to six months of her maternity leave to the father (or husband, civil partner, or partner): *Work and Families Act 2006* and *Additional Paternity Leave Regulations 2010*. Specifically, once the baby is 20 weeks old and the mother wishes to return to work, the father will be able to take between two and 26 weeks' additional paternity leave (APL). Under the statutory scheme this is reimbursed at the same rate as that which the mother would have received – i.e. either £124.88 per week or unpaid. However, the leave must end by the child's first birthday (or first anniversary of placement for adoption).

A woman who is on maternity leave and who decides that she **does not want to return** to work at the end of it should resign by giving whatever notice her contract states she should.

Maternity pay

To get Statutory Maternity Pay (SMP), a woman has to fulfil four requirements:

◆ she has to have worked for her employer for at least 26 weeks by the 15th week before the baby is due;

◆ in the eight weeks (or two months if monthly paid) prior to the 15th week she has to have had average earnings of at least £97 a week;

◆ by the 15th week before the baby is due, she has to have given her employer medical evidence of her pregnancy and told them when she intends to stop work and start claiming SMP; and

◆ she must have actually stopped work.

She will then get six weeks pay at 90% of average earnings (higher rate SMP) and 33 weeks' at a flat rate of £124.88 (2010-11) (or 90% of average earnings if this is less). SMP starts in the first week of maternity leave and continues until 39 weeks have passed or the employee returns to work, whichever happens first.

SMP is paid by the employer through the normal pay packet. The employer then reclaims most of it back through the national insurance scheme.

If a woman is refused SMP and believes she is entitled to it she should write to the employer or make a formal complaint. If no agreement can be reached the local HM Revenue and Customs Office can be asked for a formal decision.

A woman not qualifying for SMP may be able to claim **Maternity Allowance** (MA) through her local Jobcentre Plus office. MA is a flat rate of £124.88 a week (2010-11) payable for 39 weeks. The condition for this benefit is that she has had at least 26 weeks' employment, which need not be continuous, within the previous 66 weeks.

Women who meet the service requirements for SMP, and who earn less than £97 a week but at least £30 a week, even from different jobs, will get 90% of their actual earnings for 39 weeks (52 weeks as of April 2010). Those with fewer than 26 weeks' employment have no entitlement to payment.

Rights to SMP are not **dependent on returning to work**. However, rights to more generous occupational maternity pay can be linked to returning to work for a specified period, and this is not unlawful according to the ECJ in the case of *Handels-og Kontorfunktionaererenes C-66/96 [1999] IRLR 55.*

The ECJ has ruled that it is not contrary to the Directive on equal treatment to pay less than full pay during maternity leave. However, the calculation of maternity pay must be based on what a woman is earning immediately before she begins her maternity leave and this must include any subsequent increase that is backdated to that period.

Michelle Alabaster went on maternity leave in January *1996.* In accordance with the *Statutory Maternity Pay (General) Regulations 1986* her statutory maternity pay (SMP) was based on her normal weekly earnings during the eight weeks immediately preceding the 14th week before the expected week of childbirth — in her case, eight weeks prior to 31 October 1995. Alabaster's annual salary was increased with effect from 1 December 1995, but this pay rise was not reflected in her SMP, which had been calculated during the relevant period prior to October.

The European Court of Justice (ECJ) held that a woman who received a pay increase before the start of her maternity leave is entitled to have it taken into account in the calculation of the earnings-related element of her SMP, even where the pay rise was not backdated to the relevant eight-week reference period. A failure to do so would be discrimination against her, since she would have received the pay rise if she had not been pregnant. *Alabaster v Woolwich plc and Secretary of State for Social Security Case C-147/02 ([2004] IRLR 486).*

As a consequence of the *Alabaster* ruling the law was changed with effect from April 2005. Pay increases between the beginning of the 15th week before the baby's expected birth and the end of the maternity leave period are taken into account.

In the case of the *North Western Health Board v McKenna C-191/03 ([2005] IRLR 895)* (see also "Occupational sick pay" in Chapter 7) the ECJ ruled that it is not discriminatory for an employer to calculate sick pay for a woman absent for a **pregnancy-related illness** in the same way as it would for a man who is absent for any kind of illness.

It can also be lawful to calculate a **bonus** on a pro rata basis by deducting any period during which a woman was absent on maternity leave — as long as nothing is deducted for the two-week compulsory maternity leave period.

However, this case was decided because of the terms of the particular bonus scheme and the result might not be the same for someone with a different contractual scheme — particularly if the scheme is discretionary (*Hoyland v Asda Stores Ltd EAT/0058/04 ([2005] IRLR 438)*).

Returning to work

Once an employee has given notice of her maternity leave, her employer must write to her within 28 days to tell her what her **return date** will be. If they do not, she can return to work whenever she wants to.

A woman returning from ordinary or additional maternity leave need do no more than turn up for work on the date already notified to her by her employer. She can also choose to return to work before her maternity leave period ends, but has to give the employer at least eight weeks' notice of her return. An employer cannot refuse to let her return to work before the end of her maternity leave period, provided she has given notice.

In a case taken to the ECJ, *Busch v Klinikum Neustadt C-320/01 ([2003] IRLR 625)*, the court ruled that there was no right to bar an employee's return. The woman's reason for returning early was that she had exhausted her maternity pay and was pregnant again; returning to work and then immediately commencing another period of maternity leave gave her a new right to maternity pay.

Provided that a woman returns to work at the end of her ordinary maternity leave, she has the right to **return to the same job** she was employed to do before her absence. The "same job" is what she was required to do under her contract.

For example, in the case of *Blundell v Governing Body of St Andrew's Catholic Primary School UKEAT/0329/06 ([2007] IRLR 652)*, the EAT said a primary school teacher did not have the right to return to teaching the reception class as under her contract she could be required to teach any year.

A woman returning from additional maternity leave has less comprehensive rights on return: she has the right to return to the **same job** she was doing **or**, if that is not reasonably practicable, to another **suitable and appropriate alternative**. She returns on **terms and conditions no less favourable** than had she not taken maternity leave, with her seniority and pension rights as they would have been had she not taken leave. Her employer cannot refuse to take her back just because her replacement is found to be a more effective worker.

The ECJ, in the case of *Land Brandenburg v Sass C-284/02 ([2005] IRLR 147)* held that even if a woman takes more maternity leave than the minimum provided by law she still has the right to have all of the leave period included in calculating her service.

The fact that a woman is **sick and unable to return** to work on the agreed date does not give the employer a right to treat her contract as terminated, according to the Court of Appeal in the case of *Kwik Save v Greaves [1998] IRLR 245*. Her period of sickness absence starts from the date she would have returned to work.

These pay, leave and return-to-work provisions are all **minimum statutory requirements**. Many women will have better arrangements, negotiated by the union, contained in the contract of employment. Under section 78 of the ERA 96, a woman who has the right to maternity leave under a contract, in addition to the statutory rights, may not exercise the two rights separately, but may take advantage of whichever right is the more favourable.

Pregnancy discrimination

If an employer refuses to hire someone because she is pregnant, this is discrimination. A woman has **protection against dismissal** for a pregnancy-related reason during the pregnancy itself and while on maternity leave, regardless of hours worked or length of service.

However, there can be no pregnancy discrimination if the employer does not know that the worker is pregnant (*Ramdoolar v Bycity EAT/0236/04*). Even if another manager knows she is pregnant, if this is not the manager who dismisses, then there is no liability as a pregnancy dismissal (*Eildon v Sharkey EAT/0109/03*).

It does not matter that there might have been other reasons for the decision to dismiss her. Provided that at least part of the reason for dismissing her was to do with her pregnancy, a woman will be regarded as dismissed for an automatically unfair reason.

Protection against dismissal also extends to **temporary workers**. Where an employer chooses to replace a temporary worker on maternity leave with a permanent employee, this will amount to unlawful discrimination. The fact that, due to the nature of her contract her employer could lawfully have replaced her at any time, is not relevant (*Patefield v Belfast City Council [2000] NICA 4 [2000] IRLR 664*).

An employer was guilty of discrimination when it failed to offer a pregnant employee alternative work when it would have offered alternative work to a male employee who was unable to perform his normal duties (*Iske v P&O European Ferries [1997] IRLR 401*). And in the following case an employer discriminated against a pregnant employee by removing her from her normal duties:

A rail company removed Mrs Quinn from her duties as duty station manager after learning that she was pregnant, citing as their main reason the risk of a physical assault while carrying out her duties. It also reduced her salary to reflect the change in duties.

The EAT held that Mrs Quinn had been discriminated against on the grounds that her employer had suspended her because of their "paternalistic and patronising attitude" and not for any real health and safety reasons.

It held that it was up to the employer to justify Quinn's suspension by providing evidence of the gravity of the risk and also their inability to avoid it by making appropriate adjustments to her hours and conditions of work, but they had not done so. *New Southern Railway Ltd v Quinn EAT/0313/05.*

Employers should not go ahead with a **disciplinary hearing** in the absence of an employee where this is due to a pregnancy-related illness (*Abbey National v Formoso [1999] IRLR 222*).

A woman dismissed during pregnancy for a pregnancy-related reason has the right to take a claim for **sex discrimination**, in addition to her right to claim unfair dismissal. In sex discrimination cases there is no upper limit on the compensation award (see "Compensation" in Chapter 6).

Even in cases of **genuine redundancy** the tribunal can still determine whether the dismissal of a particular employee is connected with her pregnancy. If a woman's job is made redundant while she is on maternity leave she must be offered any suitable available vacancy.

If she is not offered alternative work when it is available this amounts to unfair dismissal. Section 92, ERA 96 states that any woman dismissed while pregnant or on maternity leave must be given a **written statement** giving reasons for her dismissal.

Paternity leave

Qualifying fathers, civil partners or partners of someone on maternity or adoption leave have the right to **paid paternity leave**. The leave is specifically to care for the new baby or to provide support for the baby's mother.

To qualify the individual must be an **employee** who has worked for their employer for **at least 26 weeks by the 15th week** before the baby is due and be earning at least £97 a week. The employee has to give the employer notice of his intention to take paternity leave before the 15th week before the expected week of the baby's birth.

Statutory Paternity Pay (SPP) amounts to a maximum of **two weeks'** paid leave. Payment is set at £124.88 (2010-11) a week, or 90% of earnings if they are less than this.

The leave must be taken as **one period** of either one or two weeks within eight weeks of the baby's birth. It cannot be taken as separate days or in more than one period.

Fathers will be eligible provided that they have responsibility for the child's upbringing, have been continuously employed by the employer for 26 weeks (by the 15th week before the baby is due), give eight weeks' notice to the employer, and have a signed declaration from the mother endorsing their application. Within 28 days of receiving the required information from the individual, the employer must confirm when the APL will start and end (this can be changed by the father by giving six weeks notice/or if less than six weeks, as much notice as reasonably practicable).

The father's terms and conditions (other than remuneration) will be unchanged both during and after APL. Also, as with women on maternity leave, fathers will be able to agree with the employer to come into work for up to ten "keeping in touch" days.

Adoption leave

An adoptive parent has the right to leave and pay broadly equivalent to those for statutory maternity leave. To qualify, the parent must be **newly matched** with a child for adoption by an approved adoption agency. They must also be an **employee** and have worked for their employer for **at least 26 weeks** by the date that they are matched.

Adoption leave must begin either from the date of the child's placement or up to 14 days before that date. An adoptive parent has the right to **26 weeks' ordinary adoption leave** (OAL) followed by **26 weeks' additional adoption leave** (AAL). They have the right to **Statutory Adoption Pay** (SAP) provided they are earning at least £97 a week. SAP is payable for 39 weeks at a flat rate of £124.88 (2010-11) (or 90% of earnings if they are less than this).

A worker also has the right to carry out up to **10 days** of work or training during adoption leave for the purpose of "keeping in touch" with the workplace.

The rights to return to work on conditions no less favourable are the same as those that apply to maternity leave. The partner of a person claiming adoption leave can claim paternity leave.

Parental and dependency leave

Employees are entitled to time off for **parental leave** under section 13 of the *Maternity and Parental Leave etc Regulations 1999* and to time off to deal with **family emergencies** under section 57A of the ERA 96. In both cases the leave is unpaid.

Parental leave

Working parents have the legal right to a period of unpaid leave of up to **four weeks** in a year and overall no more than **13 weeks** within the first five years of their child's life. For adopted children the leave is available in the **five years** from the time of adoption, provided that the child is still under the age of 18. If the **child is disabled** (meaning that s/he is entitled to disability living allowance), up to 18 weeks' unpaid leave in total can be taken up to the child's 18th birthday.

Parental leave is available to parents who have worked for their employer for **at least a year**. Unless there is an agreement to the contrary, leave must be taken in **blocks of no less than a week**. The right applies to each parent and for each child. Employees taking less than a week off lose a week of their entitlement.

In one case an employee who requested a day's parental leave to look after his son and was subsequently disciplined for taking the leave after receiving no response was not covered by the parental leave regulations. The Court of Appeal held that as the regulations only gave the right to leave in blocks of a week, his request for a day's leave could not have been made under them (*Rodway v South Central Trains [2005] EWCA Civ 443 ([2005] IRLR 583*).

An employee who wants to take parental leave has to give at least **21 days' notice**. Where taking the leave at a particular time would cause undue disruption to the business, the employer can make the employee postpone the leave for a period of up to six months, except in the case of leave immediately after the child's birth.

Family emergencies

Leave for urgent family reasons gives employees the right to reasonable unpaid time off to deal with family emergencies involving parents, children, a spouse or cohabitee, or anyone who looks to the employee for assistance. There is no qualifying period of service for emergency leave.

A family emergency is defined as sickness, accident, criminal injury, death, funerals, absence of the carer for a family member or serious problems at the child's school. In the case of *Qua v John Ford Morrison EAT/884/01 [2003] IRLR 184*, the EAT made it clear that the right to time off is either to deal with a variety of **unexpected or sudden events** involving a dependant or to make arrangements for their care.

The amount of leave is what is "reasonable in the circumstances" and is likely to involve relatively short periods of absence (*Uzowuru v LB Tower Hamlets EAT/0869/04*).

The law covers time off following a dependant's death to make funeral arrangements and to attend the funeral. However, according to the EAT in the case of *Forster v Cartwright Black Solicitors UKEAT/0179/04 [2004] IRLR 781*, it does not extend to the right to compassionate leave as a result of bereavement.

An employee who requests time off for urgent domestic reasons under section 57A, *Employment Rights Act 1996* should provide sufficient information for their employer to know that the leave is for those purposes (*Truelove v Safeway Stores EAT/0295/04*). Employees are protected from suffering a detriment or dismissal for exercising or seeking to exercise their rights to parental or domestic leave.

Shortly after he started his job as a delivery and collection driver, Thomas Palen had to take a day off to be with his wife, who had been taken to hospital. He returned to work the following day and was dismissed — his employer told him they were such a small company they could not afford such incidents.

The EAT held that Palen had been dismissed for a reason related to the right to take time off under section 57A, which made his dismissal automatically unfair and not subject to the one-year qualifying service. He was awarded £3,835 in compensation for unfair dismissal, which included a 30% uplift because of the employer's failure to comply with the statutory disciplinary and dismissal procedures (*RKS Services v Palen EAT/0300/06*).

On 8 December 2006 Ms Harrison's child-minder told her that she wouldn't be available on 22 December. On 13 December Ms Harrison, being unable to make alternative arrangements, told RBS that she would need to take that day off. Although RBS refused, Ms Harrison took the day off anyway and was subjected to disciplinary action. Ms Harrison brought a claim, to which RBS responded that her request for time off was not protected by the *Employment Rights Act* (on the basis that she had time to make other arrangements).

The EAT decided that Ms Harrison's request was (as required by the legislation) "necessary" and in response to something "unexpected". Requests for time off to care for dependents are therefore not (provided the possibility of making alternative arrangements has been explored) limited to last-minute incidents. *Royal Bank of Scotland v Harrison UKEAT/0093/08/LA.*

Flexible working

An employee with responsibility for the upbringing of a child under the age of 17 (18 in the case of a disabled child) has the right to request, **in writing**, a flexible working pattern **to enable them to care for the child** (sections 80F-80I, ERA 96).

To qualify for the right, the employee must have been continuously employed by their employer for at least 26 weeks.

Since April 2007, the right to request flexible working also applies to carers (the 26 weeks' qualifying service also applies to carers). A carer is defined as an employee who **is or expects to be caring for a person** aged 18 or over and who:

- is married to, or the partner or civil partner of, the employee; or
- is a relative of the employee; or
- living at the same address as the employee.

The request has to set out the employee's **desired working pattern** and include an explanation of how the employer could accommodate the request. Employers have a statutory duty to consider the application seriously, rejecting it only if there are **clear business reasons** for doing so.

In the case of a request to care for a child, it must be made no later than two weeks before the child's cut-off age. In either case, once an employee makes a formal request for flexible working, s/he cannot make another one for 12 months.

Once a request has been made the employer has to **arrange a meeting** within a specified time scale to hear the employee's reasons for the request. The employee has the right to bring a workplace companion, who is entitled to paid time off to attend (regulation 14 of the *Flexible Working (Procedural Requirements) Regulations 2002).*

The employer must then write to the employee within 14 days, agreeing to the new work pattern or providing clear business grounds for rejecting it. There is a **right to appeal** but there is nothing specifically in the law to say that the same manager who turned down the request cannot also hear the appeal. If the employer fails to comply with any of these requirements an employee can go to an employment tribunal, or alternatively to voluntary arbitration (see "Binding arbitration" in Chapter 1).

Compensation of up to eight weeks' pay can be awarded if the employer unreasonably turned down a request for flexible working and up to an additional two weeks' pay if there was no meeting or if the employee was not allowed to bring a companion. Pay is capped at a maximum, currently £380 a week. The right to request flexible working was considered by the EAT in the case of *Commotion Ltd v Rutty EAT/0418/05 ([2006] IRLR 171)*:

Warehouse assistant Mrs Rutty made an informal request to reduce her hours so that she could look after her grandchild. When this was turned down she made a formal request to move to a three-day week under the ERA 96. Her employer refused, saying that it would have a detrimental impact on performance in the warehouse.

The EAT held that a tribunal is entitled to consider whether the employer's refusal to grant a flexible working request was based on correct facts. It said that this included looking at the effect of granting the request — including whether the employer could have coped without disruption, what other staff felt about it and whether they could make up the time. The EAT found that the employer's claim that letting the claimant work a three-day week would have a detrimental effect on the performance was not supported by the evidence. Rutty's claim was successful. *Commotion Ltd v Rutty EAT/0418/05 ([2006] IRLR 171).*

Both the employee and companion have the right not to be victimised or dismissed for a reason concerned with a request for flexible working (sections 47E and 104C, ERA 96).

A refusal to allow a worker to reduce their hours could also amount to **indirect sex discrimination** (see Chapter 6). The Court of Appeal held that an employer's refusal to allow an employee to work on a job-share basis amounted to sex discrimination and could not be justified when it had failed to show that the job could not be done on that basis (*Hardys & Hansons plc v Lax [2005] EWCA Civ 846 ([2005] IRLR 726)*).

And in the case of *Shaw v CCL Ltd UKEAT/0512/06*, the EAT held that the refusal to allow part-time work was both direct and indirect discrimination and amounted to a breach of contract that allowed the employee to resign and claim constructive dismissal.

In the case of *Mitchell v David Evans Agricultural Ltd EAT/0083/06*, the EAT said that when deciding whether an employer was justified in refusing an employee's request to work part-time, the tribunal should have undertaken a proper analysis of the needs of the business, and considered whether the proposal for a full-time worker was "reasonably necessary".

> **More information:** See the LRD booklet *Working parents* (£4.25). LRD's *Workplace Report* has regular quarterly updates on discrimination law which cover the legal rules on pregnancy and maternity discrimination.

9. Industrial action

The law relating to industrial action covers not just **strikes** but **lockouts**, **go slows**, **working to rule**, and **refusing to cross picket lines**, regardless of whether or not industrial action is in breach of an agreed procedure. **Overtime bans** (even where overtime is voluntary) are normally considered as industrial action since the aim of those carrying it out is to put pressure on the employer to do, or not to do, something.

However, there are some rare circumstances where an overtime ban, called in response to an industrial dispute, nevertheless falls outside the definition of action in breach of contract. In one case, the Privy Council (the highest appeal court for many Commonwealth countries) held that industrial action which involved the union refusing to make up overtime gangs to serve on the docks, could not be viewed as industrial action in breach of contract taken by the dockers themselves. The workers had played no role. They had not been asked to work and therefore could not be said to have refused (*Burgess v Stevedoring Services [2002] UKPC 39 ([2002] IRLR 810)*).

In the UK there is **no positive legal right to strike**. Instead workers are protected by "immunities" if taking specific forms of industrial action that would otherwise be unlawful. How these immunities operate is explained below, although some workers — merchant seafarers, post office workers, the police, soldiers and some apprentices — may be excluded.

The European Court of Justice (ECJ) has held that unions have a fundamental right to strike under European law, but also that industrial action may have to be "justified" by balancing it against employers' rights to the freedom of movement of goods and services.

Viking Line shipping company tried to re-flag the ferry Rosella to replace its Finnish crew with cheaper Estonians. The Finnish seafarers' union and the International Transport Workers' Federation (ITF) organised a boycott of Viking, who claimed it was a breach of its right to the freedom of movement of goods and services. The ECJ held that the right to take collective action is a fundamental right but can constitute a restriction on the freedom of goods and services so must be justified. The case was sent back to the domestic court to decide whether the threat to the workers' jobs was such that the action was needed to protect them. *ITF & FSU v Viking Line ABP Case C-438/05.*

In *Laval un Partneri Ltd v Svenska Byggnadsarbetareförbundet and others Case C-341/05*, a Latvian building company won a contract to build a school in Sweden and brought in Latvian workers. The Swedish building union blockaded the firm in order to get them to sign an agreement to bring their wages up to Swedish levels.

The ECJ said again that the right to take collective action is a fundamental right but that it must not go beyond what is suitable for attaining its objectives. Furthermore, it held that action to give workers rights beyond those already given by the Posted Workers Directive cannot be justified.

In *Rüffert v Land Niedersachsen C-346/06*, a German company won the contract to build a prison. The contract specified that wages were to be paid at the level collectively agreed for the region. However, the German company sub-contracted the work to a Polish company which paid their workers less than half of the German workers on the site. On discovering this, Land Niedersachsen terminated the contract and imposed financial penalties.

The ECJ decided that the requirement for a minimum salary level was capable of constituting a restriction on trade and was not justified on the grounds of protecting workers, balancing the cost of the social security system or protecting the independence of trade unions. In addition to Article 49 (freedom of establishment), the Posted Workers Directive prevented the requirement for higher wages on contracts for public work where there was no corresponding requirement for private sector contracts.

The *Employment Relations Act 2004* places a legal obligation on employers to seek to resolve disputes where conciliation or mediation has been agreed. A person who has authority to resolve the dispute must represent employers at such meetings.

The immunities

Section 219 of the *Trade Union and Labour Relations (Consolidation) Act 1992* (TULRCA) establishes the "immunities". It says that an act done **"in contemplation or furtherance of a trade dispute"** is not actionable in the courts just because it makes someone break a contract or interferes with a contract.

For example, a union **leafleting campaign** aimed at persuading consumers not to buy a product, in the context of a dispute, does not fall within the definition of interference with a contract (*Middlebrook Mushrooms v TGWU [1993] IRLR 232*).

The first test is to establish whether or not a **"trade dispute"** exists. This is defined in section 244 of TULRCA as a dispute that relates "wholly or mainly to" terms and conditions; recruitment, suspension or dismissal; work allocation; discipline; facilities for union officials; or the machinery of negotiation.

A dispute over the impact of the national curriculum in schools on the working conditions of teachers, for example, falls within the definition (*LB Wandsworth v NASUWT [1993] IRLR 344*). So too does a dispute by teachers over the refusal to teach a disruptive pupil (*P v NASUWT [2003] UKHL 8 ([2003] IRLR 307)*).

Where the industrial action is in furtherance of a "trade dispute" unions and members **do not risk civil legal action** provided that, if the action is authorised by the union, a ballot conforming to the requirements listed below has approved it.

The dispute has to be with an **employer in the UK**. And it must be a dispute **between workers and their employer**. The fact that the law refers to "workers" and not just "employees" (see Chapter 2) means that it covers all those employed under personal contracts.

The fact that industrial action has to involve a dispute with the workers' own employer has given employers the option of preventing industrial action by **reorganising** so that there is more than one employer. In a case taken in 1999, the train operating company Connex was able to get an injunction to stop industrial action by railworkers protesting about rail safety on the grounds that responsibility for safety lay with Railtrack, a separate company (*Connex SE v RMT [1999] IRLR 249*).

A dispute that is purely for **political ends** is not covered by the section 244 definition and therefore cannot come within the section 219 immunities.

A dispute over a **transfer to another employer** was a trade dispute, according to the Court of Appeal in the case of *Westminster City*

Council v UNISON [2001] EWCA Civ 443 ([2001] IRLR 524). It said that a dispute about the identity of a new employer was not a political dispute. However, a dispute about the terms and conditions of **future workers** is not covered.

In 1999, the Court of Appeal held that employees calling for industrial action to win guarantees on the terms and conditions of future workers were not protected by section 244.

The union took the claim to the European Court of Human Rights which, while accepting that a total ban on industrial action would be in breach, upheld the right of the state to impose limits on the right to take industrial action, provided these were proportionate (*UNISON v UK [2002] IRLR 497*).

Under TULRCA, **unions can be taken to court** for calling or endorsing unlawful action not covered by the immunities.

Overall, the definition of a trade dispute is very narrow. There are good grounds for believing it violates international standards set by the **International Labour Organisation** (ILO).

The following forms of industrial action are **denied the protection of the immunities**: action that seeks to enforce union membership (section 222); action in protest at a dismissal following earlier unofficial action (section 223); secondary action (see below); and action intended to pressurise the employer to impose a union recognition requirement on a supplier or contractor (section 225).

Under section 235A of TULRCA, an individual who claims that the **supply of goods or services** has been affected by unlawful industrial action (for example, action carried out without a fully complying ballot) may apply to the High Court for an order against the union to discontinue its authorisation or endorsement of industrial action.

Such individuals, who do not have to show that they would have been entitled to be supplied with the goods or services in question, can be assisted by the **Certification Officer** (see "Internal union matters" in Chapter 5).

Unions are not allowed to discipline workers who refuse to support industrial action.

Workplace reps

In theory, any **individual worker**, including a representative, can be sued by the employer for breaking a contract by taking industrial action. In practice, this is unlikely to happen since the employer can only claim **damages limited to the actual loss** caused by that employee and this is difficult to prove.

Workplace representatives can claim the section 219 immunities. They are **protected** if they induce someone to break or interfere with a contract (not just a contract of employment), or threaten to do so, provided that they are acting "in contemplation or furtherance of a trade dispute" (see above). They can picket their workplace, persuade others to strike, and ask workers not to deliver goods.

A more likely response from the employer to industrial action is **dismissal** (see "How the law aids employers" below), but even this is relatively rare. Furthermore, there is a **right to be protected** against unfair dismissal in at least the first 12 weeks of strike action. Any days when employees are "locked out" by their employers are excluded from the calculation of the 12 weeks (*Employment Relations Act 2004*).

Most employers want the dispute to end (to their satisfaction if at all possible) and work to resume, so use of the law by employers is not usually the main problem for representatives.

The most important thing is to ensure that any action taken is **well organised** and that **union solidarity is maintained**. Experience also demonstrates that employers are more likely to use the law when they perceive workplace organisation to be weak.

However, this is not to say that representatives will never be threatened with legal action. Employers have threatened writs and in some cases issued injunctions (see "How the law aids employers" below).

"Official" or "unofficial" action

The law describes a strike or any other kind of industrial action as "official" where the employee is a member of a trade union and the union has **authorised or endorsed** the action in question; or the employee is not a member of a trade union but there are among those taking part in the industrial action members of a trade union, which has authorised or endorsed that action.

Section 20 of TULRCA states that the action shall be taken to have been authorised or endorsed by a trade union where it was taken by:

◆ a person **empowered by the rules** to do, authorise or endorse acts of the kind in question;

◆ the **principal executive committee** or the president or general secretary; or

◆ **any other committee** of the union or any other official of the union (whether employed by it or not).

And where a **group of people** organises or co-ordinates the industrial action, any decision taken by the group or an individual of the group comes within the definition of "any other committee".

Section 21 also makes unions **legally responsible** for all industrial action, including that authorised by local representatives, even if the union views their action as unofficial because it is contrary to union rules. However, the union may **"repudiate"** (disown) the action. Once unofficial action has commenced, if the union wishes to make it official, it must first repudiate it and then hold the ballot.

The union must, as soon as the action comes to its attention, do its best to give a copy of the repudiation, in writing, to every member taking part, or likely to take part in the action. A copy must also be given to the employer (section 21, TULRCA).

If the union has not repudiated unlawful action, or if it itself has authorised action not in compliance with all the legal rules, it leaves itself open to legal action brought by the employer or a customer or supplier of the employer. This can be by way of an **injunction** (see below). The dispute at in-flight catering company Gate Gourmet in the summer of 2005 highlighted the defects in the UK law:

Gate Gourmet had been in discussion with the T&G general union over proposed changes to staffing levels and working practices. While permanent staff were facing redundancy the company brought in around 130 seasonal workers without consulting the union. Employees assembled in the canteen for a meeting to find out what was happening, but managers told them that if they did not return to work within three minutes they would be sacked. The company then sacked 677 workers.

Because there had been no ballot or notification procedure, the action was unofficial and the employees were not protected by unfair dismissal laws. Balloting after the event would not have made the action lawful.

Employers may lawfully victimise unofficial strikers by dismissing selected individuals taking **unofficial action** (see below). Any subsequent strike action in support of an individual dismissed for taking part in unofficial action automatically loses the protection of the immunities, even if the later action is official and has been balloted on.

Balloting

Sections 226-235 of TULRCA **remove the immunities**, even where the action otherwise is not unlawful, where there has not been a ballot which complies with all of the following requirements:

◆ it must fulfil the **notice requirements** to employers (see below);

◆ it must be a **secret postal ballot**, with the ballot paper sent to the member's nominated address and specifying the address and date for return (sections 227-230, TULRCA);

◆ **at least seven days** must be allowed for its return if first class (14 days if second class);

◆ an **independent scrutineer**, responsible for the eventual preparation of a report on the ballot arrangements, must be appointed and named on the ballot paper in all ballots of more than 50 workers (section 226);

◆ the form must specify who is **authorised to call the action** (section 229);

◆ **voters must be asked** whether they support strike action or action short of a strike. If being asked to vote on both, this must be in the form of two separate questions (section 229);

◆ if action **short of a full strike** (e.g. an overtime ban) is to be called, but may be followed by full strike action, workers must be asked two separate questions, one relating to the limited action and the other to the full strike action;

◆ members must be able to indicate by **"yes"/"no"** their views on the action proposed (section 226);

◆ he forms must be **numbered consecutively**;

◆ the form must tell employees of their rights not to be **unfairly dismissed** (see below);

◆ the form must **contain the statement**: "If you take part in a strike or other industrial action, you may be in breach of your contract of employment", regardless of whether or not there would be a breach (section 229); ˙

◆ only those that the union is **calling on to take action** need to be balloted (section 227);

◆ **separate ballots** must be held for **separate workplaces**, unless the dispute involves only common terms. Where there is at least one individual who is affected by the dispute in each of the workplaces, the ballots can be **aggregated** into a single ballot. Ballots can also be aggregated where linked by occupation and employer(s) (section 228);

◆ where there have been separate ballots only those **workplaces with a majority** for strike action can be called out;

◆ as soon as possible after the vote, members should be **informed of the number of votes cast**, as well as those in favour, those against and those spoilt — one of the grounds used by British Airways in its attempt to prevent Unite members from taking industrial action (section 231); and

◆ industrial action must **commence within four weeks** of the last day of voting, counting that day as day one (*RJB Mining v NUM [1995] IRLR 556*). Employers and unions can agree to extend this period by an **additional four weeks**. If the date when the action should have begun is delayed due to legal proceedings, it has to be called within an overall 12-week period (section 234).

Those being balloted must be **told on the ballot paper** that any dismissal during an official, lawful dispute "will be unfair if it takes place fewer than 12 weeks after you started taking part in the action". They will also be told that a dismissal outside the 12 weeks can still be unfair.

It is important that all these rules are complied with. It is particularly important that the union ballots **all those who should be included**, because they are likely to be called on to take industrial action.

In the case of *RMT v Midland Mainline [2001] EWCA Civ 1206 ([2001] IRLR 813)*, the Court of Appeal ruled that a ballot was invalid because not everyone had been balloted. The union was not aware that a group of workers was in the appropriate grade and had therefore not included them in the ballot.

The case of *London Underground v RMT [1995] IRLR 636* also dealt with who should be balloted. The Court of Appeal held that the fact that the union had not balloted employees who were not its members prior to the ballot, but joined subsequently, did not invalidate the ballot.

Those being balloted are those whom the union considers will be called upon to take industrial action, but they do not all have to be directly affected by the issue over which the ballot is being called.

In the case of *BT v CWU [2003] EWHC 937 ([2004] IRLR 58)*, the High Court held that the union had not breached the law when, in a dispute over a new productivity scheme, some of the members it balloted would not have been party to the new scheme.

There has to be a **dispute in existence**. The London Underground workers' union NUR (now RMT), was held by the High Court to have lost its protection by including matters which were not yet the subject of an industrial dispute in its strike ballot (*London Underground v NUR [1989] IRLR 341*).

The ballot does not have to define every single issue of the dispute (*Associated British Ports v TGWU [1989] IRLR 399*).

Where the ballot paper contains two separate questions, a "yes" majority is determined in relation to the numbers voting "yes" to that question. The fact that they may not represent a majority of all those completing the ballot paper is not relevant (*West Midlands Travel v TGWU [1994] IRLR 578*).

A union is entitled to **campaign for a "yes" vote** in a ballot. This does not amount to an unlawful call for, or endorsement of, industrial action before the date of the ballot (*LB Newham v NALGO [1993] IRLR 83*).

Although the law states that the ballot paper must specify, in the event of a "yes" vote, **who can call action**, the courts have stressed that common sense permits a certain amount of delegation.

In a dispute called by the TGWU general union the ballot paper indicated that the general secretary was the officer authorised to call the strike. However, the fact that the actual call was made by another official, after consultation with the general secretary, did not invalidate the ballot (*Tanks & Drums v TGWU [1991] IRLR 372*).

The High Court has ruled that a union is not expected to achieve 100% perfection in conducting ballots, so long as it has in place **structures which enable it to properly ballot** all the relevant workers (*RJB Mining v NUM [1997] IRLR 621*). Additionally, section 232B of TULRCA says that where a union makes **"accidental mistakes"** in terms of those who are balloted, on a scale unlikely to affect the outcome, this will not invalidate the whole procedure.

The **"place of work"** for the purpose of ballots is not narrowly defined as the building occupied by the employee, according to the Court of Appeal in the case of *Intercity West Coast v RMT [1996] IRLR 583*.

This meant that a single ballot covering all staff working at Manchester Piccadilly railway station was valid even though it covered two rail operating companies that had separate administrative buildings at the station.

The fact that **more than one employer** is involved does not mean that different ballots have to be organised, provided that all those being balloted share common terms and conditions (*University of Central England and Kingston University v NALGO [1993] IRLR 81*). This is also the case where they comply with the requirements regarding aggregated ballots (see above).

The four-week rule for commencing industrial action does not prevent a union **suspending action** and then re-imposing it (*Monsanto v TGWU [1986] IRLR 406*).

However, the gap between the suspension and re-imposition of the action should not be too long, or indicate a change in tactics by the union; otherwise it might find that the subsequent action is not covered by the ballot (*Post Office v UCW [1990] IRLR 143*).

Alternatively, there can be **agreement over the length of any suspension** of action. Under section 234A of TULRCA, unions can suspend industrial action for talks and then resume it without having to go through the balloting procedure again, provided there is agreement from the employer for this course of action, normally with the aim of trying to restart negotiations.

Where this happens the union has to agree not to re-authorise industrial action before an agreed date.

Individual union members can use section 109 of TULRCA, to take legal action against their own unions where ballots have not been held before official action. They can use the services of the Certification Officer to do this (see "Internal union matters" in Chapter 5).

Requirements to notify employers

To comply with the legislation, a union must also **give notice to employers** at four key stages as set out below. These are contained in section 226A of TULRCA, as amended by the ERA 04.

The provision for information about employees to be balloted was amongst the final provisions of the ERA 04 to come into force and became effective on 1 October 2005. The DTI (now the Department for Business, Innovation and Skills (BIS) Code of Practice, *Industrial action ballots and notice to employers*, also came into force on that date and provides further information.

Notification stages

Stage 1 — when taking a decision to ballot for industrial action, a union must first **notify the employer in writing** at least seven days before the ballot that the **union intends to hold a ballot**, the **date** when it believes the ballot will begin, and either (a) a list of the categories of worker and workplaces, with numbers or, (b) if the employer makes deductions for payments to the union, a **check off list**, either the same list as in (a) above, or such information as to enable the employer to identify the employees concerned.

Stage 2 — no later than **three days** before the ballot commences, the employer must have received a sample copy of the ballot paper.

Stage 3 — as soon as possible after the ballot result has been declared, the union has to **notify the employer of the outcome**.

Stage 4 — after the stage 3 notice, and at least seven days before the industrial action (which has been the subject of the ballot) begins, the union has again to **notify the employer in writing** giving information on the **number, category or workplaces** of the employees being called upon to take action; the date when the action will begin, or the date of each if planning a series of stoppages; a **statement** that it gives notice under section 234 of the 1992 Act; and the **lists** of categories of workers and workplaces as for Stage 1.

The notice must also specify whether the action planned is **continuous** (giving the intended date when it will commence) or **discontinuous** (giving the intended dates when it will occur).

Picketing

Under section 220 of TULRCA, workers "in contemplation or furtherance of a trade dispute" (see above) can **lawfully picket** at or near their place of work, provided that the purpose is only peacefully to obtain or communicate information or persuade a person not to work.

But, as is the case with industrial action, the **immunities** only protect them from being sued for breach of contract. They do not provide protection for activities like trespass, or from action under criminal law (see below). If workers are not able to picket immediately in front of their workplace, the requirement that it is **"at or near"** allows some leeway.

Workers dismissed by a company sited on a trading estate were unable to picket their own workplace so they mounted a picket on the entrance to the estate. The Court of Appeal ruled that this was "at or near" their place of work (*Rayware v TGWU [1989] IRLR 134*).

Union officials representing members can picket their members' place of work. Those working from a number of different locations can lawfully picket any work location or alternatively their work headquarters, as long as they have actually worked from those different locations. If they were merely "occasional ports of call" they would not be regarded as the individual's place of work (*Union Traffic v TGWU [1989] IRLR 127*). Workers **dismissed while on strike** have a continuing right to picket lawfully at their former place of work.

The law does not lay down the **number who can picket**. Often the police try to limit it to six, but they should issue a warning to this effect. This figure comes from the DTI (now BIS) Code of Practice on picketing which says: "Pickets and their organisers should ensure that in general the number of pickets does not exceed six at any entrance to, or exit from, a workplace; frequently a smaller number will be appropriate."

Although this Code, like others, is only advisory, a 1985 case gave police additional support in attempts to reduce numbers to six.

During the 1984-85 miners' strike, pickets were posted at a pit in South Wales. Although six pickets stood outside the colliery gates, about 60 demonstrated across the road. The court ruled that the mass demonstration was a common law nuisance (*Thomas v South Wales NUM [1985] IRLR 136*).

In the 2005 Gate Gourmet dispute (see page 187), the court granted an injunction to limit pickets outside the company's offices but not at other locations:

Following an application by the company, the High Court granted an injunction limiting the number of pickets outside the company's Heathrow offices to six and limiting picketing so that the workers could not approach employees going to and from work. However, it refused the application to limit the number of pickets near the entrance to the nearby Gate Gourmet plant at Beacon Hill.

The injunction was made against the union as well as individuals because, although there had been no ballot, union officials were present at the pickets and aware of what was going on, and the union had not repudiated (disowned) the action. *Gate Gourmet London Ltd v TGWU [2005] EWHC 1889 (QB) ([2005] IRLR 881).*

Pickets are more likely to face the **criminal law** (see below) than have their picket declared outside the section 220 protection. The criminal law is operated by the police and usually involves obstruction or breach of the peace offences. However, in the majority of cases pickets take place without the intervention of the law.

Supporting other workers

Solidarity has always played an important role for trade unionists, but this unity among workers has been undermined by the legislation introduced since 1980 and still in force. This outlawed "secondary picketing".

Under section 224 of TULRCA, a person inducing or threatening another to break a contract of employment, which is not with the employer party to the dispute, is not protected by the immunities. If a union threatens to picket other places of work this will be unlawful.

The only form of solidarity action permitted is where workers picketing **at or near their place of work** persuade other workers not employed there not to deliver goods or to enter the work premises.

How the law aids employers

The use of the courts by an employer is **still uncommon** and the success or failure of a dispute usually depends more on the level of workplace union organisation than on any legal threat from the employer. Nevertheless trade union reps need to understand how employers can use the law.

Injunctions

The injunction (interdict in Scotland) is the most popular legal remedy sought by employers. An injunction is a court order **to do or to refrain from doing something**. It may be granted where:

◆ there is an allegation of **unlawful action**;
◆ a **serious issue** is to be tried;
◆ the **employer alleges a harm greater** than that which the employees would suffer by having to call off their action; and
◆ where the employer alleges that **damages** awarded at a subsequent full trial would not adequately compensate for the harm suffered.

In employment matters an injunction is generally used to try to halt industrial action and is given in the form of an **"interlocutory injunction"** — that is an injunction intended as an interim measure until the case comes to trial.

In practice, however, very few cases come to trial because the granting of the injunction itself serves the employer's purpose of stopping the action.

Failure to comply with injunctions can lead to **contempt of court** proceedings, and in some circumstances, to **sequestration** (seizing) of the union's assets. This can occur where a union has called, or not repudiated, unlawful action. If the union does repudiate the action, union funds are safeguarded, but members are then at risk of selective dismissal.

Normally unions are the targets for injunctions, but they can be taken out against **one or more named individuals**, although failure to name an individual properly can result in the injunction failing.

If an injunction is served, those receiving it have to decide whether to comply or risk contempt of court. There have been few cases of contempt of court proceedings against individual union members and it should be noted that section 236 of TULRCA says that no court can compel an individual employee to do any work or to attend work.

Section 221 of TULRCA puts some limitations on the granting of injunctions. It says that where **one party is not present**, and it could be argued that the action is in furtherance of a trade dispute, the court should give every opportunity for that party to attend before granting the injunction. In practice, however, the courts have sometimes ignored this principle and granted injunctions in the union's absence.

Dismissal

Section 238A of TULRCA gives employees **protection from dismissal** during the first **12 weeks** of any lawful, balloted, official industrial action. During these 12 weeks the protection is absolute, provided that no other unlawful act, other than the employee's breach of contract, has occurred. Any dismissal, **regardless of how long the employee has worked**, or their age, is automatically unfair unless a tribunal decides that the dismissal was not to do with the industrial action. Information about these rights must be included on the industrial action ballot paper.

The 12-week period **can be extended** if employees are still taking action but, in the view of the tribunal, the employer has not taken reasonable procedural steps to seek to resolve the dispute. This could be, for example, where there was an offer to re-open negotiations, or of mediation or conciliation that was offered and unreasonably refused. For further information, see "Dismissal while on strike" in Chapter 10.

Deducting pay

Employers are generally entitled to deduct pay for any days when a worker is on strike, as a worker has no general right to be paid if s/he does not perform her/his contractual duties.

The amount that can be deducted for each day's pay **may be specified** in the employment contract, or a collective agreement. If so, it is calculated according to those terms. In some cases there may be specific provision for the rate of deduction during industrial action.

In the case of teacher Abigail Smith the issue was whether the rate of a day's pay should be calculated according to the collective agreement (the Burgundy Book), which was incorporated into the teachers' contracts, or the statutory provisions governing teachers pay. The local authority had deducted 1/195th of her annual pay for each day of strike action and the High Court ruled that the maximum deduction should have been only 1/365th in accordance with the Burgundy Book. *Smith v Kent County Council [2004] EWHC 412*

If there is no contractual term, you can argue that the amount of a day's pay should be based on the **number of working days** (rather than calendar days). This would be in line with the EAT's decision in the case of *Leisure Leagues UK Ltd v Maconnachie EAT/940/01 [2002] IRLR 600* (as confirmed by the case of *Yarrow v Edwards Chartered Accountants EAT/0116/07)* that this method of calculation is good industrial relations practice.

If the strike action is for **less than a full day**, or there is industrial action short of full strike, such as a boycott of some work, the employer may still be able to deduct a full day's pay, but not necessarily. It will depend partly on whether the employer has made it clear that they are allowing the employee to carry out only part of their duties.

In the case of *Wiluszynski v LB Tower Hamlets [1989] IRLR 259*, the Court of Appeal held that the employer could deduct a full day's pay even though the worker only refused to perform some of his duties.

And in *BT v Ticehurst and Thompson [1992] IRLR 219*, the court said the employer could send the workers home without pay when they refused to sign a statement saying that they would carry out their full duties, when industrial action was still ongoing.

However, in the case of *Sim v Rotherham MBC [1987] IRLR 391*, the High Court said that the employer was only allowed to deduct a part of Sim's salary that fairly represented the part of the work she refused to do.

In the case of *Cooper and others v Isle of Wight College [2007] EWHC 2831 (QB)* the High Court said that the amount of pay an employer can deduct can only be as much as the **amount the employee could sue** the employer for if they had not been paid for that period.

Pay deductions because of industrial action are not protected under section 16 of the *Employment Rights Act* (ERA 96) (see "Deductions and underpayments" in Chapter 4) and regardless of whether a deduction is "lawful", a tribunal cannot rule on deductions from wages resulting from industrial action. However, it can make a finding of fact as to whether what has taken place amounted to industrial action, rather than just relying on an allegation by the employer that industrial action did occur (*Gill v Ford Motor Co & others EAT/1006/03 ([2004] IRLR 840)*).

Lockouts

Employers may try to anticipate a dispute by locking out workers. A lockout is defined in section 235(4) of the ERA 96 to **include closures or suspensions** by the employer with a view to forcing workers to accept specific terms or conditions.

Establishing when a lockout has taken place can present difficulties, but it may be important where individuals are claiming unfair dismissal, as employees who have been locked out may have a slightly better chance of pursuing a claim successfully.

The *Employment Relations Act 2004* extends the period of protection from unfair dismissal to include any time when employees are locked out. So if a group of workers wants to return to work after being on strike for 12 weeks and their employer refuses to let them back, they will still have dismissal protection. Locked out workers are treated in exactly the same way as strikers as far as state benefits are concerned (see below).

Criminal law

There are a few instances where the criminal law can be used against workers taking industrial action. In these circumstances the police may instigate the prosecution. Workers who are picketing may face **obstruction or breach of the peace** charges.

These can include unreasonable obstruction of the highway and/or wilful obstruction of a police officer. Under the *Public Order Act 1986*, individuals may be charged with disorderly conduct, threatening behaviour, riot, violent disorder or affray.

But the standard of proof required to convict on these charges is "beyond reasonable doubt", a much higher requirement than applies to civil law cases.

There are **four offences** that may be committed by people involved in picketing. They are: the use of violence; persistent following; hiding tools; and picketing a person's home. Although the law is rarely used, it was relevant in a 1984 "work in".

Laboratory staff employed by Fife Health Authority occupied their lab and began a "work in" as part of a long-running dispute. The "work in" ended when the police smashed down the door, arrested them and charged them. The court ruled that the workers were not protected by the immunities because these only applied to civil action. *Galt v Philip and Others [1984] IRLR 156.*

Section 15 of TULRCA makes it unlawful for the union to **pay an individual's fines** for criminal activity or contempt of court. Section 16 gives individual members a right to go to court if union trustees permit the application of union funds for "unlawful purposes".

Conspiracy is another criminal charge available under the *Criminal Law Act 1977*. Conspiracy involves the agreement by two or more people to pursue a course of action which would necessarily involve the committing of an offence. The penalty for conspiracy cannot be higher than for the offence itself, and under section 1, unlawful civil action in the course of a dispute does not give rise to a conspiracy charge.

State benefits for strikers

Although strikers are **mostly excluded** from claiming state benefits, they should be able to continue to receive Working Tax Credit and Child Tax Credit.

For all other benefits, anyone taking industrial action loses entitlement to claim. This also applies to anyone **laid off** because of industrial action, unless it can be shown that they have no direct interest in the dispute at their place of work. If, by custom and practice, any pay increase obtained by those on strike would be given to those laid off, they too will be disqualified from benefits.

The **dependants of strikers** or those laid off and disqualified have an entitlement to claim benefit. However, in calculating their "personal allowances" for the purpose of assessing entitlement to means-tested benefits (for example, Employment and Support Allowance), **a deduction of £35.00 a week** will be made (2010-11). This is supposed to represent the amount the striker would be receiving in union strike pay, but is deducted regardless of whether or not any strike pay is actually received. Any strike pay over that amount is classed as income and taken fully into account when assessing entitlement. The dependants of non-union members who are on strike have the same amount deducted.

> **More information:** for full details of entitlement to benefits, see the LRD booklet *State benefits and tax credits 2010* (£6.45)

10. Dismissal

Unfair dismissal accounts for the largest single category of claims coming before tribunals, with thousands of people pursuing claims every year. The right to claim unfair dismissal applies only to those defined as **"employees"** (see Chapter 2) and, except for most of those dismissals that are deemed to be "automatically" unfair (see page 227), the employee must have been continuously employed by their employer for **at least a year**.

What is a dismissal?

A dismissal occurs where:

◆ the **employment contract is terminated**, with or without notice;
◆ a **fixed-term contract** is not renewed;
◆ the employee resigns but claims this is as a result of the employer's conduct (constructive dismissal);
◆ a **redundancy** takes place;
◆ a woman is not allowed to **return to work after maternity leave**; or
◆ there is a refusal to re-employ after a **takeover** (see page 282).

The first criterion therefore is that the **employment contract has to have ended**. A dismissal is still judged to have taken place even if the employee might have anticipated the contract would end, as in the case of a fixed-term contract (see below).

A resignation by the employee will bring the contract to an end, usually after the period of contractual notice the employee has to give, but this is not normally dismissal.

In the case of *McLoughlin v Sutcliffe Catering EAT/0932/01*, an employee who tendered her notice was put on garden leave (told to stay at home with pay until the notice period ended), as allowed under her contract. She changed her mind but was not allowed to withdraw her notice, so she brought an unfair dismissal claim. However, the Employment Appeal Tribunal (EAT) held that she had not been dismissed and therefore could not bring a claim.

But if an employee has been **forced to resign**, this will be treated as a dismissal, as happened in the following case:

Mr Sandhu was asked to attend a meeting without being told what it was about. When it became clear that the meeting's purpose was to dismiss him over allegations of misconduct (which had not been investigated or reported to him), he negotiated terms on which he would leave the company.

The Court of Appeal held that where an employee's only choice is between resigning or being dismissed, this is viewed as a dismissal; whereas if the employee chooses to resign because she/he has negotiated beneficial terms, this may count as a genuine resignation. Sandhu had no option but to salvage what he could; there was no free negotiation and he was therefore dismissed. His unfair dismissal claim was upheld. *Sandhu v Jan De Rijk Transport Ltd [2007] EWCA Civ 430.*

A resignation must have been **communicated to the employer** — an employee who has drafted a letter of resignation cannot be said to have resigned until the letter is sent (*Edwards v Surrey Police [1999] IRLR 456*).

Once an employee has handed in their notice, s/he may **not be able to withdraw it without the employer's consent**, unless it was given in the "heat of the moment". In *Martin v Yeoman Aggregate Ltd [1983] IRLR 49*, the EAT held that if an employer dismisses, or an employee resigns, in the heat of the moment, the dismissal or resignation can be withdrawn provided it is done almost immediately when tempers cool.

Termination with/without notice

Under section 86 of the ERA 96, both employees and employers have a **statutory right to minimum notice** if the contract is terminated.

An **employee** is entitled to notice of at least:

◆ **one week**, if their length of service is between one month and two years; or
◆ **one week for each year**, if they have between two and 12 years' service; up to a maximum of
◆ **12 weeks**, if they have at least 12 years' service.

This is the statutory minimum, and the employment contract can provide for more notice than this. If the contract does not specify the notice period, the courts can imply "reasonable" notice, taking account of the employee's length of service and seniority.

If the employer has **not given proper notice**, the employee can bring a claim for wrongful dismissal in an employment tribunal (see

"Wrongful dismissal" below). But if an employee waives their right to notice — as happened in the unusual case of *Baldwin v British Coal [1995] IRLR 139* — there is no breach of contract:

Mr Baldwin accepted voluntary redundancy, and waived his right to notice so that he could qualify for enhanced redundancy terms that were about to expire. The High Court said it was clear that he was waiving his notice by accepting the terms, and this was not a breach of contract.

An employer can choose to make a **payment in lieu of notice** (PILON) if it has a clause in the contract allowing it to do so. This usually means that the employer can choose to exercise that option, but the employee does not have a right to demand it (see the case of *Cerberus Software v Rowley [2001] IRLR 160* in "Wrongful dismissal" below).

The minimum notice an **employee has to give** the employer is **one week**. Again, the contract can provide for longer notice. If the employee fails to give proper notice, this too amounts to a breach of contract — but does not give the employer the right to withhold wages:

Mrs Sands-Ellison failed to give proper notice when she resigned. As a result, her employer refused to pay her the commission and holiday pay that she was due. The EAT held that this amounted to an unlawful deduction from her wages, as there was no contractual authority on which the employer could rely. *Sands-Ellison v Call Insurance EAT/0002/02/ST.*

Under some peculiar provisions of the ERA 96, an employee who is on **sick leave during any part of their notice period** is entitled to be paid their full weekly pay, even if they have exhausted any contractual sick pay (section 88), unless their contractual notice is at least one week longer than the statutory minimum (section 87(4)). In the case of *Scotts Co (UK) Ltd v Budd EAT/823/01 ([2003] IRLR 145)*, an employee was denied full pay because his employer had failed to make its new sick pay policy contractual:

Mr Budd was entitled to three months' notice, but his employer introduced a new staff handbook which stated that the maximum notice period was 12 weeks. After taking more than two years' sick leave and exhausting his contractual entitlement to sick pay, Budd was dismissed; his employer wrote to him saying that he was entitled to 13 weeks' notice, during which he was not paid. Budd argued that he was entitled to full pay during his notice period, by virtue of section 88. But the EAT held that his contractual notice had not been varied and that he was entitled to 13 weeks; as this was one week more than the statutory minimum, he lost (under section 87(4)) the right to full wages during his notice.

Non-renewal of a fixed-term contract

When a temporary (fixed-term) contract comes to an end, this is **still regarded as a dismissal** and the employee can claim unfair dismissal if the qualifying conditions are met (see below). It is unlawful to ask employees on fixed-term contracts to agree to waive their rights to this protection.

Constructive dismissal

A constructive dismissal is one where the **employee resigns** but claims that the **employer's conduct** left no alternative. The conduct must amount to a serious breach of an express or implied contract term (see "Contract changes" in Chapter 3), and the resignation must be on account of the breach.

To claim constructive dismissal, three elements must be present:

◆ the employer must have **fundamentally breached the contract**;
◆ the employee must have left **as a consequence** of that breach; and
◆ there has to have been **no significant delay** between the breach and the employee's departure.

An employee who does delay may lose the right to claim constructive dismissal, but it will depend on the reason for the delay. In the case of *El Hoshi v Pizza Express Restaurants EAT/0857/03*, the EAT held that the reason for the delay was that the employee was sick, and this did not prevent him bringing a claim.

If the employee fails to tell the employer the reason for the resignation at the time, it may be more difficult to claim constructive dismissal but does not prevent the employee from doing so. Before pursuing a constructive dismissal claim, the employee is advised to **submit a grievance** in order to comply with the Acas code.

A **threat to dismiss** can be a breach of contract, allowing an employee to resign and claim constructive dismissal — even if this was not the sole reason for the resignation (*Jones v Mid Glamorgan CC [1997] IRLR 685*). For other examples of fundamental breaches of contract which could lead to constructive dismissal see Chapter 3.

The breach of contract can be either one act by the employer, if it is sufficiently serious, or a **series of actions** which cumulatively amount to a breach; these are often referred to as "last straw" cases, and are common in situations of bullying and harassment or where there has been a breach of trust and confidence in other ways. It does not matter if none of the incidents in themselves would amount to a serious breach, as long as cumulatively they destroy the contractual relationship. However, any incident that could be seen as "reasonable" or "justifiable" is unlikely to qualify as a "last straw" (*LB Waltham Forest v Omilaju [2004] EWCA Civ 1493 ([2005] IRLR 35)*).

An employee can still request **reinstatement or re-engagement** in a constructive dismissal claim without jeopardising their claim.

Other types of dismissal

A **redundancy** is always a dismissal (see Chapter 11). A refusal to allow a woman the right to return to work after maternity leave is also a dismissal (see "Returning to work" in Chapter 8).

There is a concept of **"self-dismissal"**, which could occur if the employee's actions indicate that they do not want the employment relationship to continue — for example, if they get another job and start working for the new employer. A similar idea is that a contract automatically terminates if the employee fails to do something expected of them. But tribunals and courts usually decide that there was a dismissal in these circumstances, so there is a right to claim unfair dismissal.

Mrs Igbo asked for extended holiday to visit her family in Nigeria. Her employer agreed, on the basis that her employment would be deemed to have automatically terminated if she did not return on the agreed day. When this happened, the Court of Appeal rejected the idea that the contract had terminated automatically and held that there had been a dismissal. *Igbo v Johnson Matthey Chemicals Ltd [1986] IRLR 215.*

In dismissals following a **transfer under** TUPE (see Chapter 12), claims should be brought against the new employer (*Thompson v Walon [1997] IRLR 343*). An employee cannot take an unfair dismissal claim against a third party for inducing a dismissal (*Wilson v Housing Corporation [1997] IRLR 346*).

Unfair dismissal

Dismissals for certain reasons are deemed to be automatically unfair because they infringe on an individual's rights under specific areas of employment law (see "Automatically unfair dismissals" later in this Chapter).

However, most unfair dismissals come under the provisions of section 98 of the ERA 96 (which were amended in 2006 to include retirement dismissals). These state that an employer cannot fairly dismiss an employee unless it can show that:

◆ it had a potentially **fair reason** for dismissal; and
◆ it **acted reasonably** in all the circumstances.

A "fair" reason is one specified in section 98, which must be one of the following:

◆ **capability** or **qualifications**;
◆ **conduct**;
◆ **retirement**;
◆ **redundancy**;
◆ to comply with a **legal duty or restriction**; or
◆ **"some other substantial reason"**.

If an employer fails to show that the dismissal was for one of the above reasons, it will be unfair.

Even if the employer has established a potentially fair reason as above, the dismissal must still be reasonable in all the circumstances.

For a dismissal to be **reasonable**, the employer must have followed a fair procedure and be able to show that dismissal was within a reasonable range of responses.

In cases related to the employee's conduct, the employer must have carried out a reasonable investigation into the conduct. However, the need for an investigation is not limited to cases of misconduct: it may also be necessary in cases of capability, for example. A tribunal will only take into account facts known to the employer at the time of the dismissal.

A dismissal can also be unfair because the employer has **failed to follow the statutory dismissal procedures**. Whether an employer has followed a fair procedure when dismissing an employee has always been part of the test of overall "reasonableness" — but since 2004 when the statutory procedures were introduced, a failure to follow the statutory procedures will make a dismissal automatically unfair (see page 227).

Under section 92 of the ERA 96, employees with at least one year's continuous service have the right to get a **written statement of reasons for dismissal**, which their employer must provide within 14 days of the request. If an employer refuses to give a statement, the employee can complain to an employment tribunal.

An employee who is dismissed while pregnant or on maternity or adoption leave is entitled to a written statement without having to request it, and does not need a year's service.

If an employer dismisses without giving any reasons, the dismissal will almost certainly be unfair (*Adams v Derby City Council [1986] IRLR 163*). Changing the reasons for dismissal at a later date may make the dismissal unfair, but only if the employer is alleging different facts — it is the facts and not the "label" that are important (*Hotson v Wisbech Conservative Club [1984] IRLR 422*).

Fair reasons for dismissal

Capability

A "capability" dismissal relates to "skill, aptitude, health or any other physical or mental quality". A worker can be fairly dismissed due to a poor sickness record, but the employer will usually have to show that it tried to establish the employee's medical condition and examined alternatives to dismissal (see "Dismissal while sick" in Chapter 7).

If the worker is disabled within the meaning of the *Disability Discrimination Act 1995*, there is additional protection (see "Disability discrimination" in Chapter 6).

The employee's capabilities are **assessed at the date of the dismissal**. The employer does not have an obligation to monitor the decision to dismiss by taking account of any change in circumstances between that date and the date of the appeal (*Two Shires Ambulance NHS Trust v Brooks EAT/0330/02*).

If a dismissal is on the grounds of **skill or aptitude**, the employer would be expected to have given warnings and explained the standards of work required and the consequences of failing to meet them. There would also be a requirement to show that alternatives, such as a transfer to another job, had been considered.

Conduct

A conduct dismissal is based on something the employee has done or failed to do. It is often more accurately described as misconduct. Employers should make clear to employees what they would regard as misconduct that would justify dismissal; a failure to do this could make an otherwise fair dismissal unfair.

Ms Goudie was dismissed for unacceptable misuse of her employer's computer facilities. Her employer had never made it clear that there was such a policy against personal use, and her dismissal was therefore unfair. *Royal Bank of Scotland v Goudie EAT/0693/03.*

Whatever disciplinary rules an employer seeks to impose, they should be **clear** and **well known**. They should also be **applied consistently** — although this does not necessarily mean that the outcome will always be the same. Because the individual circumstances, such as the employee's record, may be different, it may be fair for an employer to impose different penalties for the same offence, as in the following case:

Solicitor Ms Dalley was dismissed on two counts of misconduct: firstly, she had failed to return to work or report in after her holiday; and secondly, she had failed to issue court proceedings in time, which amounted to professional negligence. She claimed that her dismissal was unfair because another solicitor had also failed to meet court deadlines but had not been dismissed.

The EAT said that this did not make the dismissal unfair because the circumstances were different; the other solicitor had co-founded a new department which was understaffed, had been inundated with claims having very short time limits, and had not been faced with other disciplinary charges. This was enough to justify the difference in treatment. *Levenes Solicitors v Dalley EAT/0330/06.*

Dismissals for a **single act of misconduct** are usually regarded as fair only in very serious cases. But the Court of Appeal has held that it was fair for an employer to dismiss an employee who was suspected of intending to breach a works rule, even though he had not done so at the time he was apprehended (*BRB v Jackson [1994] IRLR 235*).

Dismissing an employee for **refusing to obey a reasonable instruction** can be fair, even if the instruction is outside the scope of the employee's duties, provided that it was issued in the genuinely mistaken belief that the employee was contractually obliged to obey (*Farrant v Woodroffe School [1998] IRLR 176*).

Employers also have a right to dismiss without warning for offences deemed to be **"gross misconduct"** — where an employer is justified in not tolerating the continued presence in the workplace of the employee who has committee the offence. However, they still have to show that they **genuinely believed** the employee to be guilty, that there were **reasonable grounds** for the belief and that they carried out a **reasonable investigation** (*Scottish Daily Record v Laird [1996] IRLR 665*).

A proper investigation may be held to have been carried out even if not all the evidence has been examined, as long as the tribunal finds that the investigation as a whole was fair and that the employer acted reasonably in dismissing the employee (*Abbey National v Morgan EAT/0403/03*).

But even where there is a clear rule that prohibits certain conduct, employers should take care before dismissing an employee:

An employer had a rule prohibiting employees from making private telephone calls, but the EAT said that this did not mean that every dismissal under the rule was fair. It said that a tribunal could consider whether, according to the ordinary standards of reasonable and honest people, the employee's behaviour was considered dishonest, and also whether the employee herself realised that what she was doing was dishonest. *John Lewis v Coyne EAT/581/99 ([2001] IRLR 139).*

A dismissal related to **drink and/or drugs** may be fair, although again it is important for the employer to communicate its policy on the issue to employees. Before any dismissal for this reason, the employer should have carried out an investigation, made it clear that there was a rule barring substance use at work, acted consistently, and consulted the employee on any dependency problem.

However, once a drugs policy is in place, any dismissal is likely to be fair. In one case the employee's defence was that his food had been "spiked" and he did not know he had taken drugs, but the EAT upheld his dismissal because the policy clearly stated that any employee found with traces of illegal drugs would be dismissed (*SW Trains v Ireland EAT/0873/01*). If there is a separate **alcohol or drugs policy**, the employee should be dealt with under that policy.

A dismissal can still be fair even if the employer is willing to consider offering alternative employment to someone dismissed for gross misconduct, but this does not invalidate the dismissal. There can be circumstances where an employer could not trust the employee to perform one job properly while believing they were able to undertake less responsible work (*Hamilton v Argyll & Clyde Health Board [1993] IRLR 99*).

Employers may also dismiss fairly for the **conduct of the employee outside work**, but only if the conduct is in some way related to work. The mere fact that an employee has been charged with an offence is not justification for dismissal without an investigation (*Securicor Guarding v R [1994] IRLR 633*).

And in some cases an employer may be expected to await the outcome of any court case, according to guidance given by the EAT in the case of *Ali v Sovereign Buses (London) Ltd EAT/0274/06*.

The rules on conducting disciplinary proceedings before any dismissal are explained in "Disciplinary procedures" below.

Retirement

When an employee's contract is brought to an end by reason of retirement, this will be a "dismissal" and will only be unfair if the employer has failed to follow the "notification" or "right to request" procedures explained below.

The law sets out the circumstances in which an employee will be deemed to have been dismissed by reason of "retirement". They are set out in the new sections 98ZA to 98ZF of the ERA 96, which were introduced by the age equality regulations (see Chapter 6).

An employee will be found to have been **dismissed for reason of retirement** if:

◆ s/he is **aged 65 or over**, the employer has given **six to 12 months' notice** of the intended date of retirement and her/his right to request working beyond it, and the **contract ends on that date**; or
◆ the employer has **set a normal retiring age below 65** which can be **objectively justified** and the employee has reached that age, the employer has **given the relevant notice** of the retirement date and right to request working beyond it, and the **contract ends on that date**.

In any of the above circumstances, the dismissal will be automatically fair.

The reason for dismissal will **not** be retirement if:

◆ the employee is dismissed **before the normal retirement age** or before their intended date of retirement; or

◆ s/he is **under 65 and there is no normal retirement age**, or there is a normal retirement age but it cannot be justified.

In those cases, the employer will have to show one of the other fair reasons for dismissal (see page 206), otherwise the dismissal will be unfair.

In other circumstances, there may still have been a retirement, but it will be for a tribunal to decide, taking into account when notice of retirement was given and whether the employer complies with its duties under the "right to request" procedure (see below).

An employee who is dismissed on grounds of "retirement" will only have been unfairly dismissed in very limited circumstances (section 98ZG, ERA 96).

If the employer has failed to do any of the following, the dismissal will be automatically unfair and there is a minimum basic award of four weeks' pay:

◆ **notify the employee** of their intended date of retirement up to two weeks before retirement;

◆ **consider the employee's request** not to be retired (which includes holding a meeting, unless this is not reasonably practicable); or

◆ **consider an appeal** against a decision to refuse a request to continue working.

If the employer has not notified the employee six to 12 months in advance of their retirement date but has notified them at least two weeks beforehand, the dismissal may still be unfair but not automatically so. In that case it will be up to a tribunal to decide.

The notification procedure

Between **six months and one year before retirement**, the employer must notify the employee in writing of:

◆ their intended retirement date; and

◆ their right to request working beyond that date.

If the employer does not do this, the employee can bring a claim in an employment tribunal for a failure to notify and the tribunal can award compensation of up to eight weeks' pay (capped at the maximum weekly amount, which is £380 for 2010-11). This claim can be brought whether the dismissal is fair or unfair (see above).

The right to request not to retire

An employee has a statutory right to request not to retire and can propose that their employment continues either for an indefinite period or for a certain length of time, or until a certain date. This request must be made in writing, and should specify that they are making a request not to retire under paragraph 5 of Schedule 6 of the *Employment Equality (Age) Regulations 2006* (in Northern Ireland, under paragraph 5 of Schedule 5 of the *Employment Equality (Age) Regulations (Northern Ireland) 2006*.

The timing of the employee's request depends on when they have been notified of their retirement date:

◆ if they have been told this six to twelve months in advance, they must make the request between three and six months before the retirement date; and

◆ if they have had less than six months notice of their retirement date, or have not been given a date at all, they can make the request at any time in the six months before their retirement date.

Unless the employer has already agreed that the employee can continue working, the employer must **hold a meeting** to discuss their request. This must be held **within a reasonable period** unless this is "not practicable", in which case the employer can make a decision without a meeting but must consider any representations by the employee.

The employer must give the employee **written notice** of its decision, which must be dated.

If the request is refused, the employee has the **right to appeal** and the employer must inform him/her of this right.

Although employers do not have to give **reasons** for refusing a request, the conciliation service Acas recommends that they should give reasons and should explain their retirement policy. Acas also says that it is **good practice** for the employer to consider the positive reasons for granting a request (in particular, the savings to the employer in recruitment and training costs, and the retention of the employee's valuable experience and knowledge), and advises employers to avoid making stereotypical assumptions about older employees' capabilities.

An employee **has the right to be accompanied** at these meetings by a worker or trade union representative employed by the same employer. Unlike in grievance and disciplinary hearings, an employee does not have a legal right to be accompanied by an external union official.

If the chosen companion cannot make the time suggested and the employee proposes an alternative time, the employer must **rearrange** the meeting to that time as long as it is convenient to the employer, employee and companion and is **within seven days** of the original suggested time.

The retirement date is not set in stone once notification has been given; employees can negotiate a different date if they change their mind.

If an employee makes a request and the **employer does not consider it**, or the employer does not consider an employee's **appeal** against their decision to refuse a request, the dismissal will be **automatically unfair**.

Redundancy

There are circumstances that could make a dismissal on grounds of redundancy unfair. A tribunal will not consider whether there was a need for redundancies or investigate the commercial reasons for them, but it can decide whether there was a genuine redundancy situation and whether the dismissal was fair or unfair for other reasons. The law relating to redundancy is set out in Chapter 11.

An individual wishing to challenge the fairness of a redundancy must bring a claim of unfair dismissal, and should specify on their claim form that it relates to redundancy.

The time limit for bringing a claim is three months, the same as in other unfair dismissal cases. If a claim is brought for a redundancy payment, there is a presumption that redundancy is the real reason for the dismissal unless the employer proves otherwise (section 163(2), ERA 96). The time limit for a claim for redundancy pay is six months.

If you are claiming redundancy pay and are unsure whether the redundancy is fair or not, the safest course of action is to claim both redundancy and unfair dismissal, and to issue the claims within three months.

Complying with a legal duty or restriction

It is fair to dismiss an employee if continuing to employ them would contravene a legal duty or restriction — in other words, **where the employer would be breaking the law** by continuing to employ them. This could apply, for example, to a lorry driver who lost their driving licence and for whom there was no alternative employment.

Some other substantial reason

It is also fair to dismiss for "some other substantial reason" under section 98(1) of the ERA 96. The act does not specify what sort of reason this may entail, except that it must be "**of a kind such as to justify the dismissal** of an employee holding the position which the employee held", and the case law shows that the term has quite a wide scope — for example, it is commonly used as a reason to dismiss employees who refuse to sign a new contract when the employer wishes to change the terms in some way. But the employer will have to justify the change, and to show that dismissal was necessary and that they acted reasonably in all the circumstances.

A breakdown in trust and confidence caused by the employee can lead to a fair dismissal for some other substantial reason (*Huggins v Micrel Semiconductor (UK) EAT/0009/04*). So can third-party pressure where, for example, the third party was the employer's only or main client (*Martin v JF X-Press EAT/0010/04*).

And refusing to sign a restrictive covenant (see page 62) can be a valid reason for dismissal even if the clause is unreasonably wide – although the dismissal may still be unfair if it was unreasonable in the circumstances (*Willow Oak Developments Ltd t/a Windsor Recruitment v Silverwood [2006] EWCA Civ 600*).

Was dismissal reasonable?

If the employer has established that it had a fair reason to dismiss, the tribunal will then go on to consider whether the employer acted reasonably in dismissing the employee, taking account of the circumstances "including the size and administrative resources of the employer" (section 98(4), ERA 96).

The role of the tribunal in assessing whether an employer has acted reasonably was affirmed by the Court of Appeal in the case of *HSBC*

Bank v Madden [2000] EWCA Civ 3030 [2000] IRLR 827. The court held that the tribunal should not substitute its own view of what is reasonable for that of the employer; its task is to establish whether the decision to dismiss the employee fell within the **band of reasonable responses** that a reasonable employer might have adopted.

The case of *British Home Stores Ltd v Burchell [1978] IRLR 379* established that, in a case of misconduct, the employer must be able to show that it had a **genuine belief** that the employee was guilty of the misconduct in question, and that its belief was based on reasonable grounds after a **reasonable investigation**.

This has become the standard starting point ("the Burchell test") in misconduct cases, but the principle of carrying out a reasonable investigation to establish the facts may apply in cases of dismissal for other reasons.

If the same person acts as the investigating, disciplining and dismissing officer, the tribunal is likely to find that the investigation is unreasonable, although it may be unavoidable in the smallest organisations. Whether dismissal is reasonable will depend on the employee's individual circumstances as well as the nature of their work.

In a case involving the dismissal of an employee for taking a milkshake without permission, the EAT noted that the offence was minor, there was an absence of deceit on the part of the employee, and the incident was isolated. Taking these factors into account, the employer's decision to dismiss was unreasonable (*Rentokil v Mackin [1989] IRLR 286*).

According to the Court of Appeal, in the case of *Strouthos v London Underground [2004] EWCA Civ 402 ([2004] IRLR 636)*, tribunals should also take **length of service** and **previous record** into account when deciding whether a dismissal was reasonable.

Failing to allow an employee the **right to appeal** will make a dismissal automatically unfair, as it will be in breach of the statutory dismissal procedure (see below). Where an employer has more stages of appeal in an internal disciplinary procedure, a failure to follow all of those stages could also make a dismissal unfair (*Stoker v Lancashire CC [1992] IRLR 75*).

Disciplinary procedures

From October 2004 to April 2009, all employers had to have a disciplinary and grievance procedure and were required to notify their employees of it, in order to comply with the *Employment Act 2002*. However, the statutory disciplinary and grievance procedures were repealed from 6 April 2009.

To replace the statutory procedures, the Advisory, Conciliation and Arbitration Service (Acas) has produced a Code of Practice which sets out what the features of a disciplinary and grievance procedure should be. The steps that the employer and employee are expected to go through are similar to those required under the *Dispute Resolution Regulations*.

The recommendations contained within the Code (not applicable to redundancy dismissals or the non-renewal of fixed-term contracts) will be taken into account by tribunals. Specifically, an employment tribunal will be able to adjust the amount of compensation (by up to + or -25%) if it has not been followed. While the Acas Code sets out the **minimum procedures** that must be followed, many employers have procedures that are more comprehensive. Some of the principal elements of the Code to bear in mind are whether:

◆ the employer has taken too long to raise the complaints (e.g. thereby meaning that witnesses' recollections are no longer reliable);

◆ the employer has sufficiently investigated that which is supposed to have occurred (e.g. has the employer failed to interview or ask relevant questions of a witness favourable to the employee);

◆ the employee has been adequately informed of the complaints against them (e.g. were new allegations raised against him or her during the disciplinary meeting);

◆ the employee was given sufficient time, bearing in mind their anxiety etc, to prepare for the hearing;

◆ at the hearing, the employee was dissuaded from raising all the points in their defence/mitigation that they could have;

◆ the employee has been able to choose and meet with an appropriate companion prior to the disciplinary hearing; and

◆ the process of how and when to appeal, has been fairly explained to the employee.

Supplementary to the code are a large amount of previous judicial decisions. Some of the points that they have established are below.

Employees facing disciplinary action should be given **adequate time** to prepare a defence, and should have the opportunity to **give and call evidence** and to **call witnesses** (*R v Securities and Futures Authority [2001] IRLR 764*). There is no absolute right to cross-examine any of the employer's witnesses, but the EAT has held that there may be circumstances in which it would be unreasonable for the employer to refuse a request to cross-examine (*Santamera v Express Cargo Forwarding [2003] IRLR 273*).

If the employer has based its case on allegations by unidentified employees, it will be for the tribunal to consider — as part of its assessment of the procedure's fairness — whether these sources must be revealed.

At the very least, though, the **substance** of the allegations must be put to the employee; the EAT has held, in the case of *Pudney v Network Rail Infrastructure Ltd EAT/0707/05*, that it is unreasonable to dismiss an employee on the basis of material not disclosed to them or on which they do not have the opportunity to comment.

Disciplinary procedures normally specify a **series of warnings** leading eventually to dismissal. Usually the warnings expire after a period of time set out in the procedure, and it would be unfair to rely on a disciplinary warning after it has expired (*Diosynth Ltd v Thomson [2006] CSIH 5 ([2006] IRLR 284)*). However, in the case of *Airbus UK Ltd v Webb [2008] EWCA Civ 49*, the Court of Appeal said there may be circumstances in which previous misconduct can be taken into account even when it was the basis for a disciplinary warning which has now expired.

A tribunal can take into account the **fairness of a final written warning** given prior to dismissal if this was relied on by the employer when making the decision to dismiss (*Digby v East Cambridgeshire DC UKEAT/522/06*).

Fixed-term employees who are offered a new contract after their current contract ends should note that any unexpired disciplinary warning can transfer to the new contract.

Even if the employer has followed the Acas code, a number of **procedural matters** could make a dismissal unfair. These include:

◆ a failure to consider a **lesser penalty** than dismissal;

◆ holding a disciplinary hearing in the **absence of the employee** (unless there are exceptional circumstances);

◆ a refusal to take account of **new evidence** presented at the appeal;

◆ a **delay** in fixing a date for the disciplinary appeal;

◆ failure to carry out disciplinary hearings in accordance with the **rules of natural justice** (*Campion v Harmsworthy Engineering [1987] ICR 966*);

◆ failure to ensure that, where possible, witnesses to a disciplinary offence are **not involved in hearing** the case (*Moyes v Hylton Castle Working Men's Club [1986] IRLR 482*);

◆ failure to obtain **sufficient proof** of the charge and an inadequate investigation (*ILEA v Gravett [1988] IRLR 497*); and

◆ giving **inadequate notice** of a disciplinary hearing (*R v BBC ex parte Lavelle [1982] IRLR 404*) in which only one hour of notice was given.

A **defective disciplinary hearing** — for example, one where the employee has not had the opportunity to prepare a case — can be put right on appeal, but on the proviso that the person hearing the appeal had not been involved in the earlier stage (*Byrne v BOC [1992] IRLR 505*). An appeal does not have to be a complete re-hearing of the case, but it must be comprehensive (*Taylor v OCS Group Ltd [2006] EWCA Civ 702*).

In some circumstances, disciplinary hearings would need to be conducted in accordance with the standards of a fair trial, laid down under Article 6 of the European Convention on Human Rights (ECHR), brought into effect in the UK by the *Human Rights Act 1998*. This would be the case if the hearing was capable of deciding whether someone could continue to practice in their chosen profession (*Tehrani v UK Central Council for Nursing, Midwifery and Health Visiting [2001] IRLR 208*).

Outside these circumstances, it is unlikely that disciplinary hearings would need to meet these high standards, but they should still be conducted in accordance with the principles of natural justice. The *Human Rights Act* also guarantees a right to privacy and is relevant in relation to unfair dismissal claims in the public sector. The Court of Appeal, in the case of *X v Y [2004] IRLR 471*, said the following factors should be taken into account:

◆ whether the circumstances of the dismissal would come within the areas covered by human rights legislation; if so
◆ whether the state has a positive obligation to secure enjoyment of the right; if so
◆ whether interference with the right is justified; or, if not
◆ whether there was a fair reason for the dismissal.

However, in the case of *McGowan v Scottish Water UKEAT/0007/04 [2005] IRLR 167*, the EAT held that an employer who hired someone to carry out video surveillance of an employee at his home was not in breach of human rights law:

Robert McGowan was dismissed for allegedly falsifying his time sheets. His employer hired someone to carry out surveillance at his home. The EAT, by a majority, held that there was no breach of his right to privacy under human rights law because his employer's actions were "proportionate". The EAT noted that McGowan's alleged activities amounted to a criminal offence, and that his employer was acting legitimately to protect its business assets.

Every employee has the **right to have a grievance dealt with**. This is a fundamental right implied in every contract (*W A Goold (Pearmak) v McConnell [1995] IRLR 516*).

The right to be accompanied

Under section 10 of the *Employment Relations Act 1999* (ERA 99), as amended by the ERA 2004, a worker who is required or invited by an employer to attend a **disciplinary or grievance hearing** has the right to bring a companion. The companion is **chosen by the worker and can be a full-time union official** (whether or not the union is recognised), a **certified lay official** (someone the union has trained to accompany individuals to hearings) or a **workplace colleague**.

Where the employee is facing grave charges which could badly damage his or her career prospects, s/he may be entitled to legal representation.

In *R on the application of G v the Governors of X School and Y City Council [2009] EWHC 504* a music assistant was accused of having an inappropriate relationship with a child. If the disciplinary charge were upheld, the secretary of state would be informed and would be likely to ban the individual from working with children in schools. Despite these implications, the employee's request for legal representation at the hearing was declined. The disciplinary charge was upheld, the employee was dismissed and the secretary of state was notified. The individual sought a judicial review. The Court of Appeal agreed that the internal disciplinary proceedings were determinant of the claimant's civil right to practise his profession. Accordingly, Article 6 of the European Convention on Human Rights (right to a fair hearing) gave the claimant a right to legal representation because legal representation might have made a difference to the outcome of this important meeting. The court commented that the right to legal representation depended less on whether it was a civil or criminal case than on the gravity of the issues.

In *Kulkarni v Milton Keynes Hospital NHS Foundation Trust and The Secretary of State for Health [2009] EWCA Civ 789* a doctor was accused of assaulting a patient. Dr Kulkarni's request to be legally represented at his disciplinary hearing was declined on the basis that such representation is not permitted under the Department of Health policy "Maintaining High Professional Standards in the Modern NHS" (MHPS). Dr Kulkarni sought a judicial review. The Court of Appeal noted that MHPS stated that doctors and dentists are entitled to be represented by (amongst others) someone retained by a trade union who is legally qualified – provided that they are not acting in a legal capacity. The Court of Appeal found that this statement provided Dr Kulkarni with a contractual right to a legal representative.

Additionally the court considered that where a doctor faces charges which are so grave that s/he may be barred from employment in the NHS, the right to a fair trial (Article 6, European Convention on Human Rights) is engaged. Specifically, if the disciplinary amounts to a criminal charge (although not involving criminal sanctions) as being dealt with internally) there is a right to legal representation.

To qualify as a disciplinary hearing, the meeting has to be one that **could result in a warning or some other action**, provided that this is held on the employee's file and represents a stage in a disciplinary procedure (*LU v Ferenc-Batchelor EAT/1039/01/PRW [2003] IRLR 252*). Whether the meeting is a disciplinary hearing (as opposed to, for example, an investigation meeting) depends on what happens at the meeting and not what the employer calls it; and if it becomes clear during the course of an "investigation" meeting that some form of disciplinary action is being considered, the worker can ask for the meeting to be adjourned (*Skiggs v South West Trains Ltd EAT/0763/03 ([2005] IRLR 459)*).

A grievance hearing has to concern "the performance of a duty by an employer in relation to a worker".

At the hearing, the companion has the right to put the worker's case, confer with the worker, sum up the case and respond on the worker's behalf to any view expressed at the hearing but s/he cannot answer questions on behalf of the worker.

The worker and the companion have **protection against any detrimental act or dismissal** in connection with exercising their section 10 rights, and can take a claim to a tribunal within three months. If working for the **same employer**, both the companion and the worker have the right to be paid. A lay official working for a different employer would be protected from detrimental action by that employer, but has no right to be paid by that employer for any time taken to deal with the hearing.

If a worker's chosen companion is not available on the date fixed for the hearing, it has to be **postponed**, provided the new date is reasonable and within five days of the original hearing. These rights are regardless of length of service.

An employee can take a claim to a tribunal if the employer refuses to let them bring their chosen companion to the hearing, and there is now a right to appeal to the EAT (introduced by section 38 of the ERA 2004).

Qualifying for unfair dismissal rights

In most cases of unfair dismissal, an individual must meet certain qualifying criteria to be able to bring a claim. They must:

◆ be an **employee** (see Chapter 2);
◆ have **been dismissed**;
◆ have been continuously employed by their employer for **at least one year** by the "effective date of termination" (see below); and
◆ present the application to a tribunal **within three months** of the date of dismissal.

There is no longer an age limit on the right to claim unfair dismissal, but employees dismissed at the age of 65 or over (or below that age, if their employer has dismissed them on grounds of retirement) should refer to the section on "retirement dismissals" on page 203 to see whether their dismissal is deemed a "retirement".

The qualifying conditions relating to length of service do not apply in most cases of **automatically unfair dismissals** (see below), with the exception of dismissal resulting from a business transfer, the employer's failure to comply with the statutory DDPs, or dismissal because of a spent conviction.

A dismissal does not take effect until it has been **communicated to the employee**.

The **effective date of termination** (EDT) is the date that the employment contract comes to an end. (For the purpose of redundancy payments this is referred to as the **"relevant date"**.) It is essential for employees to establish what the EDT is if they are to bring a claim within the time limit.

In a case of **summary dismissal** (dismissal without notice), the EDT is the date that the dismissal takes effect — usually the date the employee was told they are dismissed.

In *Gisda Cyf v Barratt UKEAT/0173/08* the employee attended a disciplinary hearing on 28 November 2006. She was told that she would be notified of the outcome by letter to be sent the following day. By the time the letter dismissing her arrived on 30 November, Ms Barratt had left to visit her sister for a few days. She did phone home while away but did not ask about the letter — Ms Barratt read the letter on her return on 4 December. She lodged a tribunal claim on 2 March but the employer argued that she was out of time (i.e. she had been notified of her dismissal when the letter arrived at her home). The EAT disagreed and found that time ran from when the letter was actually read (or at least from a time when the employee had had a reasonable opportunity of reading it). The EAT commented that the situation would be different if an employee deliberately did not read, or went away to avoid receiving, a dismissal letter.

For a **dismissal with notice**, the EDT is usually the date when the notice period expires, even if the employee is paid in lieu of notice so that they do not have to work their notice period. However, a payment in lieu of notice may bring forward the EDT in some cases, and employees and reps should be aware of this if the employer indicates that it intends the employment to finish straight away.

The EDT is not necessarily the date on the **P45**, although this can be used as evidence in establishing the date. Neither is a P45 proof of a dismissal, and an employee does not have to wait to receive one before bringing a claim. If fact, if they do wait they may be beyond the three-month time limit and lose the right to pursue a claim (*LB Newham v Ward [1985] IRLR 509*).

The Court of Appeal has held that the employer and employee cannot agree on a date of termination retrospectively — the date is determined by what has happened in practice:

Maureen Fitzgerald was offered early retirement by letter dated 2 March. She accepted the offer, which said her retirement would take effect on 28 February — two days earlier. She subsequently brought an unfair dismissal claim within three months of the date of the letter but past the deadline if her date of dismissal had been 28 February. The Court of Appeal held that it was not up to the parties to agree the EDT — this was something that was determined in accordance with statute (the ERA 96). If they were allowed to agree a different date, individuals could be deprived of their statutory rights and this was not permissible. *Fitzgerald v University of Kent at Canterbury [2004] EWCA Civ 143 ([2004] IRLR 300).*

If an employee is dismissed for a reason other than genuine gross misconduct (or another reason that would justify summary dismissal) and has not been given the **statutory minimum notice** (see page 25), the EDT is extended to the date when that notice would have expired (section 97(2), ERA 96).

This means that an employee dismissed within a week of the end of their first year in employment will still be entitled to bring a claim for unfair dismissal. But the extension of the EDT does not apply to contractual notice — so an employee entitled to a month's contractual notice will not be able to claim unfair dismissal if they are dismissed two weeks before the end of the year. This has been confirmed by the Court of Appeal in the case of *Harper v Virgin Net Ltd [2004] EWCA Civ 271 ([2004] IRLR 390.*

If there is an **appeal hearing** and the dismissal is confirmed, the EDT is still the **date of the original dismissal**. If the dismissal is overturned and the employee is reinstated, the dismissal "vanishes" and there can be no unfair dismissal claim (*Roberts v West Coast Trains [2004] EWCA Civ 900 ([2004] IRLR 788)*).

The tribunal has discretion to extend the time limit for submitting a claim if it was "not reasonably practicable" to present the claim in time, but this test is strictly applied.

In one case, the fact that the employee did not find out until some time later that the reason given for her dismissal — redundancy — was a sham made it "not reasonably practicable" to present the claim within the three-month limit.

In the case of *Marley v Anderson [1996] IRLR 163*, the Court of Appeal held that, where the facts emerge over time, an employee is not automatically time-barred in making a second claim just because the first claim was out of time. It is up to the tribunal to determine what is a reasonable time within which the employee should have presented a claim, having discovered the relevant information that formed the basis for the claim.

Continuous employment

Workers who have broken or irregular service with the same or an "associated" employer may still be able to show that they have the necessary continuity of employment to claim unfair dismissal (and other statutory rights).

Continuous employment is calculated in accordance with sections 210 to 219 of the ERA 96.

A gap of less than a week does not break continuity even if, within that week, the employee goes to work for another employer and then returns. Under section 210, employment is **presumed to be continuous** unless the contrary is shown — for example, where it was clearly intended that a series of temporary contracts would not be regarded as continuous (*Booth v USA [1999] IRLR 16*). Under section 212, the following circumstances do not break continuity of service:

◆ incapacity through sickness or injury of 26 weeks or less;
◆ a "temporary cessation of work"; or
◆ absence that "by arrangement or custom" is regarded as continuing the employment.

Home tutor Margaret Prater was employed by a local council to teach pupils as and when needed. She could choose not to take on particular pupils if she wished, but she never did so, and she taught the pupils for as long as necessary — which could be up to five years.

The Court of Appeal held that she had been an employee for the entire time she had worked for the council. There was a mutuality of obligation — once she accepted a pupil she was obliged to teach them, and the council was obliged to pay her — and the gaps between the contracts were "temporary cessations of work" which did not break continuity of service. *Cornwall CC v Prater [2006] EWCA Civ 102 ([2006] IRLR 362).*

An employer and employee cannot agree that weeks will not count toward continuous service if they meet the statutory criteria under the ERA 96:

In the case of *Carrington v Harwich Dock Co [1998] IRLR 567*, the employee agreed to resign, breaking his continuity, so that he could take advantage of a favourable early retirement package. He immediately returned to a new job with the same employer. But the EAT said that his continuity was not broken, because he could not sign away his statutory rights.

However, continuity of service can be preserved by agreement. In particular, reps should examine any **career break schemes** to ensure that individuals taking advantage of them do not then forfeit future employment rights, in light of the Court of Appeal's ruling in the case of *Curr v Marks & Spencer [2002] EWCA Civ 1852 ([2003] IRLR 74):*

Cheryl Curr had worked for the same employer for 20 years when she took a career break. She returned to work at the end of it, and worked for another five years before being made redundant. Curr had assumed her redundancy pay would take account of all of her service, but the Court of Appeal ruled that it did not: there was no agreement or custom by which she could have been regarded as an employee during her career break, and therefore her continuity was broken.

However, in the case of *Unwin v Barclays Bank EAT/0273/02, the* EAT held that an employee on a career break did have continuity of employment, so that her service prior to her career break was included when she was made redundant a year after returning to work.

The following examples show the circumstances when the rules operate to **preserve continuity**:

◆ employment on a **series of fixed-term contracts** (*Pfaffinger v City of Liverpool Community College [1996] IRLR 508*) (note that, under the *Fixed-Term Employee Regulations*, an employee who has worked on a series of fixed-term contracts for four years or more will be deemed to be a permanent employee unless the employer can justify keeping them on a fixed-term contract — see "Temporary employees" in Chapter 2);

♦ dismissing and then **reinstating** an employee (*Ingram v Foxon [1985] IRLR 5*);

♦ gaps between employment which are **relatively short** in comparison to the period of employment (*Sillars v Charringtons Fuels [1989] IRLR 152*);

♦ a period of **work abroad** followed by one in the UK with the same employer (*Weston v Viga Space Systems [1989] IRLR 429*);

♦ a break for **sickness of fewer than 26 weeks**, even if the employee worked elsewhere in that period (*Donnelly v Kelvin International Services [1992] IRLR 496*);

♦ a two-week gap during which the employee continued to work for the old employer before being **transferred** to the new employer under the TUPE regulations (*Tuck A & G v Bartlett [1994] IRLR 162*); and

♦ a week during which the employee received unemployment benefit in the period between his employment **shutting down and reopening** (*Justfern v D'Ingerthorpe [1994] IRLR 164*).

In *Da Silva v Composite Mouldings and Design Ltd EAT 0241/08* the same owner, through a different set of companies, took over from an undertaking which had gone into **voluntary liquidation**. Even though the employee had been unemployed for a six-week period, he was found to have retained continuity. Continuity is also preserved following a **business transfer** under the TUPE regulations (see Chapter 12).

If an employee is **on strike** for any part of a week, continuity is not broken. However, that week does not count in calculating continuous length of service. Women on maternity leave preserve their continuity of employment, and the period of the leave itself is counted.

Dismissal while on strike

Employees have the right not to be dismissed in the first 12 weeks of taking lawful, **official industrial action** (see "How the law aids employers" in Chapter 9). This is the protected period, but beyond this period there may still be some protection from dismissal.

In a case taken to a tribunal by workers at automotive company Friction Dynamics, who were dismissed after eight weeks had expired (until the *Employment Relations Act 2004* came into effect, the protected period was only eight weeks), a tribunal ruled that the workforce still had protection. It gave two reasons for this:

◆ threatening letters to workers were sent within the protected period, which made it clear that the employer had **already taken a decision to dismiss** the workforce; and

◆ the employer **refused to take any steps to resolve the dispute** after the protected period — a breach of the legal obligation to take reasonable procedural steps to resolve a dispute.

The ERA 04 has also extended the protected period to include any time when employees are locked out. After the 12 weeks, an employer that wants to dismiss some strikers has to **dismiss all of them**; it cannot pick and choose. After three months from the date of dismissal, employers can take back who they want without the risk of unfair dismissal claims.

In the case of *Crosville Wales v Tracey [1997] IRLR 691*, the House of Lords said that, where all the employees had taken industrial action, it would not be possible to judge whether one employee was to blame without referring to the conduct of the other employees. This meant, in practice, that all had the right to damages for unfair dismissal.

Whether an individual is taking part in a strike is decided objectively. The test is what the employee did, not why it was done.

Mr Britton was instructed to drive a van without a heater. He refused and was dismissed. At the end of the day's work, his colleague Mr Lewis attempted to intervene on his behalf and informed the employer that no one would work unless the dismissal was reversed. All the other drivers were then dismissed. On application to the tribunal, the EAT upheld a finding that they had been "taking part in strike action" and that the tribunal had no jurisdiction to hear their case. *Lewis v E. Mason and Sons [1994] IRLR 4.*

In one case, an employee only took part in a strike to enable him to report back to the company on what the strikers were up to. When everyone else was dismissed, he was not, and the company tried to argue that he had not really been taking part in the strike. The EAT disagreed, saying his motive for taking part was irrelevant.

Workers must actually be taking industrial action when dismissed. If they have already **returned to work** and are then dismissed, they are not barred from taking unfair dismissal claims. Whether or not they were taking the action is a question for the tribunal, not the employer, to decide (*Jenkins v P & O Ferries [1991] ICR 652*). In cases of **unofficial action** there is no protection against dismissal, even if it is selective. The **International Labour Organisation** (ILO), the body responsible for regulating employment law worldwide, has repeatedly condemned UK law for allowing the dismissal of strikers, saying that it breaches international standards.

Automatically unfair dismissals

Dismissals for certain reasons are automatically unfair and there is no need to go on to consider whether dismissal was reasonable. In these cases it is for the employee to prove that the reason for the dismissal fell within one of the automatically unfair categories.

In the case of *Povey v Dorset CC EAT/209/01* the employee claimed his dismissal was due to his health and safety activities. However, he could not prove this. His employers successfully argued that he had been dismissed for refusing to obey a legitimate order.

The list of automatically unfair dismissals continues to grow as employees gain statutory employment rights. The different types of automatically unfair dismissals are described below. Except for dismissals relating to business transfers or dismissal because of a spent conviction, there is no service qualification for the right to claim unfair dismissal on one of the automatically unfair grounds (see "Qualifying for unfair dismissal rights" above).

Pregnancy and parental rights

Dismissing a woman because she is pregnant or on maternity leave, or for any reason connected with her pregnancy, is contrary to both the *Sex Discrimination Act 1975* (SDA) and section 99, ERA 96. The dismissal of an employee due to a pregnancy-related illness is also unlawful (*Brown v Rentokil [1998] IRLR 445*). However, a woman undergoing IVF treatment whose ova have been fertilised but not yet implanted, is not entitled to the protections afforded to pregnant women (*Mayr v Bäckerei und Konditorei Gerhard Flöckner, C-506/06*). Dismissal of employees for exercising their parental, paternity or adoption leave rights (see Chapter 8) is automatically unfair.

Business transfers

A dismissal connected with the transfer of business is unfair under the *Transfer of Undertakings Regulations 2006* (TUPE) (see Chapter 12).

Trade union membership

Section 152 of the *Trade Union and Labour Relations (Consolidation) Act 1992* (TULRCA) protects those dismissed because they are, or propose to become, a member of an independent trade union or **take part in its activities** at an "appropriate time", i.e. outside working hours or inside those hours with the employer's consent. In the case of *Britool v Roberts [1993] IRLR 481*, individuals dismissed because of their trade union activities, including their involvement in the preliminary planning stage of a strike, were protected under section 152. A management-grade employee, who was also a rep and was dismissed for advising new employees that their only safeguard lay with the union, was also held to have been unfairly dismissed.

Employees are protected by section 152 if they are dismissed for invoking the assistance of the union in relation to their employment (*Speciality Care v Pachela [1996] IRLR 248*). However, this does not include organising or taking part in industrial action — see "Dismissal while on strike" on page 207.

Anyone dismissed for trade union reasons should immediately use the **interim relief** procedures in section 161 of TULRCA (see "Victimisation" in Chapter 5).

This must be done **within seven days** of the dismissal and the application must include a certificate, signed by a union official, which says that the dismissal is on account of union membership. The tribunal will, if it believes there are grounds for the claim, make a continuation order which means that the employer must continue paying the employee pending the full tribunal hearing.

Representation rights

Employees have protection from dismissal where they are exercising their right to be accompanied or are acting as a companion in disciplinary and grievance hearings (see "The right to be accompanied" above).

Protected industrial action

During the period of protected industrial action (see "Dismissal while on strike" above) employers are barred from dismissing employees taking industrial action.

Enforcing a statutory right

It is automatically unfair to dismiss someone because they have attempted to enforce a relevant statutory right, such as a claim for holiday pay (section 104, ERA 96). It does not matter whether the employee actually has the right, or whether it has been infringed, as long as they acted in good faith (*Mennell v Newell and Wright [1997] IRLR 519*).

In the case of *Pearce and Pearce v Dyer EAT/0465/04*, the EAT held that the dismissal of employees because they had alleged their employer had made **unlawful deductions** from their wages was a dismissal for enforcing a statutory right and therefore automatically unfair. Dismissal for a reason relating to **jury service or working tax credits** is also automatically unfair, as is dismissal for a **spent conviction** (see page 48).

Part-time or fixed-term employees

It is unlawful to dismiss a part-time worker or fixed-term employee because of their employment status or for exercising their rights to no less favourable treatment.

Health and safety reasons

Under section 100, ERA 96 if an employee who is acting as a safety rep is dismissed for carrying out those duties, the dismissal is automatically unfair. So too would be the dismissal of any worker leaving or proposing to leave work in circumstances where they believed there to be a **"serious and imminent"** danger. However, in the case of *Balfour Kilpatrick v Acheson EAT/1412/01 ([2003] IRLR 683)* staff who walked out over being made to wear damp clothing were not able to show that there was an imminent risk justifying their action without a prior ballot.

An employee who leaves work due to threats from another employee may be able to claim protection if dismissed (*Harvest Press v*

McCaffrey [1999] IRLR 778). And the right extended to an employee leaving a kitchen where he worked because he believed that health standards were putting customers at risk (*Masiak v City Restaurants [1999] IRLR 780*).

Refusal to work on Sundays

Dismissal of a protected shop or betting worker because they refuse to work on Sundays is automatically unfair.

Employee representatives and pension fund trustees

Under section 103, ERA 96 an employee representative, or a candidate for such a position, who is dismissed because they have performed, or proposed to perform, functions of such a representative will be regarded as having been unfairly dismissed.

Similar protection applies to trustees of occupational pension funds under section 102 ERA 96. The dismissal of an employee for activities as a member of a European Works Council (EWC) is also automatically unfair, as is dismissal in connection with information and consultation rights.

Whistleblowing

Under the *Public Interest Disclosure Act 1998* (PIDA), an employee who makes a **protected disclosure** ("blows the whistle") about their employer's fraudulent or criminal activities has protection against **victimisation**, **detriment** and **dismissal**.

Even if it turns out that the allegation was wrong, provided that the employee had a reasonable belief and was reasonably mistaken, the law will protect them from detrimental treatment (*Darnton v University of Surrey [2003] IRLR 133*, upheld by the Court of Appeal in *Babula v Waltham Forest College [2007] EWCA Civ 174 ([2007] IRLR 346)*. However, the employee's reasons for making the disclosure must be **motivated entirely by the public interest** and not by personal antagonism.

Frances Street made a number of allegations against her manager. An investigation revealed that her motivation for making the allegations was malicious and Street was dismissed. She took an unfair dismissal claim. The Court of Appeal dismissed the claim. It held that even if an employee believes the disclosure to be true, they would not be acting in good faith unless motivated entirely by public interest. *Street v Derbyshire Unemployed Workers' Centre [2004] EWCA Civ 964 ([2004] IRLR 687)*.

Employees are protected even if the whistleblowing relates to something that happened before the 1998 Act came into force, provided that the victimisation itself occurred after the law came into force (*Miklaszewicz v Stolt XA108/01 [2001] IRLR 656*). The types of wrongdoing that are covered are also wide:

In the case of *Hibbins v Hesters Way Neighbourhood Project UKEAT/0275/08*, the employee was a female teacher who having interviewed a prospective male student for a place on the project, read a media report that indicated that he was wanted for rape. Ms Hibbins immediately contacted the police and provided certain information. She also informed her male manager, who responded (in Ms Hibbins' view) very unsympathetically, which caused her to submit her resignation. Ms Hibbins brought a claim on the basis that she had been constructively dismissed for having made a protected disclosure. The EAT decided that her claim could proceed. PIDA protects individuals making disclosures (giving the suspected criminal's contact information to the police) about the wrongdoing of a third party, not just the wrongdoing of their employer.

The EAT has held that the Act also covers workers who complain about breaches of any **legal obligations** their employers have under their individual employment contracts. However, the whistleblowing protection applies to a "disclosure of information", not merely to a statement of position.

Employees who write to their employers, complaining about breach of contract and threatening to resign, (even if done through solicitors) are not making protected disclosures under PIDA. They are simply stating their position, not conveying "information": *Cavendish Munro Professional Risks Management Ltd v Geduld [2010] IRLR 38*.

In the case of *Parkins v Sodexho [2002] IRLR 109* an employee used the Act successfully to complain about lack of adequate supervision, amounting to a breach of the health and safety obligations. Compensation in whistleblowing cases can include an award for **injury to feelings**.

Minimum wage and working time

The regulations guaranteeing minimum wage and imposing working time restrictions for health reasons (see Chapter 4) provide protection for anyone dismissed for trying to pursue their rights to pay, hours or holidays in accordance with the law.

Union recognition

Dismissing employees for seeking rights to trade union recognition comes within the definition of automatically unfair dismissals.

Retirement

If an employer fails to comply with the following legal requirements under the *Employment Equality (Age) Regulations 2006* before dismissing an employee on grounds of retirement, the dismissal will be automatically unfair: notifying the employee of their retirement date two weeks in advance; hearing the employee's request not to retire; hearing the employee's appeal against a decision not to let them continue working beyond the retirement date.

Successful claims

An employee bringing a claim for unfair dismissal is entitled to ask for their job back. However, in the vast majority of cases tribunals do not award reinstatement or re-engagement. Most get financial compensation and less than 1% of those who win are reinstated or re-engaged.

Reinstatement or re-engagement

Under sections 113 and 114, ERA 96 tribunals can order an employer to reinstate (give the employee their old job with compensation for lost earnings) or **re-engage** (give the employee a suitable alternative job with compensation for lost earnings). But they cannot be ordered to give an employee a better job than the one held prior to the unfair dismissal (*Rank Xerox v Stryczek [1995] IRLR 568*). A reinstatement **restores the original contract** and preserves continuity.

Mr Kirkpatrick was dismissed and two months later reinstated after an internal appeal. A month later his employers reneged on the decision to reinstate and restored the original decision. They then argued that Kirkpatrick could not bring an unfair dismissal claim because his continuity of service had been broken by the original dismissal.

The EAT rejected the employer's submission. The decision to reinstate meant that as a matter of contract Kirkpatrick was regarded as not having been dismissed. To hold otherwise would allow employers to dismiss employees (for example prior to a redundancy), reinstate them and then claim they had no service upon which their redundancy pay could be based. *London Probation Board v Kirkpatrick EAT/0544/04 ([2005] IRLR 443)*.

Employers cannot avoid their obligations to reinstate or re-engage simply by showing that they have already hired a replacement. When deciding whether to order the re-employment of unfairly dismissed employees, the tribunal has to make a provisional assessment of the practicability of the employer complying with the order. A final decision is only made if the employer refuses to comply (*Port of London Authority v Payne and Others [1994] IRLR 9*). The usual test is whether, despite the dismissal, the fundamental relationship of **trust and confidence has broken down**. In the case of *Cruikshank v LB Richmond [1999]* (unreported), the fact that the employee had made allegations about the employer while presenting his tribunal claim was not enough to show that this fundamental relationship had been destroyed. However, if a tribunal has already found that the employee was partly responsible for the dismissal it is very unlikely to order re-engagement.

In *Abimbola v Central and North West London NHS Foundation Trust UKEAT/0452/08* a psychiatric nurse was dismissed for gross misconduct after allegedly holding an agitated patient in a headlock. His claim for unfair dismissal was successful and an employment tribunal ordered that he be reinstated. The employer did not wish to have the employee back and appealed to the EAT. The EAT noted that employment tribunals have a wide discretion on reinstatement but must take into account three factors under section 116(1), *Employment Rights Act 1996*: (a) whether the claimant wants to be reinstated, (b) whether it is practicable for the employer to reinstate, and (c) where the claimant caused or contributed to his dismissal, whether it would be just. The loss of mutual trust and confidence could make it not practicable for the employer to reinstate, and on the facts of this case, the reinstatement order was overturned.

Compensation

Compensation has two main elements — a **basic award** and a **compensatory award**.

The basic award depends on length of employment and age prior to dismissal. The government decided to keep the age bands after the age equality laws came into place, despite expectations that they would be abolished. However, it did remove the upper age limit and the "tapering provisions" that reduced compensation for employees over the age of 64.

The basic award is calculated as a number of "weeks' pay" according to age and length of service, as follows:

◆ aged **under 22** — half a week's pay for each complete year worked under this age;

◆ aged **22 to 40** — one week's pay for each complete year worked between these ages; and

◆ aged **41 and over** — one and a half weeks' pay for each complete year worked from this age onwards.

The **"week's pay"** is capped at the statutory maximum of £380 (2010-11). It is based on **gross pay** and, where earnings are irregular, is averaged over a 12-week period. However, **overtime** will only be taken into account if there is a contractual obligation on the employer to offer it and on the employee to work it (*British Coal v Cheesbough [1990] IRLR 148*).

The "week's pay" cannot be calculated at less than the national minimum wage, even if the employee was not receiving it (*Paggetti v Cobb EAT/136/01 ([2002] IRLR 861)*).

The **maximum number of years of work** that can be taken into account is 20. This makes the maximum basic award £10,500.

In cases of **dismissal for trade union duties and activities**, for carrying out the duties of a health and safety rep, an employee rep, a rep for the purposes of the *Working Time Regulations*, or of a trustee of a pension scheme, the minimum basic award is **£4,700** (2009-10). There may also be an entitlement to an additional award (see below).

If the dismissal is automatically unfair under the dispute resolution procedures or age equality regulations, there is a minimum basic award of four weeks' pay.

The **compensatory award** (section 123, ERA 96) is based on any loss sustained as a result of the dismissal, although the tribunal has the discretion to award an amount that it considers "just and equitable". It can include:

◆ expenses incurred by reason of the dismissal;

◆ loss of wages;

◆ loss of pension rights;

◆ loss of accrued statutory protection (normally given a notional value of around £300);

◆ cost to employee of time and effort in seeking new work (e.g. travel to interviews); and

◆ future loss (the length of period claimed should reflect the ease with which the employee can find alternative work in their chosen profession — six months out of work is typical, but can be significantly longer especially if economic conditions are poor).

If the claimant has not found alternative work quickly, the largest part of his or her compensation claim is likely to be for actual and projected loss of earnings. Employees working in some sectors may also be able to claim extended loss of earnings for being stigmatised for having brought a claim against their employer.

The case of *Chagger v Abbey National PLC & another [2009] EWCA Civ 1202; [2010] IRLR 47* concerned a man of Indian ethnic origin, who had been dismissed for redundancy. Mr Chagger's allegation that the employer's redundancy scoring system discriminated against him on the grounds of his race, was upheld. On appeal, reviewing the loss of earnings awarded, the Court of Appeal noted that Mr Chagger had unsuccessfully applied for 111 jobs and that it had been assessed that he would never again find employment in the financial services industry.

The Court of Appeal rejected the employer's argument that Mr Chagger's loss of earnings should not be calculated on the basis of the rest of his working life. The court found that Mr Chagger would only have left Abbey National to take up a similar or better paid job. The Court of Appeal decided that, in principle, claimants can claim compensation for stigma loss (normally by extending damages due under the head of loss of earnings).

Loss of pension rights amounts to more than just the money the employer would have paid into the pension fund. It is the amount of pension an individual would have been entitled to had it not been for the unfair dismissal (*Clancy v Cannock Chase Technical College [2001] IRLR 331*). If they were in a final salary scheme this is likely to be significant.

A claimant can only recover losses that are attributable to the employer's actions. A hospital consultant was not entitled to recover earnings from private work he took on externally because these were not earnings he was entitled to under his contract with the NHS Trust.

And the EAT, in the case of *Schlesinger v Swindon & Marlborough NHS Trust EAT/0072/04*, held that even if the dismissed employee could establish that his additional earnings were dependent on the existence of his substantive post, he could not claim for the loss.

It is not possible to claim for **injury to feelings** in unfair dismissal cases following the ruling by the House of Lords in the case of *Dunnachie v Kingston upon Hull City Council [2004] UKHL 36 ([2004] IRLR 727)*.

An example of a future unanticipated loss comes from a case taken against Strathclyde Buses:

Unfairly dismissed employees who were required to sell shares allocated under a share-option scheme were able to claim for the fact that the value of the shares rose after their dismissal but prior to the tribunal hearing. *Leonard v Strathclyde Buses [1998] IRLR 693.*

Employees have an obligation to **"mitigate (lessen) their losses"** by, principally, looking for alternative work. In order to be able to evidence the efforts that they've made, employees litigating against their former employer should keep a job-search diary (i.e. record where, and in what publications, they've looked for work together with details of applications made). Of course, if an individual successfully obtains new employment, their overall compensation entitlement will normally be correspondingly reduced.

The case of *Norton Tool Company Limited v Tewson [1972] ICR 501* established that where an employer dismisses an employee without notice, the employee need not give credit in unfair dismissal compensation for sums earned from a new job, during the notice period. However, the situation is different with claims for wrongful dismissal (i.e. a breach of contract by not giving notice) and also constructive dismissal (i.e. where an employee resigns).

In the situation where an employee has been constructively dismissed, and goes on to find new work during his or her notice period, s/he is not entitled to double-recover (i.e. s/he cannot claim compensation for the entire notice period and must account for his or her additional earnings): *Stuart Peters Ltd v Bell [2009] EWCA Civ 938*.

When looking for alternative work an employee should try to replicate their earnings in their previous job. However, they will not lose compensation if they were unable to achieve these earnings or could not get the same level of employment benefits, such as a comparable pension scheme.

The tribunal will take account of any earnings they have achieved. However, it will not look at **earnings from a second job** an employee already had prior to the dismissal.

An employee may be able to show mitigation in other ways. For example, in the case of *Orthet v Vince-Cain EAT/0801/03 ([2004] IRLR 857)*, the EAT ruled that a dismissed employee had mitigated her loss by attending a university course, since it was unlikely that she would get a comparable new job to the one she had lost without further qualifications.

The **burden of proof** that the employee has failed to mitigate their losses rests with the employer (*Fyfe v Scientific Furnishings [1989] IRLR 331*). An unreasonable refusal of an offer of re-employment can amount to a failure to mitigate. The tribunal will consider whether the employee acted unreasonably in refusing the offer, taking into account all the circumstances (*Wilding v BT [2002] EWCA Civ 349 ([2002] IRLR 524)*).

Any earnings in the period between the dismissal and the tribunal hearing will be taken into account in assessing the compensatory loss. This means that if the employee gets higher-paid work, there is no claim for loss of earnings. However, it they get but then lose a better-paid job before the date of the tribunal hearing, the loss of wages can be taken into account. What cannot be claimed is for any period of unemployment that the tribunal assesses is due to the employee's incapacity rather than due to the dismissal.

In the case of an employee who had been unable to work due to ill-health as a result of an unfair dismissal, the tribunal was entitled to award compensation for whatever period it decided the employee was out of work as a consequence of the dismissal (*Devine v Designer Flowers [1993] IRLR 517*).

In *Adey-Jones v O'Dowd UKEAT/0098/08*, a care home worker with 17 years' service was unfairly dismissed after having been accused (without proof) of stealing from a resident, Ms O'Dowd struggled to hold down a subsequent job due to poor health partly (but not wholly) brought on by her dismissal. Ms O'Dowd won a claim in the tribunal but the amount of her compensatory award was disputed. The EAT ruled that Ms O'Dowd should have received compensation from her former employer which reflected the level of responsibility that the employer bore. In other words compensatory awards should not be calculated on an "all or nothing" basis.

> If the employee has been unfairly dismissed without notice pay, they do not have to give credit for any earnings during what would have been their notice period (*Voith Turbo v Stowe EAT/0675/04 ([2005] IRLR 228*). However, they are only entitled to be compensated for the amount they would have earned had they not been dismissed:

Nanny Ana Burlo was dismissed after a row about a pay rise and was told she had to work her notice. During the notice period she was involved in a car accident and was unable to work for four months, after which her employers told her she would not be required to work her notice. Her contract only entitled her to statutory sick pay (SSP). Burlo won her claims for unfair and wrongful dismissal and a tribunal awarded her full pay for her eight-week contractual notice period. But the Court of Appeal said that she was only entitled to compensation equivalent to SSP for her eight weeks' notice because that is all she would have received had she not been dismissed. *Burlo v Langley [2006] EWCA Civ 1779 ([2007] IRLR 145).*

> The **maximum compensatory award** that can be made in most cases is **£65,300** (2010-11). However, there is no maximum in cases of dismissal for health and safety reasons or for whistleblowing cases. If the dismissal is discriminatory then compensation for loss of earnings can be claimed under the relevant discrimination/equality act and there is no limit on the amount of compensation that can be awarded (see Chapter 6).
>
> If the tribunal thinks the employee's conduct **contributed** to the unfair dismissal it can reduce the compensatory award to reflect this (section 123(6), ERA 96). However, to justify a reduction in compensation, the conduct has either to be a breach of contract or conduct properly capable of being described as "perverse, foolish, bloody-minded or unreasonable in all the circumstances" (*Ceesay v Securicor Security EAT/0105/04*).
>
> In addition, the tribunal can reduce the amount of the basic award because of any conduct of the employee before their dismissal (section 22(2), ERA 96). If the employee has already received some money from the employer (for example an ex-gratia payment) paid as a consequence of the dismissal, the amount already paid would be deducted from the compensation.
>
> If money has been paid by a permanent health scheme, where only

the employer had made contributions, that too can be taken into account in assessing the compensation (*Atos Origin IT Services UK v Haddock EAT/0100/04 ([2005] IRLR 20)*). Employment and Support Allowance paid to the employee can also be taken into account (*Morgans v Alpha Plus Security EAT/0438/04*).

Compensation can also be reduced to reflect a finding on the facts that there was a chance that, even if a fair procedure had been followed, the employee would have been dismissed. This is known as a **Polkey reduction**. The upper limit is applied after any such reduction (*Walter Braund v Murray [1991] IRLR 100*). Compensation cannot be reduced to take account of the size of the employer. Small employers cannot use the argument that they have fewer resources to avoid paying the level of compensation that reflects the employee's loss.

Compensation can be increased or decreased because of the employer's (or employee's) failure to follow the ACAS Code of Practice. The amount awarded can be increased or decreased by up to 25%: new Section 207A, *Employment Rights Act 1996*.

Jobseeker's Allowance is normally offset against the compensatory award, however, incapacity benefit is not automatically deducted (*Sheffield Forgemasters International Ltd v Fox UKEAT/0143/08/MAA*).

Redundancy payments (*Digital Equipment v Clements [1998] IRLR 134*) are offset against the compensatory award, but only if the tribunal finds that there was a redundancy. In the case of *Boorman v Allmakes [1995] IRLR 553*, the employers terminated Boorman's employment, paying him an ex-gratia payment, which was said to incorporate statutory redundancy pay. However, the tribunal found there had been no redundancy, therefore the ex-gratia payment was not offset.

An **additional award** applies in trade union membership (or non-membership) cases and in cases of unlawful discrimination and dismissal for health and safety reasons where the employee asked for reinstatement or re-engagement but the employer refused to comply with the tribunal order. It gives between 26 weeks' and 52 weeks' pay. Section 160 of TULRCA gives the tribunal power to order that the compensation award be paid by the union instead of the employer in cases where the tribunal decides that the union induced the employer to dismiss.

If the sum awarded remains **unpaid 42 days after** the tribunal decision, interest is payable on amounts outstanding. In cases where the employer is insolvent and unable to pay compensation, the secretary of state for Department for Business, Innovation and Skills (BIS) assumes responsibility, but only for some of the money due.

The right to payment from the secretary of state covers basic awards for unfair dismissal, arrears of pay (to a maximum of eight weeks) and holiday pay (six weeks maximum). But in these cases a "week's pay" is calculated as for the basic award for unfair dismissal with a maximum of **£380** (2010-11). The employee receives a net sum after tax and other deductions (*Titchener v Secretary of State for Trade and Industry [2002] IRLR 195*).

Contractual layoff pay is not payable by the secretary of state as it does not come under the definition of pay, according to the case of *Benson v Secretary of State EAT/633/02 ([2003] IRLR 748).* A payment made by the secretary of state **breaks continuity**. Even if employees subsequently transfer to a new employer, they will have lost their right to count previous service. If the secretary of state fails to make any payment a claim should be submitted to a tribunal **within three months**. If any other money is due from the employer it is dealt with either as a priority debt or an unsecured debt.

An important ruling by the European Court of Justice may mean that the current system for dealing with money due to employees in insolvency is unlawful and may need to be changed. Although the case is based on Spanish law, the basic rules are the same. Under Spanish law, like UK law, employees can only claim partial compensation when their employer is insolvent. The ECJ held that this rule is in breach of equal treatment laws (*Rodriguez Caballero v Fondo de Garantia Salarial [2004] EWCA Civ 1657 ([2003] IRLR 115)).*

A payment received as compensation for unfair dismissal under a compromise agreement is **tax free** up to £30,000, even if the employee is reinstated, where it is for loss of the job rather than payment for services (*HM Inspector of Taxes v Clayton [2005] IRLR 108).*

Wrongful dismissal

Employees who do not meet the qualifying conditions for unfair dismissal rights, usually because they have not worked for at least a year and whose dismissal is not "automatically unfair", may be able to claim wrongful dismissal or seek an injunction. As a minimum, a person who shows that they have been wrongfully dismissed will receive compensation at least equal to the pay they would have received had the employer lawfully dismissed them.

A wrongful dismissal is one in **breach of a contract** and generally means dismissal without proper notice. Usually the contract will specify the notice that the employer and the employee must give to end the contract. Employees who are wrongfully dismissed without proper notice can take a claim for any rights they would have had during the period of the notice, according to the Court of Appeal in the case of *Silvey v Pendragon [2001] EWCA Civ 784 ([2001] IRLR 685)*.

Where employees have the benefit of a contractual entitlement to a disciplinary or appraisal procedure they will be entitled to be paid for the time it would have taken to operate the procedure where the employer, in breach of contract, had not done this. Dismissing in breach of procedure, so that the timing means the employee does not have enough service to claim unfair dismissal, may give the employee the right to claim monetary damages for wrongful dismissal.

For employees on **high earnings** there could be circumstances where a claim for wrongful dismissal would yield a higher level of compensation because, unlike claims for unfair dismissal, there is no maximum limit. However, the **maximum** an employment tribunal can award for breach of contract claims is **£25,000** so in those cases, the claim should be brought in the civil courts.

Additionally, if an employee has a fixed-term contract they may be able to claim damages equivalent to the pay they would have received to the end of the contract if there is no provision in the contract to terminate it early. Employees who have a contract clause stating that their pay will be reviewed annually may have their damages assessed to take account of future pay increases they might have had, if they had not been wrongfully dismissed (*Clark v BET [1997] IRLR 348*).

In a breach of contract claim, an employee has a duty to **mitigate (lessen)** their loss. This includes a claim for notice pay. If the employee has been dismissed this means that they must make reasonable efforts to find alternative work. This is the case even if there is a contractual term that allows the employer to make a payment in lieu of notice.

Mr Rowley was entitled to six months' notice. He was dismissed (unjustifiably as the tribunal found) and found another job around five weeks later. He claimed wrongful dismissal and argued that he should be entitled to the balance of the six months' notice. But the Court of Appeal rejected his claim. It held that the PILON clause gave the employer the right to make a payment in lieu if it chose — it did not give Rowley an automatic right to the payment. They then dismissed him in breach of contract and his claim was therefore one for damages for breach of contract, in which a claimant has a duty to mitigate his or her losses. *Cerberus Software v Rowley [2001] EWCA Civ 78 ([2001] IRLR 160)*.

Following Ms Ridley's unfair dismissal she found new work as a self-employed TV journalist. Initially she was able to produce two shows a week (for a period of thirty weeks) but thereafter she only had one show a week to produce. When she produced two shows a week, she earned more than she had done when she was employed — but when she only produced one show a week, she earned less. When the tribunal came to award compensation it decided that Ms Ridley did not have to give credit for the excess earnings in the first 30 weeks of her work. The employer appealed but the EAT decided that it was up to the tribunal to calculate compensation in a way which it considers just and equitable. This may entail looking at the whole period, adding up all the lost earnings and deducting all sums earned — or it may entail drawing a line between past and future losses. *Islam Channel Ltd v Ridley UKEAT/0083/09*.

Injunction

In some cases it may be possible to seek an injunction to **stop the employer dismissing**. Anyone contemplating this course of action would need to seek **expert advice** before proceeding. The general rule is that the court will grant an injunction to order the employer to revoke a dismissal where it is believed that there is continued mutual trust and confidence between employer and employee and monetary damages would not be an adequate remedy.

More information: See the LRD booklets *Disciplinary and grievance procedures* (£4.20) and *Unfair dismissal — a legal guide* (£5.10). LRD's *Workplace Report* has quarterly updates on dismissal law.

11. Redundancy

What is redundancy?

An employee is dismissed for redundancy, and may be entitled to redundancy pay, if either of the following occurs (section 139 of the *Employment Rights Act 1996* (ERA 96)):

◆ the employer has **ceased, or intends to cease, to carry on the business** for which the employee was employed, or to carry on that business in the place where the employee was employed; or

◆ the **requirements of the business for employees to carry out work of a particular kind**, or to carry it out in **the place** in which they are employed, have ceased or diminished or are expected to cease or diminish.

For collective consultation purposes only, there is a different definition of "redundancy" (see below).

A redundancy can therefore occur where the workforce is reorganised and there is less work; when changes in conditions mean that the old job is quite different from the new one; where the business relocates, or when an employer decides to put work out to contract.

The test for redundancy is whether the employer requires **fewer (or no) workers** to do work of a particular kind and not just whether the work itself has ceased or diminished. The expiry of a fixed-term contract can also amount to redundancy.

A job change as a result of reorganisation does not necessarily amount to redundancy — it depends on the nature of the work the employee is required to do before and after. The test is always whether the statutory definition (above) has been met.

The hospital where Dr Shawkat worked decided to merge two departments. As a result Dr Shawkat was required to carry out cardiac surgery as well as thoracic surgery. He argued that he had been made redundant because the result was that he would be required to do less thoracic surgery. The Court of Appeal disagreed and said that although the reorganisation had changed Dr Shawkat's work there had been no cessation or diminution of the requirement for the hospital to carry out thoracic work and therefore the definition of redundancy had not been met . *Shawkat v Nottingham City Hospital [2001] EWCA Civ 954 ([2001] IRLR 555).*

A general manager of a hotel was not made redundant when a new area manager post was created because the hotel group still had a requirement for the same work to be done. In fact, the EAT held, the work had increased. However, the manager was unfairly dismissed because his employer had failed to show a fair reason for dismissal (*Corus & Regal Hotels v Wilkinson EAT/0102/03*).

The employer does not have to show that there is any **economic justification** for the decision to make redundancies or that there are financial problems that have led to the reduction of work (*Polyflor v Old EAT/0482/02*). If an employee has always worked in one place and is no longer required to work in that place this can be a redundancy even if there is a **"mobility clause"** in their contract saying that they can be required to work in other locations (*High Table Ltd v Horst [1997] EWCA Civ 2000 ([1997] IRLR 513)*). But in the case of *Home Office v Evans & Laidlaw [2007] EWCA Civ 1089* the Court of Appeal said the Home Office **could** invoke a mobility clause in order to avoid redundancies.

It is very rare to be able to challenge an employer's decision to make redundancies because a tribunal will not generally interfere in what it considers are "business decisions". However, a redundancy may be unfair because of the selection process or the procedure, including whether there was adequate consultation and an offer of alternative work (see "Unfair redundancy" below). The law does not treat voluntary and compulsory redundancies differently — either will be a dismissal for redundancy reasons.

Consultation

An employer has a legal obligation to consult over **collective redundancies** if it proposes to dismiss as redundant **20 or more employees** at one establishment **within a 90-day period**. The law was introduced by the *Collective Redundancies and Transfer of Undertakings (Protection of Employment) (Amendment) Regulations 1995* and is set out in Chapter II (section 188 onwards) of the *Trade Union and Labour Relations (Consolidation) Act 1992* (TULRCA). In Northern Ireland they are contained in Part XIII of the *Employment Rights (Northern Ireland) Order 1996* (article 216 onwards).

The TURLCA provisions on collective redundancies do not apply to **Crown employees** (those working for a government department or carrying out its functions). However, civil servants will have consultation rights under their civil service redundancy policy.

However, even if there is no duty to consult over collective redundancies because fewer than 20 employees are affected, the employer must consult with any individuals who are at risk of redundancy. A **failure to consult an individual** at risk of redundancy can make their dismissal unfair. This is the case even on the **expiry of a fixed-term contract** (*University of Glasgow v Donaldson and McAnally EAT/951/94*).

To calculate whether the proposed number of redundancies is 20 or more, you can only take account of the numbers **employed in that establishment**. According to the ECJ, an "establishment" is the unit to which workers are assigned to carry out their duties, whether there is a separate management or not (*Rockfon v Specialarbejderforbundet i Danmark C-449/93 [1996] IRLR 168*).

In the case of *MSF v Refuge Assurance plc & another EAT/1371/99 ([2002] IRLR 324)*, the EAT held that field staff in an insurance company were assigned to their local branch office; therefore, the duty to consult would only arise if 20 or more redundancies were proposed within one office.

However, in the case of *Mills & Allen v Bulwich EAT/154/99*, the EAT held that the direct sales team nationwide was one establishment, even though sales staff worked out of different offices around the country. Therefore, when it proposed 24 redundancies nationwide, it had a duty to consult the union. It does not matter if in the end fewer than 20 employees will be made redundant because some employees would be offered alternative employment — the obligation to consult still exists:

Sarah Hardy was one of 26 employees who were told that they would be made redundant when their office was closed. Her employer claimed that because it expected to redeploy most of the staff and only 12 would be made redundant, the collective consultation requirements did not apply. The EAT rejected that argument. It held that an employer "proposes to dismiss" if it proposes to withdraw the existing contracts. Even though new jobs would be offered to some staff they would be at a different location and involve different duties. This amounted to a proposal to dismiss and the duty to consult did arise. *Hardy v Tourism South East UKEAT/0931/04 ([2005] IRLR 242.*

The **definition of redundancy** for the purposes of collective consultation is different from the statutory definition under the ERA 96 given above. It is "a dismissal for a reason not related to the individual concerned".

This means that the union may have a right to consultation over dismissals even if they do not meet the definition of redundancy under the ERA.

In the case of *GMB v Man Truck and Bus UK Ltd EAT/971/99 ([2000] IRLR 636)*, the EAT held that the dismissal of employees and their **re-engagement on new terms and conditions** gave rise to collective redundancy consultation rights, even though there was no proposed reduction in the number of employees.

Collective consultation

Where there is a proposal to dismiss 20 or more employees for redundancy the employer must consult the **appropriate representatives** of any employees likely to be made redundant.

Where the **union is recognised** the appropriate representatives are representatives of the union(s). Trade union representatives have the right to **paid time off** to take part in consultation.

Consultation must be with all recognised unions even if members of one union will not be affected (*Governing Body NI Hotel and Catering College v NATFHE [1995] IRLR 83*).

Where there is no recognised union the appropriate representatives can be either:

◆ representatives of affected employees appointed or elected generally for consultation and information purposes; or
◆ employee representatives elected by affected employees **solely for the purpose** of redundancy consultation.

The employer must invite employees likely to be made redundant to elect employee representatives "long enough before the time when the consultation is required" and must comply with the rules set out in section 188A of TULRCA.

Employee representatives elected for the purposes of redundancy consultation have **statutory protection against dismissal**. The protection from any detrimental action extends to representatives and candidates for election.

Employee representatives are also entitled to reasonable time off to perform their functions as reps or candidates. They must be allowed **access to employees** and must be provided with accommodation and other **appropriate facilities**.

When does consultation begin?

Consultation must take place "in good time". If **100 or more employees** at one establishment are to be dismissed, consultation must begin at least 90 days before the redundancies take effect. If the numbers involved are **more than 20 but less than 100** the minimum consultation period is reduced to **30 days**.

But these are the **minimum** periods laid down by law. Sometimes employers will need to start consultation earlier than that; they should not wait until the statutory time clock starts ticking (*Elkouil v Coney Island EAT/0520/00 ([2002] IRLR 174)*).

Even if the employer is looking at two options and only one of them involves redundancies, there is still an obligation to consult (*Scotch Premier Meat v Burns [2000] IRLR 639*).

Consultation must take place when **proposals are still at a "formative stage"** (i.e. before decisions have been taken): this is so that the union can genuinely exercise its influence and has time to respond to proposals/make counter-suggestions (*Amicus v Nissan Motor Manufacturing (UK) Ltd EAT/0184/05*). Employers should consult as soon as redundancies are contemplated.

Irmtraud Junk was employed as a care assistant by a company that employed around 430 people providing domestic care services. The company began insolvency proceedings and all employees were notified that their employment would terminate in three months, which was the end of the collective consultation period. The ECJ held that the obligation to consult arises before the employer has made a decision to terminate the contracts of employment, while the employer is still "contemplating". Notifying an employee that their contract of employment has been terminated, albeit at the end of notice, means that a decision has already been made. By then it is too late to consult and this goes against the purpose of consultation, which is to avoid or reduce redundancies. *Junk v Kuhnel C-188/03 ([2005] IRLR 310.*

This important decision is also authority for the proposition that an employer cannot **give notice** of redundancy **before the consultation process has been completed**.

As a result of the introduction of the local government "single status" agreement at a local council, hundreds of employees were dismissed and re-engaged on less favourable terms. The dismissals amounted to redundancies, so there was an obligation for the council to consult the union.

Although there had been discussions with the union at an earlier stage, the employer had broken them off, and no consultation had taken place before the decision to dismiss was announced at a meeting.

The Court of Appeal held that the duty to consult arises before any decision to terminate contracts arises, because its aim is to avoid the need for dismissals.

As the tribunal had found that the announcement at the meeting simply confirmed a decision already taken, the obligation to consult had already arisen, and the council had failed to do so in breach of its duty (*UNISON v Leicestershire County Council [2006] EWCA Civ 825 ([2006] IRLR 810)*).

The case of *Akavan Erityisalojen Keskusliitto AEK ry and others v Fujitsu Siemens Computers Oy (C-44/08)* concerned a multinational company's decision to make redundancies. On 7 December 1999 the board of the parent company was asked to consider a proposal to cease operating a Finnish factory. On 14 December the board approved the plan. On 14 December a consultation exercise was also approved — which started on 20 December. The trade union complained that the decision about the factory had been taken before the "consultation" had started, and so the process was a sham.

The ECJ noted that the obligation to consult is triggered when an employer is contemplating or drawing up a plan for collective redundancies. It also arises when a group of undertakings adopts strategic decisions or changes in activities which compel the employer to contemplate or plan for collective redundancies.

The obligation on the employer to consult is triggered even if (as here) the decision on collective redundancies is made by an undertaking controlling the employer. Also, the time when consultation should start is not dependent on whether the employer is already able to supply to workers' representatives all the required information: employers can and must add to the information supplied during the consultation process.

The employer must also **notify the secretary of state** (in practice this is done by completing an HR1 form and sending it to the Redundancy Payments Office) of all proposed redundancies of 20 or more employees.

This notification must take place **before notice** of dismissal has been given to comply with the ECJ's decision in the *Junk* case above; the law was changed to reflect this (*Collective Redundancies (Amendment) Regulations 2006*).

The consultation process

Employers are obliged by law to consult about ways of:

◆ **avoiding dismissals**;
◆ **reducing the number** of employees to be dismissed; and
◆ **mitigating the consequences** of the dismissals.

Consultation should be undertaken "with a view to reaching agreement with the appropriate representatives" and the employer must consider representations and reply to them.

According to the EAT in the case of *UK Coal Mining Ltd v NUM & BACM UKEAT/0397/06*, an employer's obligation to consult with the unions to avoid redundancies **includes consultation over the reasons** for the proposed closure. This overrules previous case law.

Consultation must be real and not a "sham", according to an EAT decision which said that issuing redundancy notices by letter half an hour after a meeting with the unions had ended suggested that the consultation was not meaningful.

The representatives consulted must have **time to consider properly** any proposals put to them (*TGWU v Ledbury Preserves [1985] IRLR 412*). If an employer has already decided to make redundancies before consulting with reps and is not prepared to consider other options, this would not amount to genuine **meaningful consultation** (*Middlesbrough BC v T&G and UNISON EAT/26/00 ([2002] IRLR 332)*).

The Court of Session in Scotland, in the case of *King v Eaton [1996] IRLR 199*, held that the mere fact that the employer had meetings with the reps was not sufficient to establish that there had been fair consultation.

In the case of *Ferguson v Prestwick Circuits [1992] IRLR 266*, the employer said that previous experience suggested employees did not like consultation. This did not, according to the tribunal, absolve the employer of the obligation to consult.

Even if employers reasonably believe there is no alternative to redundancy, they must still consult; the employee may know something that alters the situation (*Heron v Citylink [1993] IRLR 372*).

In the case of *R v British Coal ex parte Price [1994] IRLR 72*, the High Court held that **fair consultation** must include:

◆ consultation when the proposals are still at a formative stage;
◆ adequate information on which to respond;
◆ adequate time in which to respond; and
◆ conscientious consideration of the response.

It also confirmed that the fact that there were **voluntary redundancies** did not invalidate the consultation.

Remedies for failure to consult

If employers fail or refuse to consult, a complaint can be made to a tribunal. This must be done by whoever should have been consulted — either the union or the employee representative. The tribunal can make a **protective award**, which is a sum of money paid to each affected employee.

The purpose of the award is not to compensate the employee for the loss they have suffered, but to provide a sanction against the employer for the failure to consult, according to the Court of Appeal in the case of *Susie Radin v GMB and others [2004] EWCA Civ 180 ([2004] IRLR 400)*.

The award can be up to 90 days' pay and the EAT has said that the tribunals should use this as a starting point and then decide whether there are circumstances to justify reducing it (*T&G v Morgan Platts EAT/0646/02*). This maximum applies even if the minimum consultation period was 30 days, as the EAT held in the following case:

A tribunal made a protective award of 80 days' pay to members of the T&G general union after their employer failed to consult over the proposed redundancy of 30-35 workers, but the employer argued that the award was too high. The mandatory period of consultation is 30 days if 20 to 99 redundancies are planned, or 90 days if the figure is 100 or more. However, the limitation of the protective award to 30 days' pay for fewer than 100 redundancies was removed in 1999.

The EAT held that a protective award of up to 90 days' pay can be awarded when fewer than 100 employees are to be made redundant. As the award is punitive and not compensatory, it relates to the seriousness of the employer's breach of its consultation duty and not the losses incurred by the workers. *Newage Transmission v TGWU EAT/0131/05.*

A tribunal should make a protective award unless the employer can show that there were **"special circumstances"** making it not reasonably practicable to consult, but that all reasonably practicable steps to comply were taken.

In a recent case where the question of what these special circumstances might amount to was examined, the EAT held that an employer could not escape the obligation to consult in good time by claiming that it did not have all the necessary information. If some information is available it must be consulted over (*GMB and Amicus v Beloit Walmsley EAT/1094/02 ([2004] IRLR 18)*).

Insolvency does not by itself constitute special circumstances. For these circumstances to apply there has to be something out of the ordinary and insolvency does not come into that category, according to the EAT in the case of *Iron and Steel Trades Confederation v ASW Holdings EAT/0694/04 ([2004] IRLR 926)*).

The employer will still be liable to pay the protective award even if its view was that consultation would have **made no difference** to the redundancies (*Sovereign Distribution Services v TGWU [1989] IRLR 334*). Even if the company goes into receivership this does not bring the award period to an end (*AEEU/GMB v Clydesdale Group [1995] IRLR 527*) nor does it allow for the award to be offset against any redundancy pay due.

Selection for redundancy

Where compulsory redundancies are to be made an employer will usually operate a formula for selecting employees. There may already be a **selection procedure** in place, but it is rare that this would have been incorporated into an employee's contract and so is unlikely to be legally binding.

The selection criteria chosen must be **objective and fairly applied** but the employer has a wide discretion to decide what the criteria will be. There is little scope to challenge the selection criteria or process as long as they would be considered "reasonable" by a tribunal. However, they **must not be discriminatory**.

If the criteria or the process discriminates on the grounds of sex, race, disability, sexual orientation, religion or belief or age, then it can be challenged under the appropriate discrimination legislation (see Chapter 6). In cases of indirect discrimination, this may be lawful if the employer can show that it was objectively justified (*Kachelmann v Bankhaus Hermann Lampe C-322/98 ([2001] IRLR 49)*).

It is also unlawful to select an individual for redundancy on grounds of their **trade union membership or activities**. Selection of individuals because they are **part-time workers** or **fixed-term employees** is also unlawful — unless the employer can show this to be "objectively justified" (see "Part-time workers" in Chapter 2).

Section 105 of the *Employment Rights Act 1996* also specifies a number of other reasons for selection that would make a redundancy **automatically unfair** (see "Unfair redundancy" below). These include exercising particular employment rights — for example, it would be automatically unfair to dismiss an employee for redundancy because they had previously made a request for flexible working.

The selection of two employees because they had been leading **strike activists** was an automatically unfair dismissal (*Britool v Roberts [1993] IRLR 481*), as was selecting someone for redundancy because they spent too much time on union activities even though the employer was not motivated to get rid of the employee because of their union activities (*Dundon v GPT [1995] IRLR 403*).

Equally, an employer cannot assess an employee based on skills demonstrated while carrying out their work as a **safety rep** (*Smiths Industries v Rawlings [1996] IRLR 656*). An employee's duties as a trade union or safety rep should neither prejudice nor advantage a redundancy selection.

However, a union rep who was given an alternative job to accommodate his trade union duties was not unfairly dismissed when he was selected for redundancy from that role even though there was still a need for work in his original post (*O'Dea v ISC Chemicals [1995] IRLR 599*).

Employers can use **sickness absence** as a criterion for selection but should consider whether adjustments need to be made in the case of disabled workers.

An employer may ask for **volunteers** first and would not need to apply the selection procedure to them, but a failure to ask for volunteers first does not make compulsory redundancies unfair (*Rogers and others v Vosper Thornycroft [1989] IRLR 82*).

Voluntary redundancies are treated as dismissals in the same way as compulsory redundancies provided there is a genuine redundancy situation. However, someone choosing to take voluntary retirement should take care — in the case of *Birch & another v University of Liverpool [1985] IRLR 165*, the Court of Appeal held that employees who accepted early retirement in the face of the threat of compulsory redundancy had terminated their contracts by mutual consent.

Many agreed redundancy procedures use the criterion of **last in, first out** (LIFO), which protects employees with longer service from being selected before those with shorter service. LIFO agreements have been questioned because they have the potential to discriminate.

Take, for example, a company that previously had no black employees but as a result of a new equality policy took positive steps to recruit. Soon afterwards, it declares redundancies. The black workers, as the most recent recruits, would fall foul of a LIFO rule, meaning that the redundancies would have a greater impact on black workers than on white workers.

Using LIFO as a criterion for selection may also discriminate on grounds of age, as it will tend to favour older employees (who are more likely to have longer service). But an employer may be able to justify this for the purpose of the age regulations, on the grounds of retaining those employees with the most skills and experience.

When claims based on this type of discriminatory outcome have come before the courts, there have been mixed views on whether the procedure is unlawful. Some tribunals have upheld LIFO selection; others have not. The clearest interpretations of the law seem to suggest that having LIFO as one criterion for selection is acceptable, but having it as the sole criterion is more open to challenge.

However, the EAT ruled in the case of *Messrs Blatchfords Solicitors v Berger EAT/207/00* that, in a situation where an employer needed to cut the number of its cashiers from three to one, having LIFO as the sole criterion did not make the dismissals unfair.

An unusual case involved knitwear company Pringle which had a LIFO procedure but was not following it in selecting for redundancy. The Court of Session in Scotland ruled that a LIFO procedure was part of the employees' individual contracts and could therefore be enforced by employees in breach-of-contract claims.

The Court took the unusual step of granting an injunction to stop the employers implementing the redundancy in breach of the contractual procedure. Injunctions against employers in these circumstances are relatively rare, but the Court said that there was no evidence that "trust and confidence" (two essential items in the employment relationship) had gone, and that compelling the employer to continue to employ those selected for redundancy in breach of the procedure was therefore possible. *Anderson v Pringle of Scotland [1998] IRLR 64.*

In *Rolls-Royce v Unite [2009] EWCA Civ 387* the union and employer had agreed a method of redundancy selection which recognised an individual's length of service. When the employer later sought to drop the length of service criterion (on the purported basis that it was discriminatory on the grounds of age) the union mounted a legal challenge.

The Court of Appeal agreed with the union that rewarding long service by employees in a redundancy selection process was held to be reasonable. Specifically, the policy was justified as a "legitimate employment policy" and "labour market objective" under Article 6 of the Equal Treatment Framework Directive. Accordingly the length of service bonus was a proportionate means of achieving a legitimate aim — to reward loyalty and maintain a stable workforce.

The Court of Appeal also went on to decide that a length of service criterion is capable of being a benefit. Specifically, a length of service criterion of more than five years does reasonably fulfil a business need, again, that of having a loyal and stable workforce.

In the case of *Alexander and Hatherley v Bridgen Enterprises Ltd EAT/0107/06 ([2006] IRLR 422)*, the EAT held that the employer must send the employee a written statement informing them that they are considering dismissing them on grounds of redundancy and inviting them to the meeting.

If they were selected using selection criteria then before the meeting the employer must provide the employee with the selection criteria and their mark, so that they have the opportunity to challenge it.

However, they do not need to provide the "threshold score" or the scores of other employees. In this case the scores had not been provided until after the decision had been made so the dismissals were automatically unfair for a failure to comply with the statutory procedures and the employees were awarded four weeks' pay.

However, they were not unfair on other grounds and the EAT upheld the tribunal's decision not to make a compensatory award because the claimants would have been dismissed anyway if a fair procedure had been followed.

In the case of *British Aerospace v Green [1995] IRLR 433*, the Court of Appeal also held that there was no legal obligation on employers to disclose the assessments of employees not selected.

Alternative work

An employer should consider offering **suitable alternative work** if it is available and this might include considering whether employment is available in **other companies within the same group**. Employers must offer alternative work, if available, to employees who are on **maternity or adoption leave**.

If the employer does not consider offering suitable alternative employment this may make redundancy unfair. Offers of suitable alternative employment are covered by section 141 of the ERA 96. This states that any such offer must be made **before the old contract ends** and begin **within four weeks** of the date of the end of the original employment.

It must be the same as, or not substantially different from, the previous work and must be suitable for the employee. The employee is not obliged to accept the alternative but if they **unreasonably refuse** it they will **lose their entitlement to redundancy pay**.

The issue of whether work is suitable is considered separately from whether an employee is acting reasonably in refusing it, although there may be some overlap.

Work would normally be considered unsuitable if it involved changes in pay, travelling time, skills and experience or status while the reasonableness of the refusal may relate more to personal circumstances such as domestic arrangements, health and housing.

Mr Ruse was made redundant and offered suitable alternative work at the same grade but in a post which he saw as of lower status. The EAT accepted this gave him the right to reject the offer and seek redundancy pay. *Cambridge Co-op v Ruse [1993] IRLR 156.*

Mr Denton was offered an alternative job that would have required him to work in a dusty environment. Even though the work was suitable, he had an obsession with the potential health hazards of air-borne dust since close relatives had died from respiratory infections. The tribunal said that even though his fears were unfounded, they were genuine and this made his refusal reasonable. *Denton v Neepsend [1976] IRLR 164 .*

As part of a redundancy exercise, Ms Ward was offered two new posts (both of which she rejected). The employer offered her amended terms for one of the posts — which Ms Ward again rejected and instead sought a redundancy payment (which the employer declined to pay). Even though the EAT considered that the third post probably just amounted to a suitable alternative, it also took into account the circumstances in which the offer was made. The EAT decided that because the employer's failings had let to a deterioration in the relationship between the parties, Ms Ward's refusal of the third post was reasonable. *Commission for Healthcare Audit & Inspection v Ward UKEAT/0579/07/JOJ.*

Employees have the right to a **statutory trial period of four weeks** in the new job. These four weeks are defined as calendar, not working weeks (*Benton v Sanderson Kayser [1989] IRLR 19*).

The employer should give the worker a written copy of the agreement specifying the terms and conditions of the new work and the date of termination of the trial period (section 138, ERA 96). If an employer refuses to offer a trial period the employee can claim unfair dismissal (*Elliot v Richard Stump [1987] IRLR 215*). If the employee agrees to a trial period in the new job they will still be entitled to redundancy pay if the post proves not to be suitable as long as they **reject it within that trial period**. If they work beyond the four weeks they will lose the right to claim statutory redundancy pay.

Mr O'Hara accepted an offer of alternative work. He then decided it was unsuitable and wrote to his employer to that effect. However, he continued working. The EAT held that his letter did not amount to a notice to terminate his employment and since he had worked beyond the four weeks he had no right to redundancy pay. *Reality (White Arrow Express) Ltd v O'Hara EAT/0447/03.*

The trial period can be extended by agreement. If it is, the terms should be clear and state that the employee still has the right to a redundancy payment if the job proves unsuitable. If an employee refuses a trial period in an alternative job, it may make it harder to show that it was unsuitable — although this will depend on how different it is from their existing job.

Looking for work

While under notice of redundancy, employees have the right to **reasonable time off** with pay during working hours to look for alternative work, provided that they meet the qualifying conditions (see below).

There is no fixed amount of time off that employers should give. If an employer refuses time off, or payment for the time off, employees can make a claim to a tribunal that can order the employer to pay (section 52, ERA 96). However, the maximum an employer can be required to pay by a tribunal is 40% of weekly earnings. The complaint must be made within three months of the employer's refusal.

Qualifying for redundancy rights

To qualify for **statutory redundancy pay** and **time off** to look for work, employees must have been employed for two years by the date of dismissal, regardless of their hours of work.

Employees do not qualify for statutory redundancy pay if:

◆ they accept suitable alternative employment;
◆ they unreasonably refuse suitable alternative employment (see above);
◆ they are dismissed for misconduct (section 140, ERA 96); or
◆ they fail to comply with a notice of extension after a strike (section 143, ERA 96). This is where the employer has given notice to end employment; the employee takes part in a strike, and the employer submits a request to extend the employment by the number of days lost.

Crown employees are not entitled to statutory redundancy pay or time off. However, civil servants are entitled to better than statutory redundancy under their civil service redundancy scheme and to time off to look for work.

Employees on a **series of fixed-term contracts** may be entitled to redundancy pay at the expiry of a contract (*Pfaffinger v City of Liverpool Community College [1996] IRLR 508*). Employers can no longer get temporary employees to sign waiver clauses and so avoid paying them redundancy pay.

Employees will lose the right to claim statutory redundancy pay if they leave work before the redundancy notice is issued. But employees under notice of redundancy can agree with their employers to extend the notice, for example, in the hope of work picking up, without jeopardising redundancy entitlement (*Mowlem Northern v Watson [1990] IRLR 500*).

However, if an employee agrees to an earlier termination date, the three-month time limit for bringing an unfair dismissal claim will run from that date (*Palfrey v Transco plc EAT/0990/03 ([2004] IRLR 916)*).

The time limit for making a claim for redundancy pay is **six months** from the date when the contract ends.

Redundancy payment

Statutory redundancy pay is calculated by taking account of the employee's age and length of employment, and awarding a number of "weeks' pay" accordingly.

Starting at the relevant date and counting backwards, statutory redundancy pay is calculated as follows:

◆ half a week's pay for each year the employee was aged below 22;
◆ a week's pay for each year s/he was aged 22 to 40; and
◆ a week-and-a-half's pay for each year s/he was aged 41 or over.

These three age bands are almost identical to those that existed before the age equality regulations were introduced in October 2006.

It had been expected that the regulations would abolish the bands, but in March 2006 the government announced that they would be maintained. The only changes to the statutory scheme were to remove the upper and lower age limits of 65 and 18 for calculating statutory redundancy pay, and the tapering provisions which meant that employees aged over 64 received reduced payments.

The Department for Business, Innovation and Skills (BIS) provides an online "ready reckoner" for calculating statutory redundancy pay, available at: www.berr.gov.uk/whatwedo/employment/employment-legislation/employment-guidance/page33157.html. This includes a redundancy table for calculating the number of weeks' pay a redundant employee is entitled to.

The **maximum amount of a week's pay** that can be taken into account is currently £380 (2010-11) and the **maximum number of years** of employment that can be taken into account is 20. This makes the maximum statutory redundancy pay £11,400 (in 2010-11).

The level of redundancy pay depends on what the employee is earning at the time of the redundancy. An employee who has previously worked full-time but has transferred to part-time work has all of his/her redundancy pay calculated at the part-time rate and will not be credited for any of the full-time service (*Barry v Midland Bank [1998] IRLR 138*).

The employer must give the employee a written statement saying how redundancy pay is calculated (section 165, ERA 96) and must also inform the representative. Employers can be fined a small amount for failure to comply with this requirement.

Employers can offer **contractual redundancy pay** that is better than the statutory scheme. Any scheme that uses age-based or length of service-based calculations has the potential to be discriminatory under the *Employment Equality (Age) Regulations 2006* (EE(A)R), but there is an automatic exemption for schemes that are based on the statutory entitlement.

Under regulation 33 of EE(A)R an employer's redundancy scheme will not amount to age discrimination if it has amended the statutory scheme in any of the following ways:

◆ by increasing or removing the maximum amount of a week's pay;
◆ by multiplying the amount for each age band; or
◆ by multiplying the total amount by a figure of more than one.

For example, it is lawful for an employer to calculate redundancy payments based on one week's pay per year of service for under-22s, two weeks' pay for each year between the ages of 22 to 40 and three weeks' pay for each year when aged 41 and over, because this maintains the ratio of 0.5:1:1.5.

But it will be unlawful to base redundancy pay on a week's pay for the under-41s and two weeks' pay for those aged 41 and over, unless the employer can show that this is justified by a legitimate aim.

The employer can also base those payments on a week's actual pay rather than the statutory maximum of **£380** (2010-11 rate), and/or multiply the amount of weekly pay by some fixed amount.

An employer is free to come up with its own redundancy scheme — but if this scheme is based on different criteria from those in the statutory scheme, the employer will have to be able to objectively justify it if challenged.

If an employer has a policy that pays the **same for everyone** — so that every employee is entitled to a month's pay for each year of service, regardless of age, for example — there is no need to justify it, as there will be no age discrimination.

Unless the contractual scheme is expressly included or incorporated into the contract, it can be difficult to establish whether it is a **contractual entitlement**. In the case of *Albion Automotive v Walker EAT/415/00*, the EAT upheld the tribunal's reasoning that for a scheme to be contractual the following criteria must be met:

◆ the terms have been **drawn to the employees' attention** and are well-known;

◆ the terms have been followed for a **substantial period of time**;

◆ these have been followed on a **number of occasions**;

◆ payments were made **more or less automatically**;

◆ the policy as communicated to staff indicated that management **intended to be bound by it**;

◆ it was adopted by **agreement** with workplace representatives;

◆ its terms were **incorporated** into a written agreement;

◆ employees had a **reasonable expectation** that they would be applied.

But if the entitlement to a redundancy payment is clearly expressed, whether in the contract or some other document, the employer must pay it, according to the Court of Appeal:

Christopher Keeley had a written statement of employment terms, which set out his main terms of employment but made no reference to redundancy. However, the statement made reference to company handbooks where staff could obtain further information. The staff handbook had a section headed "Employee benefits and rights", which included the redundancy policy and stated: "Employees with two or more years' continuous service are entitled to receive an enhanced redundancy payment." Even though the whole handbook was not contractual, the Court of Appeal held that a written term "put in clear terms of entitlement" can be part of the contract, even if other terms in the same document are not. The court said that a redundancy entitlement is an important part of an employee's remuneration package, and this made the statement particularly "apt for incorporation", which meant that it was a contractual entitlement and Keeley was entitled to the enhanced pay. *Keeley v Fosroc International Ltd [2006] EWCA Civ 1277.*

If an employer has on previous occasions paid redundancy at an enhanced rate, but never included it in the terms of their contracts, there is no custom and practice to guarantee the right to the payment in a later round of redundancy (*Quinn v Calder Industrial Materials [1996] IRLR 126*).

It is also the case that where a redundancy pay scheme requires a decision on each occasion, it is not an incorporated term in the employee's contract.

The Court of Appeal held that a collective agreement containing a "no compulsory redundancy" clause did not make an employee's redundancy unfair. It found that the clause was "aspirational" only and was not a contractual entitlement (*Kaur v MG Rover [2004] EWCA Civ 1507 ([2005] IRLR 40)*). Employers cannot try to avoid paying contractual redundancy pay by dismissing employees for another reason instead.

Mr Jenvey was dismissed for asserting his statutory right to a written statement of his terms after his employer tried to reduce his hours. His employer argued that because they had dismissed him for another reason (albeit unfair) he had no right to redundancy pay. The High Court rejected the argument. It held that if an employer was intending to dismiss for redundancy (which it found it was in this case) it cannot dismiss for another reason without very good cause. It suggested the only likely such cause would be gross misconduct. *Jenvey v Australian Broadcasting Corp [2002] EWHC 927(QB) ([2002] IRLR 520).*

In determining entitlement to redundancy pay, employers cannot impose criteria that discriminate on unlawful grounds. A contractual redundancy scheme that excluded employees over state retirement age was discriminatory because it excluded more women than men and was unenforceable (*McKechnie v UBM [1991] IRLR 283*). In certain circumstances workers may also have redundancy pay offset against periodic occupational pension entitlement (section 158, ERA 96). The pay rights of employees on **annualised hours** contracts are sometimes called into question when the contract ends during the year of calculation.

In the case of *Ali v Christian Salvesen [1997] IRLR 17*, the Court of Appeal ruled that employees on annualised hours could not have their salary, for redundancy pay purposes, calculated to take account of the fact that they would have averaged more than 40 hours a week had their employment lasted the full year. For **local government employees** there is a separate statutory scheme, which is set out in the *Local Government (Early Termination of Employment) (Discretionary Compensation) (England and Wales) Regulations 2006* (which replaced the 2000 regulations). It allows for a maximum of 104 weeks' pay based on actual earnings and not the £380 maximum.

When the age regulations came into force, the government removed the option for employees aged over 50 to have years added to their pension entitlement instead. However, under regulation 52 of the Local Government Pension Scheme the employer still has the power to award added years (now up to 10 additional years). Redundancy pay (both statutory and contractual) is **tax free up to £30,000**. However, employees and reps should be aware that if a negotiated settlement is seen to include "emoluments" (such as wages or fees) it will be taxable — only a payment made in connection with termination of employment is tax free up to that limit.

Mr Delaney had a contractual right to 18 months' notice. His employers told him that they wanted to end his contract and, following negotiations, they agreed to pay him a lump sum of £75,000 "in compensation for the termination of his employment and loss of office". Delaney thought that this amounted to a redundancy and that the whole of the first £30,000 would be tax free. The Inland Revenue won a ruling in the High Court that it had the right to tax him on the whole amount. *Richardson (Inspector of Taxes) v Delaney [2001] IRLR 663.*

If the employer cannot pay redundancy compensation because of insolvency, it becomes payable, under section 182 of the ERA 96, by the secretary of state.

Unfair redundancy

There are circumstances in which redundancy is unfair and the employee can bring a claim for unfair dismissal. A redundancy dismissal is automatically unfair under section 105 of the ERA 96 if the individual has been selected because they have exercised rights or undertaken duties in relation to the following:

◆ jury service;
◆ leave for family reasons;
◆ refusal of Sunday work by a shop or betting worker;
◆ working time;
◆ trustees of occupational pension schemes;
◆ acting as or being elected as an employee representative for collective redundancy or TUPE purposes;
◆ protected disclosure;
◆ assertion of a relevant statutory right;
◆ national minimum wage;
◆ tax credits;
◆ flexible working;
◆ participating in official industrial action;
◆ transnational information and consultation of employees regulations (European Works Councils);
◆ part-time workers regulations;
◆ fixed-term employees regulations;
◆ European public limited-liability company regulations; and
◆ information and consultation of employees regulations.

In the above automatically unfair cases, the one-year service **qualifying condition does not apply**.

A redundancy may also be unfair if there is no genuine redundancy situation, and if the employer fails to show an alternative fair reason for dismissal. And it may be unfair on the grounds that it is **unreasonable** in the circumstances. This could be because there was a lack of consultation, an unfair selection procedure or a failure to offer alternative employment. In these cases the usual unfair dismissal **qualifying conditions do apply** — so the employee must have been continuously employed for a year.

A decision to make a long-standing employee redundant when a job he was doing on a temporary basis ended, was held by the EAT to amount to an unfair selection. The employer should have considered selecting other similarly graded employees with less experience or qualifications (*Balfour Beatty Construction v Baird EAT/120/00*).

If an employee succeeds in a case of unfair dismissal then their redundancy payment will be **offset** against the basic award (which means that they will receive only one or the other). If they received a contractual redundancy payment that is more than the statutory minimum the balance of this will be offset against any compensatory award (*Digital Equipment v Clements [1998] IRLR 134*).

The time limit for a claim of unfair dismissal on grounds of redundancy is **three months** from the date of termination, with discretion for the tribunal to extend this if it was not reasonably practicable to issue it within that time. This is the same as for any other case of unfair dismissal. The six-month time limit only applies to claims for the redundancy payment.

An employee who brings a claim for their statutory redundancy pay will be deemed to have been dismissed on grounds of redundancy and there will be no opportunity to challenge the reason for dismissal. It is important therefore that if you wish to challenge the reason for dismissal, or believe that the redundancy was in other ways unfair, you bring a claim for unfair dismissal as well as redundancy pay.

State benefits

Workers who have lost work either through unfair dismissal or redundancy may be entitled to Jobseeker's Allowance or Employment and Support Allowance.

More information: See the LRD booklets *Redundancy law* (£5.25) and *State benefits and tax credits 2010* (£6.15). LRD's *Workplace Report* has regular quarterly updates on redundancy law.

12. Business transfers and contracting out

If a business is sold (other than through a share transfer) or if a service is privatised or contracted out, the employees who work in that business are protected by the *Transfer of Undertakings (Protection of Employment) Regulations 2006* (TUPE). These replaced the 1981 regulations with effect from 6 April 2006. The effect of the TUPE regulations is to make sure that when a business changes hands all its **employees transfer with it** and that their **terms and conditions stay the same**. However, there are some exceptions — occupational pensions do not transfer, and some changes may be allowed for an economic, technical or organisational reason or in cases of insolvency (see below). TUPE applies to "employees" only (see Chapter 2):

Agency worker Mr Summers met the definition of a "worker" under the *Working Time Regulations 1998* and was entitled to be paid holiday pay by the agency. However, the EAT held he was not an employee and did not come within the protection of the TUPE regulations. *Drivertime Manchester Ltd v Summers EAT/0073/04.*

The TUPE regulations can apply to transfers outside the UK, as in the following case in which the union brought a claim for failure to consult:

Newell Ltd in Tamworth, which made tracks, poles and blinds, sold the track and pole manufacturing part of its business to Holis Metal Industries, which is based in Israel. Without any consultation, 107 employees were told they could either move to Israel or be made redundant. They were all made redundant. The EAT said TUPE can potentially apply to a transfer from the UK to a non-EU company; regulation 3 says they apply to a transfer of a business "situated immediately before the transfer in the United Kingdom" so it is the location of the transferor that decides it. The EAT said that this would also meet the purpose of the regulations, which is to protect the rights of workers in the event of change of employer. *Holis Metal Industries Ltd v GMB & another UKEAT/0171/07 ([2008] IRLR 187).*

There is **no time limit** to protection under TUPE. In the case of *Taylor v Connex South Eastern EAT/1243/99*, the Employment Appeal Tribunal (EAT) held that an employee who was dismissed two years after a transfer could still claim protection under TUPE. His employers wanted him to agree to a change to his terms and conditions to harmonise them with those of other workers who had not transferred. He refused and was dismissed. The EAT ruled that the dismissal was automatically unfair because it was related to a TUPE transfer.

Relevant transfers

For employees to be protected by TUPE there must be what is termed a "relevant transfer". Under the 2006 TUPE regulations there will be a relevant transfer in either or both of the following circumstances:

◆ where there is a transfer **of an economic entity which retains its identity**; and

◆ where there is a **service provision change** in which the employer's activities are either contracted out, given to a different contractor or brought in-house.

A transfer can take place in **more than one stage** and still be covered by TUPE. In the case of *Re Maxwell Fleet [2000] IRLR 368* the employer tried to avoid TUPE through a series of transfers prior to the eventual transfer. The High Court said that the series of transfers should be seen as one.

An economic entity

The TUPE regulations define an economic entity as "an organised grouping of resources which has the objective of pursuing an economic activity, whether or not that activity is central or ancillary".

This means that there must be a business activity that is capable of having its own identity. This can be identified by a number of factors including: its workforce; its management; the way in which work is organised; its operating methods; or its operational resources. It does not mean that the business has to be making a profit. The TUPE regulations apply to the charity, voluntary and non-profit sectors as well as commercial enterprises.

Transfers of **franchises**, **leases** and **dealerships** are covered and transfers between subsidiary companies within the same group can also come within the definition, as happened in the case of *Allen v Amalgamated Construction C-234/98 ([2000] IRLR 119)*. This means that companies cannot restructure in advance of a transfer in order to avoid TUPE.

Retaining its identity

For TUPE to apply, the economic entity has to retain its identity after the transfer. Whether or not it has done so, depends on a number of factors. The EAT in the case of *Cheesman v R Brewer Contracts Ltd*

EAT/909/98 ([2001] IRLR 144) came up with the following checklist of factors that need to be taken into account (which was based on the principles established by the European Court of Justice (ECJ) in the case of *Spijkers v Gebroeders Benedik Abbatoir CT C-24/85* and is sometimes referred to under that name):

◆ the **type of undertaking** (the importance of the various aspects will depend on the type of business carried out);

◆ whether its **tangible assets** are transferred;

◆ the value of its **intangible assets** at the time of transfer and whether they transfer;

◆ whether the **majority of its employees** are taken over by the new company — and if not, why not;

◆ whether its **customers** are transferred;

◆ the degree of similarity between the **activities** carried on before and after the transfer;

◆ the period, if any, during which the activities are **suspended**; and

◆ whether there is a **contractual link** between the transferor and transferee (although there does not need to be such a link in order for there to be a transfer).

No single factor is decisive — the importance of each will depend on the nature of the business. Even if no staff or significant assets have been transferred there could still be a relevant transfer.

In *RCO Support Services v UNISON [2002] EWCA Civ 464 ([2002] IRLR 401)* the in-patient service of a hospital was moved to another hospital. The contract for cleaning and catering was awarded to the company RCO, who said that TUPE did not apply and offered to take on the staff only if they resigned from their existing employer. In the event, RCO did not take on any of the cleaners or catering staff and there was therefore no transfer of assets or staff. The Court of Appeal said the failure of staff to transfer was relevant but not conclusive — the key question was whether the cleaning and catering functions had retained their identity, and this was one of the factors to be considered. There had been a relevant transfer, it ruled, and the staff should have been taken on.

There can be a TUPE transfer even if there is **only one employee**.

The courts have distinguished between labour-intensive undertakings and other transfers that are more reliant on assets, particularly in the form of equipment needed to carry out the work. In asset-reliant undertakings, whether assets transfer is likely to be an important factor — in the case of *Oy Liikenne Ab v Liskojarvi C-172/99 ([2001]*

IRLR 171), which involved the replacement of a contractor providing a bus service, the ECJ found that there was no TUPE transfer because the buses had not been transferred. However, that is not always the case. In *P&O Trans European Ltd v Initial Transport Services Ltd [2003] IRLR 128*, the EAT held there had been a TUPE transfer even though P&O had not taken over all the vehicles from another contractor when it took over the delivery contract for Shell.

These cases show that each case is very much dependent on its own facts. However, although whether or not TUPE applies is something that can only be decided by a tribunals, unions need to be aware of the factors that could indicate a TUPE situation and seek clarification.

A service provision change

There will be a service provision change if an employer:

♦ **contracts out** certain activities;

♦ ends a contract with one contractor to carry out certain activities and **gives it to another**; or

♦ brings certain activities **in-house**.

It does not matter whether the activities have already been contracted in or out on previous occasions. TUPE will apply to a service provision change if there is an **organised grouping** of employees whose **principal purpose** is to carry out the activities concerned before the transfer. This means there must be employees whose main job is to do that work.

For example, a company has a contract to clean offices and the same group of cleaners cleans the offices every day (except during holiday and sickness absences, when cover is provided by other workers). If the contract is then given to a different firm, this will be a service provision change that is protected by TUPE. But if the first cleaning contractor sent in different cleaners every day, according to whoever happened to be around, there would not be an organised grouping of employees who could transfer and therefore TUPE would not apply.

Migrant Helpline had a contract with Churchill Dulwich to provide accommodation for asylum seekers. Before that contract expired, Migrant Helpline entered into a replacement contract with Metropolitan Resource Ltd for such provision at a different location. Apart from a few remaining asylum seekers who could not be moved, Churchill Dulwich received no more asylum seekers. When the Churchill Dulwich contract expired, its employees claimed there had been a service provision change under regulation 3(1)(b) of the TUPE regulations. The EAT considered the definition of a "service provision change". Tribunals are likely to be faced with arguments that the "activities" carried out by the new contractor are not identical to those carried out by the old contractor, and therefore there has been no service provision change. But minor differences in the tasks carried out before and after the transfer should not mean the concept does not apply. The tribunal should ask itself whether the activities carried on by the alleged transferee are fundamentally or essentially the same as those carried out by the alleged transferor. A change of location or the carrying out of some additional duty was unlikely to mean the same service had not transferred. *Metropolitan Resources Ltd v (1) Churchill Dulwich (in liquidation) (2) Cambridge & others UKEAT/0286/08; [2009] IRLR 700, EAT.*

The company fulfilled a catering contract at a car plant (by providing cooked breakfasts, hot meals at lunchtimes, sandwiches and drinks). Ms Jones and Ms Ciliza, who were employed as chefs/supervisers, spent a good deal of their time preparing hot meals. However, in April 2007, the catering contract was taken over by MIS — which decided to only sell pre-prepared salads and sandwiches (i.e. no more hot food preparation). Was there a service provision change? The tribunal thought not, but the employees appealed. The EAT identified that the key issue is whether the activities carried on by the new contractor are fundamentally the same as those carried out by the old contractor. In this case, there had been a change from a full catering contract (involving the preparation of hot or cold cooked food) to one which only involved the selling of pre-prepared sandwiches and salads: the tribunal's decision was upheld. *OCS Group UK Ltd v Jones and Ciliza UKEAT/0038/09.*

TUPE can still apply even if the work is split up between different contractors or only part of it is contracted out. For example, suppose that the cleaning contractor is also responsible for recycling and has a team of employees who carry out that particular task. Then the contract is terminated and a new contractor (B) is taken on to do the office cleaning but a separate contractor (C) is given the contract for recycling. Both are covered by TUPE because each activity had a dedicated group of workers — the cleaners would transfer to contractor B and the recycling staff to contractor C.

The case of *Clearsprings Management Ltd v Ankers and others UKEAT/0054/08/LA* concerned the provision of accommodation and support to asylum seekers. Clearsprings (which employed 17 people) lost its contract to three other companies. The three companies acquired leases of properties and gradually took on responsibility for the asylum seekers (who were distributed to the companies randomly). Were Clearsprings' staff right that there been a service provision change? The tribunal thought not, but the employees appealed. The EAT noted that the allocation of service users (i.e. asylum seekers) showed no discernible pattern of reallocation to the incoming contractors. On the facts, the tribunal was entitled to conclude that Clearsprings' activity was so fragmented that no transfer took place — the appeal was dismissed.

TUPE can apply even if there is **only one employee** doing the activity. However, there are two circumstances in which TUPE will not apply to the transfer of services. These are:

◆ where the new service provider is only intended to carry out those activities in connection with a **single specific event or task of short-term duration**; or

◆ where the activities consist wholly or mainly of the **supply of goods** — TUPE will not apply to a contract simply to supply food to a company, for example, but will apply if the contractor is also responsible for running the company's canteen.

On the issue of short-term contracts, the Department for Business, Innovation and Skills (BIS) publication, *A guide to the 2006 TUPE regulations for employees, employers and representatives*, gives the example of a security contract for the Olympic Games. If the organisers engage a contractor to give security advice for several years running up to the event, this is a one-off event but is not short-term so TUPE will apply. But if the contractor is hired just to provide security staff during the Games themselves, TUPE will not apply because the contract is only for a short period.

Transfers within public administration

Generally TUPE applies to both the public and private sector and includes transfers to and from the private sector. However, the regulations specifically exclude an **administrative reorganisation or the transfer of administrative functions** within public administrative authorities. This means that most transfers within central or local government are not covered by TUPE. However, they are covered by the Cabinet Office's *Statement of Practice: Staff transfers in the public sector*, which gives TUPE-like protection to these staff.

Consultation and collective rights

TUPE provides for collective information and consultation in regulations 13 and 14. Where there is a recognised union, consultation takes place with representatives of that union. If there is no union, consultation takes place with either reps who have been appointed or elected generally for consultation and information purposes, or reps elected specifically for TUPE purposes.

If no representatives are elected the employer should inform and consult employees directly (*Howard v Millrise Ltd & S G Printers t/a Colourflow EAT/0658/04 ([2005] IRLR 84*). Representatives should be allowed access to employees and appropriate facilities.

All employees who could be affected by a change of employer have the right to be informed in advance of what is happening. This includes both employees working for the **old employer (the transferor)** and those working for the **new employer (the transferee)**. Employers have a duty to inform representatives of the following:

◆ the fact that the transfer is taking place, the reason why, and the proposed date;
◆ the likely legal, economic and social consequences for the employees; and
◆ what measures are likely to be taken in relation to employees.

This information must be provided **long enough before the transfer** to allow consultation to take place.

In *Cable Realisations Ltd v GMB Northern [2010] IRLR 42* the transfer of a business was completed on 3 September 2007. On 15 August 2007, GMB Northern was given the required information and told that no measures would be taken. No consultation was therefore compulsory under TUPE. The factory was closed for its annual shutdown from 17–31 August, so the GMB could not get in touch with its members. It complained that the employer had breached regulation 13(2) as it had not given the information "long enough" before the transfer for meaningful consultation, albeit voluntary, to take place.

The EAT said that the obligation to inform under regulation 13(2) TUPE arises not just for compulsory consultation, but also in respect of voluntary consultation. A responsible employer would not limit consultation to the compulsory requirements. To engage in meaningful consultation, it was essential that the union representatives could speak to their members, and that was not practicable during the shut-down. The information had therefore not been provided "long enough" in advance of the transfer.

If it is envisaged that **measures will be taken** (for example, that jobs may change) the employer also has an obligation to consult the reps, to consider any representations they make and to reply to them, stating reasons for objection where appropriate.

Unlike in a collective redundancy consultation (see Chapter 11) there is **no minimum number of affected employees** required for TUPE consultation to take place. And there is no specified minimum period of time over which it must take place.

If the employer **fails to inform or consult** the appropriate reps (or the individual employees if there is no rep) a complaint can be made to the employment tribunal. This must be made **within three months** of the date of the transfer.

The tribunal can make an award of up to 13 weeks' pay. According to the EAT, this should be determined in the same way as for a protective award in cases of redundancy, which means it should reflect the seriousness of the employer's failure and the maximum amount should only be reduced if there is mitigation (*Sweetin v Coral Racing EAT/0039/05 ([2006] IRLR 252)*).

The case of *Royal Mail Group v CWU [2009] EWCA Civ 1045* involved the conversion of post office branches to privately-run franchises. Royal Mail staff were offered redeployment or voluntary redundancy. However, the union believed that TUPE applied and that the staff should have transferred. A claim was brought arguing that the employer, by stating that there was no transfer, had failed to inform and consult— specifically, Royal Mail had not advised staff of the legal, economic and social implications of the transfer. The courts could find no evidence that Royal Mail didn't genuinely believe, that TUPE did not apply. The Court of Appeal decided that employers do not have to warrant the accuracy of their view about the legal implications of a change. That is not to say that employers can abdicate their responsibilities by shutting their eyes to legal problems — rather, they must consider the legal implications and pass on to the union a considered and genuine view.

The 2006 regulations make the transferor and the transferee **jointly and severally** liable for compensation for a failure to consult. This means that if the transferor fails to pay, the transferee must pay. However, the transferee does not have to consult with the employees after the transfer has taken place (on the basis that the new employer may not take any measures in relation to transferred staff): *Amicus v Glasgow City Council UKEATS/0007/08/MT*.

Collective agreements made by a recognised union with the old employer transfer to the new one under regulation 5. They are treated in the same way as if they had been made with the new employer so any transferred employees continue to benefit from the terms in that agreement (except in respect of occupational pensions). Under regulation 6, trade union recognition also transfers but only when the group of employees who transfer retain a distinct identity.

Identifying employees who transfer

All employees who are **employed immediately before the transfer** and are assigned to the business or part of business that transfers will transfer with it, unless they object. This includes employees **who would have been employed** immediately before the transfer but were dismissed because of it. This is the case even if the transfer takes place in more than one stage and the employee is dismissed before the first stage. An employee who is off sick when the transfer takes place will still transfer (*Fairhurst Ward Abbots v Botes Building [2004] IRLR 304*).

Identifying the employees who are assigned to the business that transfers is not always straightforward. An employee may have more than one role; the section that transfers could be part of a large department, or the employee could even work sometimes for different companies in the same group. The EAT has said that what is important is looking at where the employee is assigned to work in practice.

A worker who is temporarily allocated to part of a business that is to transfer will not transfer, as the EAT confirmed in the case of Mr Bademosi, an employee who was temporarily transferred to another site following an injury. When that site transferred under TUPE, he did not have to transfer with it but had the right to stay with his existing employer (*Securiplan v Bademosi EAT/1128/02*).

A full-time shop steward did not transfer when the department he was paid to work in transferred. Mr Gaston, who was a full-time union rep at Birmingham City Council, continued to be paid as a plumber. The only plumbing work he did was on an out-of-hours rota and the EAT found that he did not transfer because he was not assigned to that department (*Birmingham City Council v Gaston EAT/0508/03*).

In the following case, two employees were dismissed before a TUPE transfer for an unconnected reason but reinstated on appeal. The EAT held that their employment transferred to the new employer:

Mr Anstey and Mr Simpson were custody officers employed by security company GSL under a contract to the Home Office and they were both dismissed for alleged gross misconduct. They appealed but before their appeals were heard the contract with GSL was transferred to G4S, who refused to hear their appeals. GSL heard the appeals instead and said they should be reinstated but had no work for them following the loss of the contract. G4S refused to reinstate them on the grounds they were not employed by GSL immediately before the transfer.

The EAT held that when a dismissal is overturned on appeal the dismissal effectively "vanishes" and continuity of employment is preserved. The claimants were therefore to be treated as having been employed immediately before the transfer and their employment transferred under TUPE. It said this was consistent with the purpose of TUPE which was to safeguard the rights of employees in the event of a transfer. *G4S Justice Services (UK) Ltd v Anstey, Simpson & GSL UK Ltd EAT/0698/05.*

However, in the case of *Dowling v Ilic Haulage and Berkeley Logistics EAT/0836/03* (which is possibly open to challenge), a shop steward was denied the protection of TUPE even though he was awarded interim relief in his trade union victimisation claim.

Mike Dowling, a shop steward, was dismissed by his employer and believed that this was for reasons related to his trade union activities. He successfully claimed interim relief at an employment tribunal, which meant that the tribunal made a "continuation order" requiring his employer to continue paying him until his victimisation claim could be heard at a tribunal.

In the meantime, the company that Dowling worked for was transferred to a new employer under TUPE. When his claim came to be heard, Dowling attempted to claim against the new company, arguing that the continuation order meant he was still in employment and had therefore transferred under TUPE. The EAT held that there was no right to claim against the new employer. Dowling was no longer an employee of the company at the time of the transfer; he was an ex-employee but with financial protection as far as his rights to be paid were concerned.

Where employees are assigned to work at more than one location it may be difficult to decide who transfers. The EAT said in the case of *Duncan Web Offset (Maidstone) Ltd v Cooper [1995] IRLR 633* that tribunals should bear in mind that the purpose of TUPE was to protect employees and should go beyond the terms of the contract to see how work was being carried out in practice.

Objecting to the transfer

An employee cannot be forced to transfer if they do not want to and can object to the transfer by informing either the old or the new employer. But if they do object, their contract of employment will be terminated and they will not be treated as having been dismissed. This means that they will **not be entitled** to redundancy and will **not be entitled** to claim unfair dismissal.

In *Capital Health Solutions v Mclean UKEATS/0034/07/MT*, an occupational health nurse did not want to transfer from the BBC to Capital Health Solutions. Accordingly, she resigned on 31 March 2006 (the transfer taking effect on the following day). However, she agreed to the BBC's suggestion that, as part of the hand-over, she work a "period of secondment" for six weeks with Capital Health Solutions (although there was no job at the BBC to which she could return). The EAT found that when an employee seeks to object to a transfer, they cannot also work out their notice if this would involve them working for the proposed new employer. In this case, Ms Mclean's objection to the transfer was ineffective and her employment transferred. However, there is an exception to that rule under regulation 4(9), which states that if the reason for the employee's objection is that the transfer involves or would involve a **substantial change in working conditions to their material detriment** they will be treated as having been dismissed. In those circumstances, the employee could claim unfair dismissal.

The effect on terms and conditions

The purpose of the TUPE regulations is to protect employees' terms and conditions when their employment is transferred to a new employer. The effect of the transfer is to treat the existing contract of employment as if it had been made with the new employer (the transferee). This means that **continuity of service** is preserved and will run from the date employment began with the old employer (the transferor) and the existing terms and conditions are maintained, except for occupational pension schemes.

In *Jackson v Computershare Investor Services [2007] EWCA Civ 1065 ([2008] IRLR 70)* in 2004, Ms Jackson, who had started work for her original company in 1999, transferred to Computershare. As Ms Jackson's employment was terminated by Computershare shortly after the transfer, she was entitled to redundancy pay. Ms Jackson argued that the amount due should be calculated under the terms of Computershare's most generous but closed scheme (only open to employees who joined the organisation prior to 2002). The Court of Appeal found that although Ms Jackson's continuity of service commenced prior to 2002 (and therefore she should be compensated for six years' service), as she was not an employee of Computershare prior to 2002, she could only benefit from their less generous, more recent package. In other words Ms Jackson could not claim a right that she did not have on transfer.

Mr Alemo-Herron and 23 of his colleagues at the London Borough of Lewisham, had their jobs outsourced to Parkwood Leisure. Although their contracts detailed that they were governed by the collective agreement, intermittently negotiated by the National Joint Council for Local Government Services (NJC), Parkwood Leisure refused to extend the benefit of new NJC collective agreement to Mr Alemo-Herron and his colleagues. (Parkwood Leisure was not a party to NJC settlements, nor did it recognise the unions involved in the negotiation process).

The employees believed that TUPE entitled them to the subsequent salary increases and so brought claims for unlawful deduction from wages. The Court of Appeal noted that it was bound by the decision of the European Court of Justice in *Werhof v Freeway Traffic Systems GmbH and Co KG (C-499/04)*. Accordingly, it found that there is only "static" protection for transferred terms and conditions under section 5(1), *Transfer of Undertakings (Protection of Employment) Regulations 1981* — as it then was.

In other words, the claimants could only enforce the pay and conditions specified under the collective agreement as it was at the time of the transfer, and TUPE protection did not entitle them to subsequent amendments. *Parkwood Leisure Ltd v Alemo-Herron [2010] EWCA Civ 24].*

In this case an employee's place of work was transferred from Camberwell to Beckenham. The employee objected to the increased journey time, the impact on her childcare arrangements and the way in which the change occurred. She resigned and claimed constructive unfair dismissal. The new employer pointed to the contract clause which stated that: "There may be occasions when you are required to perform your duties, either temporarily or permanently, at other locations within the Trust." It argued that that reference to "the Trust" was (following the transfer), a reference to it.

The EAT disagreed — the mobility clause only allowed a transfer to locations operated by the original trust (i.e. the entity with which the contract had been made). The EAT also commented on Ms Tapere's argument that the change of location represented a substantial change which was to her material detriment (sufficient to justify resignation under regulation 4(9) TUPE). The EAT decided that the impact of the proposed change should be considered from the employee's point of view and then it should be decided whether the employee's position was a reasonable one to adopt. Here, the change of location meant potential disruption to childcare arrangements and a longer or altered journey involving travel on the M25, which Ms Tapere did not find attractive. The EAT therefore decided that, on this basis too, Ms Tapere had been dismissed (*Tapere v South London and Maudsley NHS Trust UKEAT/0410/08*).

Legal liabilities also transfer, for example, liability for acts of discrimination or for personal injury. This means that an employee can bring a claim against the new employer for things that happened before the transfer.

Maintaining terms and conditions

If the new employer attempts to make any changes to the employees' terms and conditions as a result of the transfer these changes will be void (unenforceable). If necessary, employees can bring a claim to enforce their right to retain their proper terms and conditions. However, changes to terms and conditions as a result of a transfer can be lawful if they are **to the employee's benefit**, according to the Court of Appeal in the following case:

Mr Power's employment contract specified that his contractual retirement age was 60. When the part of the business in which he worked was transferred to a new employer, he agreed to change his contractual retirement age to 65. But his new employer then forced him to retire at 60, so he claimed unfair dismissal. His employer argued that because changes resulting from a business transfer are unenforceable under TUPE, Power could not enforce the right to retire at 65.

But the Court of Appeal said that the purpose of the TUPE legislation was to safeguard the rights of employees when they transferred, not to prevent them from benefiting from new terms that they have agreed. It found that Power's original right to retire at 60 had transferred — and he had also acquired a new right by agreement to retire at 65. When this happens, it said, the employee can choose between enforcing the transferred acquired right or the newly obtained right. *Regent Security Services Ltd v Power [2007] EWCA Civ 1188.*

In the following case a change to the method of payment amounted to a breach of TUPE even though the employee received the same pay overall:

Mr Bates worked a three-week shift system of 18, 45 and 60 hours. His basic pay was based on an average 41-hour week, and so was the same each week. He was then entitled to overtime at time-and-a-half for any additional hours that he worked. When Chubb took over the business in a TUPE transfer, it paid him monthly and for the hours he actually worked: he still worked the same shifts and ended up with the same amount over a three-week period, but his wages varied each month. Bates said he should be entitled to overtime in any week that he had to work more than 41 hours, because those were his contracted hours.

The EAT held that, by changing the method of payment, Chubb had chosen not to comply with the TUPE arrangements; this amounted to a unilateral variation of contract. Because Chubb was now paying him for the hours he actually worked, Bates was entitled to overtime for the two weeks out of three that he was working more than 41 hours. *Chubb Security Personnel v Bates EAT/0358/04.*

In another case, the EAT held that employees continued to be entitled to profit-related pay based on their old employer's scheme. The effect of the transfer was that the right to participate in the scheme was deemed to have been made with the new employer and therefore the right transferred (*Unicorn Consultancy Services v Westbrook EAT/892/98 ([2000] IRLR 80)*).

Terms contained in a collective agreement which is incorporated into the contract will also transfer. These have been found to be binding on the new employer even when recognition has ended:

In the case of *Whent v T Cartledge Ltd [1997] IRLR 153*, the EAT held that employees transferred under compulsory competitive tendering had the continued right to benefit from terms negotiated with their old employer.

heir contracts stated that their pay would be as laid down in the NJC agreement and this right transferred even though their new employer was not a party to that agreement.

But in the following case a subsequent change to the collective agreement did not apply to the transferred employees:

Ms Ackinclose and her colleagues worked for the school meals service, and their employment was transferred when this was contracted out. Five years later, they were transferred back to the council, but by that time the collective agreement governing their terms and conditions had been abolished and replaced with a new agreement relating to all staff. The EAT held that it was only the original agreement that had been incorporated into their contract; their terms and conditions could not be determined by any other agreement or document. *Ackinclose & others v Gateshead Metropolitan BC EAT/0087/04 ([2005] IRLR 79.*

The ECJ has held that it is only rights and obligations in force at the time of the transfer that are transferred (*Werhof v Freeway Traffic Systems Gmbh & Co KG C-499/04 ([2006] IRLR 400)*).

Redundancy terms can also transfer, as confirmed by the EAT in *Lansing Linde Severnside v Spiers EAT/1490/01*; see also *Solectron Scotland v Roper and others EAT/0305/03 ([2004] IRLR 4)*. But in one case, an employee who accepted promotion after a transfer was found to have accepted a new contract and lost his entitlement to an enhanced redundancy scheme which otherwise would have been protected by TUPE (*Barry v Bateman Catering EAT/1515/00*).

There is **no time limit** on the right to maintain terms and conditions under TUPE. An employee who has a contractual term that has transferred from the old employer continues to have the right to benefit from that term until it is lawfully changed.

However, it is only changes that are proposed for a reason related to the transfer that are invalid. The more time that has elapsed since the transfer the more difficult it will be to establish that the transfer is the reason for the change.

In the case of *Celtec Ltd v Astley C-478/03 ([2005] IRLR 647)*, the ECJ held that a transfer cannot take place over a period of time but occurs **on a particular date**. This is the date when the new employer becomes responsible for carrying on that business. When the ECJ's decision was applied to the facts of that case, the employees were found to have transferred from the time of their secondment:

A large number of civil servants were seconded from the Department of Education to a new training and enterprise council (TEC) in early 1990. The TEC opened for business in September of that year, and in 1993 the workers were given the option of transferring to the TEC and resigning from the civil service, which they did. When they were subsequently made redundant, they argued that their years in the civil service should be taken into account, but the TEC said that their continuous service dated back only to 1993.

The House of Lords held that the TUPE transfer had taken place in September 1990, even though all the claimants had believed they were just on secondment from the Department of Education. Because this was the legal date of transfer, it could not be changed by agreement or by the understanding of the parties at the time. The employees were entitled to have the full length of their employment with the DofE taken into account when their redundancy payments were calculated. *Celtec v Astley and others [2006] UKHL 29 ([2006] IRLR 635)*.

The time limit for a claim that relates to an occupational pension provided by the original employer (the transferor) runs from the date of the transfer. This is because occupational pension rights do not transfer. This was confirmed by the House of Lords in the long-running case of *Powerhouse Retail Ltd v Burroughs [2006] UKHL 13 ([2006] IRLR 381)*:

A number of part-time employees in the electricity industry were transferred under TUPE following privatisation. They brought equal pay claims because they had been excluded from joining their original employer's occupational pension scheme, but they issued these more than six months after the transfer. A claim under the *Equal Pay Act* must be brought within six months of the end of the employment to which it relates. Because occupational pension rights do not transfer under TUPE, the only liability for the claim arises from the original contract prior to transfer. The House of Lords held that the time limit for equal pay pensions claims following a business transfer runs from the date that employment with the old employer ended. The claims could not succeed. *Powerhouse Retail Ltd v Burroughs [2006] UKHL 13 ([2006] IRLR 381).*

Changes that are allowed

Variations to the contract that are **unconnected with the transfer** are allowed, although they must be agreed in the same way as they would in any non-transfer situation. Changes can now also be agreed for a reason connected with the transfer if they are for an **economic**, **technical** or **organisational reason** (usually referred to as an "ETO reason").

Until the 2006 regulations came in this was a defence only available to an employer who had dismissed an employee as a result of a transfer. The government extended this to allow for contractual changes even though this is not permitted by the Directive because it believed it was inconsistent to allow employees to be dismissed for an ETO reason but not allowed to accept changes to their terms and conditions.

The ETO reason must be a reason **entailing changes in the workforce**. The key case in defining what "entailing changes in the workforce" means is *Delabole Slate Ltd v Berriman ([1985] IRLR 305)*:

Mr Berriman was a quarryman with a guaranteed weekly income. The new employer proposed a change to his pay to bring it into line with the terms of the existing collective agreement. He refused the accept the change (which would have involved a substantial cut in his pay) and resigned, claiming constructive dismissal. The Court of Appeal upheld Berriman's claim for unfair dismissal because, although the employer had established an ETO reason, it did not entail changes in the workforce — the reason for the pay cut was to standardise terms and conditions and not to reduce the workforce. The Court of Appeal held that there was not a change to the workforce if the numbers or functions of the workforce do not change.

A change in the workforce cannot amount to one person leaving and someone else taking their job. Even if an employer dismissed all its employees and replaced them with new ones, this would not be a change to the workforce because there would still be the same number of workers doing the same jobs. If, however, the employer proposed redundancies or redeployed staff into different jobs, this could entail an ETO reason entailing a change in the workforce.

As can be seen from this case, the **harmonisation of terms and conditions** between workforces does not entail a change to the workforce and will therefore be **unenforceable**. This was confirmed recently in the case of *London Metropolitan University v Sackur & others EAT/0286/06*.

There is no obligation on an employer to offer new workers the same terms and conditions as those who are protected by TUPE. This can create a two-tier workforce, with colleagues working alongside each other on different terms and conditions, which undermines union organisation and collective rights.

In the public sector, extensive campaigning by unions resulted in the government issuing the Code of Practice on workforce matters in local authority service contracts to cover local authority transfers to the private or voluntary sector. In 2005, this was extended to cover the wider public sector including the civil service, NHS and maintained schools. It provides that new recruits must be employed on terms and conditions that are no less favourable overall than those of existing employees.

Insolvency

The 2006 regulations introduced new provisions to encourage the "rescue" of failing businesses (regulations 8 and 9). This is achieved in part by ensuring that some of the business's debts, including redundancy payments and outstanding wages, do not transfer to the new business. Instead they become payable by the secretary of state through the National Insurance Fund, in the same way as they would if a business closed but there was no transfer. Any remaining debts not met by the fund then transfer to the new owner.

The provisions apply where insolvency proceedings have been started, except where the proceedings consist of the liquidation of assets. Secondly, the regulations allow for changes to terms and conditions after the transfer to take place. The normal restrictions do not apply and more limited restrictions apply in their place.

Under regulation 9, variations to terms and conditions can be agreed with the union representative or other appropriate representatives. Union reps are entitled to paid time off for this purpose. It applies to variations that are made as a result of the transfer but not for an ETO reason, but they must be designed to **safeguard employment opportunities** by ensuring the business's survival.

Once the variation has been agreed by the representative it becomes a part of the employees' contractual terms and conditions of employment.

Where employees are represented by non-trade union reps, the agreement must be in writing and signed by each rep or someone authorised to sign it on their behalf. The employer must provide a copy of the agreement and any guidance necessary to all employees to whom it applies.

In November 2005 Mr Da Silva started work for Andream Ltd (75% owned by Mr Greenwood). On 1 December 2006 all staff were dismissed — and within three weeks a liquidator had been appointed. A new business (100% owned by Mr Greenwood) which had been incorporated on 20 November 2006 acquired some of Andream's assets and staff. Mr Da Silva started work for the new company on 14 January 2007, but was dismissed on 17 August 2007. Mr Da Silva brought an unfair dismissal claim — to which the employer responded that he didn't have one year's continuous service.

The EAT considered that the key issue was whether Andream was still under Greenwood's control at the date Mr Da Silva started work for the new company. The EAT believed it should take a purposive approach to the meaning of "control", that is, it should follow Parliament's intention that employees' rights are protected on changes of employer, and not destroyed by manipulation of the employment relationship. Even though, throughout the period of liquidation, Andream spoke through the liquidator, practical control (if not directly, then indirectly) remained with its main shareholder, Mr Greenwood. Accordingly Mr Da Silva could bring his claim. *Da Silva Junior v Composite Mouldings & Design Ltd UKEAT/0241/08.*

Mr Oakland worked for a fruit and vegetable wholesaler (Oldco) that was in financial trouble. Due to the scale of Oldco's debts, it could not be rescued as a going concern. Administrators were appointed on 6 December 2006 and on the same day a new company (Newco) took on Oldco's staff and the lease of its premises. Mr Oakland was dismissed in November 2007: did he have the one year's continuous service that he needed to bring an unfair dismissal claim? The tribunal thought not, but Mr Oakland appealed.

The EAT did not accept Oakland's argument that the appointment of joint administrators cannot by definition amount to the institution of insolvency proceedings with a view to liquidating a company's assets. It thought that only applied where there was a creditor's voluntary winding-up or a compulsory winding-up by the court. In the case of joint administrators, it all depended on the facts and circumstances.

Here the tribunal had found that the administrators had decided not to continue trading, but to sell the assets with a view to the eventual liquidation of Oldco. The rejection of Mr Oakland's claim was consistent with the policy behind regulation 8(7) TUPE, that is, to promote a rescue culture whereby potential purchasers of Oldco were not put off by TUPE protection (*Oakland v Wellswood (Yorkshire) Ltd UKEAT/0395/08*).

Pensions

Any provisions relating to old age, invalidity or survivors' benefits under an occupational pension scheme are specifically excluded from TUPE by regulation 10 and **do not transfer**.

More limited protection of pension rights is provided instead by the *Pensions Act 2004* and the *Transfer of Employment (Pension Protection) Regulations 2005*. Under these regulations if the old employer provided a pension scheme, the new employer must provide some form of pension for those who were eligible to join. It does not have to be equivalent but must be of a minimum standard.

Employees in the public sector who transfer are covered by the Cabinet Office statement of practice on staff transfers in the public sector and *A fair deal for staff pensions*. The government's policy is that public sector employees who transfer to the private sector should continue to have a "broadly comparable" pension. Local government employees are covered by the Code of Practice on *Workforce matters in local authority service contracts.*

Early retirement provisions do, however, transfer according to a landmark ruling by the ECJ in the case of *Beckmann v Dynamco Whicheloe Macfarlane C-164/00.* The case concerned rights for over-50s. The NHS scheme provided that those aged over 50 who are made redundant would receive an early retirement pension. The ECJ held that early retirement benefits are not old-age, invalidity or survivors' benefits and were not covered by the pensions exclusion, which, it said, must be narrowly interpreted.

The principle was applied again by the ECJ in the case of *Martin and others v South Bank University Case C-4/01 ([2004] IRLR 74):*

Staff at Redwood College of Health Studies were entitled to enhanced benefits and compensation in the event of redundancy under their NHS scheme. When they transferred to a new employer they had to move their pension, but the new scheme did not provide the same benefits when they were later made redundant.

The ECJ held that the employees were entitled to the same early retirement benefits as they would have been under the NHS scheme. It said that only benefits paid when an employee reaches the end of his or her working life can be classified as old-age benefits. Even agreeing to accept lower benefits in return for early retirement would not affect this entitlement because an employee cannot agree to changes that have only been made as a result of the transfer.

Protection against unfair dismissal

If an employee is dismissed because of the transfer or a reason connected with it, their dismissal will be regarded as automatically unfair unless the employer can show that the dismissal was for an **economic, technical** or **organisational** (ETO) reason (see below). It does not matter whether they are employed by the transferor or the transferee or whether they were dismissed before or after the transfer. However, unlike most other classes of automatically unfair dismissals (see Chapter 10) employees need to have at least **a year's service** to be able to exercise the right.

Where the employee is dismissed for an ETO reason, the dismissal is potentially fair for either redundancy or some other substantial reason. However, the dismissal must still be reasonable in accordance with section 98(4) of the *Employment Rights Act 1996* as in any standard case of unfair dismissal (see Chapter 10).

There is no time limit for the protection against dismissal under TUPE, although the more time that passes the more difficult it will be to demonstrate a link between the transfer and the dismissal. However, in the case of *Taylor v Connex South Eastern EAT/1243/99* (see page 265), a dismissal two years after the transfer was still related to the transfer and therefore automatically unfair. The new regulations have made it easier to bring a claim of constructive dismissal resulting from an intended change to terms following a transfer. It used to be the case, following the Court of Appeal's decision in *Rossiter v Pendragon Plc [2002] EWCA Civ 745 ([2002]IRLR 483)*, that an employee could only succeed in a claim based on a substantial change in terms and conditions if the change amounted to a breach of contract, as is the case in a normal constructive dismissal claim.

Norman Rossiter was a car salesperson employed by Lex Ford. He received commission and basic pay but his employer reserved the right to change or remove the commission scheme at any time. Pendragon acquired the business and altered the rate of commission. Rossiter resigned, claiming constructive dismissal on the grounds that there had been a substantial change to his working conditions to his detriment. The Court of Appeal held that a change to conditions as a result of TUPE must still amount to a breach of contract if it is to be a constructive dismissal. In Rossiter's case there was no breach because his employer was contractually entitled to change his pay.

However, a claim such as Rossiter's could succeed under TUPE 2006, regulation 4(9), as an employee is now entitled to pursue a claim of unfair dismissal if a transfer involves or would involve **a substantial change in working conditions to their material detriment**. This means that an employee does not need to show that the change amounts to a fundamental breach of contract. But an employee is specifically prevented under the 2006 regulations from bringing a wrongful dismissal claim (a claim for notice pay) if they do not work their notice in those circumstances (regulation 4(10)).

This rule does not affect an employee's right to claim constructive dismissal in response to a breach of contract in the usual way. This could apply, for instance, if there was a fundamental breach of trust and confidence but no "material detriment". In that case the normal rules for constructive dismissal apply (see page 203). Likewise, an employee could bring a wrongful dismissal claim if there is a breach of contract.

In either case employees will need to consider whether the best course of action is to resign or refuse to transfer and claim constructive dismissal or stay and enforce their right to maintain their existing terms and conditions.

Dismissal for an ETO reason

A dismissal will not be automatically unfair if it is related to the transfer but is for an **economic, technical or organisational (ETO) reason entailing changes in the workforce**. If the employer can establish this, then that will be a potentially fair reason for dismissal for either redundancy or some other substantial reason. However, they must still go on to show that dismissal was reasonable in all the circumstances.

The key case in defining what "entailing changes in the workforce" means, as for changes to terms and conditions above, is *Delabole Slate Ltd v Berriman ([1985] IRLR 305)* (see page 280).

That case established that a change in the workforce cannot amount to one person leaving and someone else taking their job. Even if an employer dismissed all its employees and replaced them with new ones this would not be a change to the workforce because there would still be the same number of workers doing the same jobs.

If, however, the employer proposed redundancies or redeployed staff into different jobs this could amount to an ETO reason entailing a change in the workforce.

If the ETO reason is **redundancy** as defined in section 139 of the *Employment Rights Act 1996*, the employee is entitled to a redundancy payment. Where the dismissal is by reason of the transfer, but the employer has demonstrated a valid ETO reason entailing changes in the workforce, the dismissal could still be unfair.

An employment tribunal would go on to consider whether the dismissal was reasonable in all the circumstances, including whether the employer has consulted with representatives and individuals in the usual way.

Who to claim against

The claim should usually be brought against the transferee (the new employer) even if the employee does not transfer. This is because liability for the dismissal will transfer to the new employer.

In *Perry's Motor Sales v Lindley UKEAT/0616/07*, the employee had, when she previously worked for the organisation to which she was due to be transferred, brought a tribunal claim against it. The transferee (Ms Lindley's prospective new employer) did not wish to have her back and so instructed the transferor (her existing employer) to terminate her employment prior to the transfer — which they did. Ms Lindley (who had less than a year's service) brought a claim under section 104, *Employment Rights Act 1996* (assertion of a statutory right) against the would-be new employer. The EAT decided that the liability which only crystallised on the transfer (the breach of section 104 being alleged against the new employer only), was capable of transferring (consistent with the objectives of TUPE).

However, in *Coutinho v Vision Information Services UKEAT/0469/07/ ZT*, the EAT considered the situation where an employee (whose employment terminated prior to the transfer) claimed for an act of victimisation after the transfer had taken effect. The EAT decided that liability for the act of victimisation did not transfer. Also, if the employee was dismissed for an ETO reason or a reason unconnected with the transfer (which would not be automatically unfair but could still be unfair under the usual unfair dismissal rules), the claim may need to be brought against the transferor.

If there is any doubt about who the employer is or whether the employment transferred it is best to claim against both and the issue will be resolved at an early stage of the proceedings.

More information: See the LRD booklet *TUPE — a guide to the business transfer regulations* (£4.25); LRD's *Workplace Report* has regular updates on TUPE.

Further information

Legal sources and publications

Throughout the booklet references have been made to the relevant statutes. Copies of these can be obtained online from the Office for Public Sector Information website at: www.opsi. gov.uk. In Northern Ireland, legislation is available online from the Labour Relations Agency website at www.lra.org.uk.

The full text of the cases referred to in this booklet is contained in the monthly Industrial Relations Law Reports (IRLR) or in the Industrial Cases Reports (ICR). Recent cases are also published on the web. EAT, Court of Appeal, House of Lords and ECJ decisions are available at: www.bailii.org.

Local libraries may have copies of the statutes and can obtain the books and law reports. Always check the date of publication to make sure that the book actually deals with the current law.

The Labour Research Department publishes booklets on specific legal issues. Relevant titles have been referred to in the "More information" box at the end of each Chapter of this booklet. LRD's monthly magazine *Workplace Report* provides up-to-date explanation of, and commentary on, all legal developments with quarterly updates on contracts, termination of employment, discrimination, TUPE and tribunal procedures. Information on LRD's publications and details of how to order are available on the website at www.lrd.org.uk or contact LRD, 78 Blackfriars Road, London SE1 8HF, tel: 020 7928 3649.

Useful organisations

Information, guidance and Codes of practice are available from the following:

Advisory, Conciliation and Arbitration Service (Acas), Euston Tower, 286 Euston Road, London W1 3SJ, helpline: 08457 474747, textphone: 08456 061600, publications: 08702 429090, www. acas.org.uk.

Central Arbitration Committee (CAC), makes awards of statutory recognition of trade unions and deals with union requests for disclosure of information (see Chapter 5). 22nd Floor, Euston Tower, 286 Euston Road, London NW1 3JJ: tel: 020 7904 2300, www.cac.gov.uk. Data protection helpline: 0845 306060.

Department for Business, Innovation and Skills (BIS), 1 Victoria Street, London, SW1H 0ET, Enquiry Unit tel: 020 7215 5000, www. bis.gov.uk.

Equality and Human Rights Commission (EHRC), www. equalityhumanrights.com. The EHRC has offices in Manchester, London, Glasgow and Cardiff and operates helplines: England 0845 604 6610 (textphone 0845 604 6620); Wales 0845 604 8810 (textphone 0845 604 8820); Scotland 0845 604 5510 (textphone 0845 604 5520).

Equality Commission for Northern Ireland (EOCNI), Equality House, 7-9 Shaftesbury Square, Belfast, BT2 7DP, tel: 028 90 500600, textphone: 028 90 500589,enquiry line: 02890 890890, www.equalityni.org.

Employment Tribunals Service, 100 Southgate Street, Bury St Edmunds, Suffolk, IP33 2AQ, www.employmenttribunals.gov. uk. Enquiry line: 08457 959775, Minicom: 08547 573722.

Information Commissioner's Office, Wycliffe House, Water Lane, Wilmslow, Cheshire SK9 5AF, helpline: 0303 123 1113, www.ico. gov.uk.

Labour Relations Agency, 2-8 Gordon Street, Belfast BT1 2LG, tel: 028 9032 1442, www.lra.org.uk

Pay and work rights helpline, including help on the National Minimum Wage tel: 0800 917 2368, textphone 0800 121 4042.

Employment rights — quick facts

Working time (for adults)

◆ Rest break at work of at least 20 minutes (if working day is six hours long or more).

◆ Break between days of work of at least 11 hours.

◆ Weekly rest of not less than 24 hours (can be averaged over two weeks — i.e. not less than two days off every two weeks).

◆ For night workers (those working at least three hours between 11pm — 6am), a maximum eight hour shift (in any 24-hour period as averaged out, normally, over 17 weeks).

◆ 48 hours (unless opt-out agreed) maximum per week — calculated by averaging out hours over 26 weeks (except in certain sectors or unless varied by agreement).

◆ 5.6 weeks holiday per year (which can include bank holidays) making a minimum of 28 days for those working five days per week.

Notice

◆ Statutory notice: after one month's service, one week per year of service up to a maximum of 12 weeks.

Minimum time limits for a collective consultation

◆ 100 or more employees: at least 90 days.

◆ 20 — 99 employees: 30 days.

Elements of a fair consultation

◆ Consultation when the proposals are still at a formative stage.

◆ Adequate information on which to respond.

◆ Adequate time in which to respond.

◆ Conscientious consideration by the employer of the response to consultation.

Other leave and pay

◆ Time off to care for dependants: unpaid time off to handle an unexpected emergency/disruption in care arrangements.

◆ Parental leave: 13 unpaid weeks in blocks of one or more complete weeks (up to age of 17, or in the case of a disabled child up to 18 years).

◆ Statutory maternity leave and pay: 39 weeks paid (six weeks at 90% of wages, 30 weeks at £124.88 per week) and 13 weeks unpaid leave.

◆ Statutory paternity leave and pay: two weeks at minimum of £124.88 per week — as of April 2011 new mothers can transfer all or part of their additional leave (i.e. the second six month period away from work) to fathers.

◆ Statutory week's pay (for calculating minimum redundancy entitlement, etc): £380 from 1 October 2009.

◆ National Minimum Wage: £5.80 an hour (unless under 22 years old): £5.93 from 1 October 2010.

◆ Statutory Sick Pay: from the fourth day off in a row onwards, statutory sick pay is payable for up to 28 weeks (£79.15 for 2010–11).

Index

Index

Index